EMANCIPATION FOR GOALPOSTS

FOOTBALL'S ROLE IN THE FALL OF YUGOSLAVIA

CHRIS ETCHINGHAM

Published by Ockley Books

First published 2023

All text copyright of the author

The moral right of the author to be identified as the author of this work has been asserted

All rights reserved. No part of this book may be reproduced in any form without prior permission in writing from the author and Ockley Books

Cover design: Steve Leard
Layout: Rob MacDonald
Edited by Adam Bushby & Rob MacDonald

Printed & bound by:
Ashford Colour Press
Unit 220, Fareham Reach
Fareham Road, Gosport,
Hampshire PO13 0FW

For Charlotte, Poppy, Georgia, Dougal & Myles

ABOUT THE AUTHOR

Chris Etchingham is a football writer and podcaster. He has been featured in *The Football Pink* magazine and on websites including *In Bed With Maradona*. He hosts a weekly football podcast called *Man On The Post* in which he discusses both football matches as well as social issues within the world of football.

A football obsessive, Chris will take in any game he can find. From the Premier and Champions League on TV, to far-flung leagues across the world on his laptop, to attending his local village team in person.

He lives in Cornwall with his wife, two children and his dog Myles.

This is his debut book.

★
CONTENTS

Introduction	11
Chapter 1: Origins and Evolution	15
Chapter 2: Fissures	43
Chapter 3: Breakup	73
Chapter 4: Almost	105
Chapter 5: Cain and Abel	139
Chapter 6: Down Under	173
Chapter 7: The Future	193
Acknowledgements	223
Bibliography	225

★
INTRODUCTION

Nineteen-year-old Zvonimir Boban strode up to take what was at that point the most important kick of a football of his life. His six-foot frame seemed reduced by his incredibly boyish face. With his pop-star hair and obvious good looks, he wouldn't have looked out of place if he had been walking to school in his hometown of Imotski in the Yugoslav republic of Croatia.

What did belie his years though was his confidence — it didn't seem to matter that he was about to take the decisive penalty at the 1987 World Under-20 Championships. If he scored, Yugoslavia were champions. Their goalkeeper, Dragoje Leković, had already saved the West German Marcel Witeczek's soft penalty low down to his left, and all the subsequent attempts had been scored. Just — Knut Reinhardt had sent the German's previous penalty gently, straight down the middle of the goal. As he dived left, Leković despairingly stuck his arm in the air and managed to get his hand to the ball, but could not prevent it crossing the line. As Reinhardt walked back to the centre circle holding his head in his hands with relief, he shot a few words back towards the penalty area, possibly in support of his own keeper, Uwe Brunn; possibly towards Leković for his futile efforts to save.

None of this seemed to deter the impeccable Boban. He had almost won the game once already, scoring what looked like an

85th-minute winner for Yugoslavia, only to see Witeczek equalise from the penalty spot just two minutes later. The teams played out 30 goalless minutes of extra time.

Boban placed the ball on the spot, turned around, and walked to the edge of the penalty area, before running up and confidently placing the ball into the bottom right-hand corner. Despite diving the right way, Brunn had no chance; Boban's penalty was perfect. As he turned and sprinted past his teammates and coaching staff in the dugout, and towards Yugoslavia's jubilant fans, one could have been forgiven for thinking that this was the start of something momentous for Yugoslavian football. Their Under-20 team were world champions and the blueprint for success seemed established for a generation of Yugoslavian footballers.

Nobody could have imagined that there was to be no future for this team of supremely talented youngsters. Within just a few years, Yugoslavia was in the grip of a brutal civil war, and there are those who think that Boban and his mercurial feet were at the centre of its origins.

***

I can't remember a time when I wasn't a football fan. The first game I can properly recall is Manchester United v Everton in the 1985 FA Cup final. This was a time before 24-hour rolling sports channels with yellow ticker feeds for transfer gossip and other meaningless nonsense. Foreign leagues and players were remote in a way that is unimaginable now, with everything from *La Liga* to the A League just a click or a touch of a smartphone away.

Diego Maradona appeared on my television for a month at the World Cup in Mexico in 1986, then disappeared from my screen in a huge puff of celebratory smoke for another four years. When I next saw him, Argentina, and the rest of the teams at Italia '90, it wasn't he who grabbed my attention, nor was it the West Germans with their relentless dominance, nor Roger Milla and his samba hips wiggling by the corner flag. My attention was taken by another team and another player: Yugoslavia, and in particular Dragan Stojković, who was five feet nine inches of class and talent.

I wanted Maradona to be the Maradona of Mexico '86. To grab games by the scruff of the neck like he did against Belgium, or score goals that were unimaginable to others, like his second in that quarter-final against England. Instead we got only fleeting glimpses of what he was, his dribble and assist for Claudio Caniggia in the last-16 against Brazil possibly the only positive moment of his whole World Cup.

Stojković, though, played with an élan and flair that was missing elsewhere. I watched him with my jaw on the floor. His two goals against Spain in the last-16 were impulsive, spontaneous and intelligent: absolute works of art. But it wasn't just Stojković; his support cast was equally capable. Robert Prosinečki was just as beautiful to watch. Darko Pančev showed on the world stage what he had been able to do for Red Star Belgrade for the previous couple of years.

For English football fans of a certain age, myself included, Italia '90 is looked upon with huge fondness. But as much as the tournament was about Gazza's tears, England's agonising semi-final defeat to the Germans, Cameroon beating Argentina and Rene Higuita's upfield dance for Colombia, Italia '90 was also about a Yugoslavia team that seemed to be maturing towards something great.

By the next World Cup in the USA in 1994, football outside England was beginning to lose its exotic distance. Italian *Serie A* matches were a weekly occurrence on the UK television screens, the Premier League (while still in its infancy) was starting to attract players from all over the world, and the Champions League was becoming richer. By the time France '98 rolled around, the internet had started to take hold of the world and players were no longer strangers to us — almost all of the elements of surprise at a World Cup had gone. The first time I saw that 1990 Yugoslav team with Stojković and Prosinečki, they gave me a moment of glee that is absent from today's familiarity. But I'm glad I had that moment, however fleeting it was — for me and for Yugoslavia itself.

This book documents what happened next. It will provide a background on the bloody wars that ripped Yugoslavia apart, and also the football, which seemed to be intertwined with the country's destruction.

From its alpine north to its drier south, Yugoslavia was a mix of ethnicities, religions and languages. It was perhaps inevitable that these diverse groups would eventually fracture, yet so much of what made Yugoslavia what it was passed from its society and into its football. Nothing I have written down is intended to glamourise any events that happened at this time; the wars were unimaginable in their horror and yet so close to home. Rather, I want to provide an insight into how sport, society and politics are inextricably linked, no matter how much they try to keep apart.

★

CHAPTER ONE
ORIGINS AND EVOLUTION

Football edged its way into what would become Yugoslavia during the latter half of the 19th century. The first documented game took place in 1873 in Rijeka, in what is now Croatia, when a group of British engineers there to construct factories and railways gave locals a demonstration of the beautiful game. The first time that locals formally participated in a game wasn't for another seven years: in 1880, in what was then the part of the Austro-Hungarian Empire but now is the eastern Croatian town of Županja, another group of Brits (foresters this time) were the opposition. In 1887, an exhibition game attended by Queen Victoria's son Alfred, the Duke of Edinburgh, took place in the port city of Zadar, also now in Croatia. It was due to the many British sailors who played football after docking in the area that football began to take hold in the region.

While it wasn't particularly unusual for the travelling British to introduce football to a country (they also introduced it to Macedonia), much of the sport's route to the rest of Yugoslavia came from mainland Europe and countries to its north. Hugo Buli, born in Belgrade in 1875, was a very keen sportsman. While studying in Germany, he played football in Berlin for BFC Germania 1888, one of the oldest German clubs still in existence. Enthused by the sport, Buli brought a ball home with him in May 1896 and introduced the game to his hometown gymnastics club SK Soko, which played its first game close to the historic Nebojša Tower, where the Sava and Danube rivers meet.

In May 1899, Buli co-founded the *Prvo Srpsko društvo za igru loptom* (First Serbian Ball Association). However, football instantly faced stiff competition from more established sports, such as gymnastics and athletics, something that was quickly evident in the lack of assistance and funding the sport received from the authorities. Indeed, those who weren't taken with football would describe it disparagingly as '*jurcati za naduvanim balonom*' ('chasing the inflated balloon') and expounded the values of cultural physical exertions of the *Soko* (Falcon) methods of gymnastics exercise. The older and more conservative elements of society felt football did little to support traditional Serb values. The sport was also hindered by the fact that it was new and thus there was little available equipment; what there was normally sold at an expensive rate.

However, by the early 20th century, younger Serbs were becoming bitten by the football bug in a time-honoured fashion. Games took place in back alleys for hours at a time, with varying interpretations of the rules depending on the players. The educated middle classes also saw football as an appealing pastime. Following in Buli's footsteps, other notable Serb émigrés who imported football to Serbia include Stevan Stefanović, who studied and played amateur football in Switzerland. Stefanović's father owned a canning factory in Belgrade, giving him the financial means to provide the expensive equipment needed to play organised matches. He joined forces with Buli at Soko, forging an early Serbian football powerhouse.

Buli became an integral figure to Serbian football over the following years. However, due to his part-Jewish heritage, he was deported to the notorious Topovske Šupe concentration camp during the German occupation of Yugoslavia in World War II. There he was one of thousands of Jews and Romany to be murdered by the Nazis and their local collaborators. The site of the camp, on the outskirts of Belgrade, is today within walking distance of the city's two clubs, Red Star and Partizan.

Other clubs appeared too in the early years of football in the area. FK Šumadija 1903 was formed in September 1903 by Danilo Stojanović, an engineer in a weapons factory. Stojanović was so versatile that he could play either in goal or on the left wing and he was soon granted time and space within the factory grounds to train a team of his fellow workers, as well as those from a nearby food production facility. They played their first official fixture on the same day that SK Soko played theirs.

SK Soko and FK Šumadija 1903 were the bedrock of things to come in Serbia. In 1905, Anastas Hristodulo, a lawyer and gymnast, translated the laws of the game from German. Until then, each team had played by local rules — Hristodulo's translation facilitated a uniform game for all teams and was key in football's development in Serbia. By the time World War I broke out, the number of clubs in Belgrade alone had reached double figures and the game had spread across the country, with many thousands of regular players.

The origins of football in Bosnia, on the other hand, are blurred. Many accounts state that a British archaeologist Sir Arthur Evans, who spent a significant amount of the late 1870s in Bosnia, wrote in May 1877 that he saw a group of Serb partisans playing football (at the time they were fighting the Ottoman Empire). According to Evans there was no goal, and they were using a ball made out of several caps from their uniforms crammed together.

An alternative version identifies a banker from Mostar named Bernard Lajhner as bringing the first actual football into Bosnia following a trip to Budapest in 1903. Lajhner gave the football to his two sons, Alfred and Oskar, to play with and before long, their friends had joined in too. With no-one to teach them the basics of the game, the children spent most of their time trying to see who could hoof the ball the furthest. The rules of the nascent game were that one team would stand behind a line on the far end of the pitch and points were gained by the opposing team if they could kick the ball across the line from a significant distance away.

The pitch on which these early games were played was in front of barracks occupied by Austro-Hungarian troops. Two of the soldiers watching had played back home and decided to intervene and show Alfred, Oskar and their friends how the game really worked. This small group of friends, along with the two soldiers, founded the first football club in Mostar, and were followed by several other clubs whose members were mainly students, such as *Đački športski klub* (Students Sports Club) and *Hrvatski radnički omladinski klub* (Croatian Workers' Youth Club). It is worth noting that ethnic names were already beginning to take hold at this incredibly early stage of football's development in Bosnia, so much so in fact that, immediately prior to the start of World War I, the Austro-Hungarian authorities banned some clubs with ethnic names.

The war forced the abandonment of many of the pre-Yugoslav leagues. Croatia abandoned its league after only a handful of matches in 1914; indeed HŠK Trgovački were so eager for the season to finish they conceded 22 goals in the two fixtures they managed to play.

Following the end of the war and the creation of the State of Slovenes, Croats and Serbs (soon to be replaced by the Kingdom of Slovenes, Croats and Serbs) football began its seasonal cycles over again. In April 1919, the first united football association, *Jugoslavenski Nogometni Savez*, was set up in the region with four sub-divisions. Attempts had been made at re-establishing clubs during the war, such as Hercegovac Football Club, which consisted of players who had previously played for the now defunct Zrinjski; however, those clubs tended to be short-lived. *Jugoslovenski Sport Klub* became Mostar's first dedicated football club in 1919 and announced themselves with a 19-0 victory over Uskok from Čapljina in south-west Bosnia.

Shortly after, *Radnički sportski klub Velež* (Velež Workers' Sports Club) was founded in Mostar in 1922 by Gojko Vuković and became renowned as a club with a strong socialist ethic; they have long been known as Velež Mostar. Vuković was a committed socialist and long-time member of the Central Committee of the Communist Party of Yugoslavia. He spent three years in prison, as well as a significant period of time under police surveillance, before coming to an untimely end in July 1934 when he fell off a roof he was working on. Zrinjski was also re-founded in 1922, winning the Mostar Championship the following year.

In Croatia, two dominant clubs emerged, HNK Hajduk Split and HŠK Gradanski. The former was founded at the U Fleků, a 15th-century inn located in Prague, taking its name from the Hajduks, who roamed the area of Europe occupied by the Ottoman Empire and were considered outlaws by some and freedom fighters by others. With the initials in the club's name meaning '*hrvatski nogometni klub*' ('Croatian football club') and with the red-and-white *šahovnica* on its club crest, Hajduk made its pro-Croat feelings clear from the beginning. Despite winning their first game against Calcio Spalato 9-0, they were quickly brought back down to earth thanks to a 13-1 drubbing by Slavia Prague. They did take part in the inaugural championship in 1923, set up as a knockout format, but lost 4-3 to SAŠK of Sarajevo in their first and only game.

There was momentum building at the club, however, as they reached the final of the King's Cup in both 1924 (when they also lost in the final of the national championship) and 1925, though they lost both times. It was unquestionably a strong side — in 1924, Yugoslavia played Czechoslovakia in Zagreb and with the exception of goalkeeper Dragutin Fridrih, every player came from Hajduk. The club peaked in the late 1920s, winning the Yugoslav league in 1927 and 1929. They also competed in the inaugural Mitropa Cup, a trophy contested by teams from central Europe, in 1927, though suffered a significant 9-1 aggregate loss to Rapid Wein of Austria. Hajduk's fortunes faltered further and even more dramatically during the 1930s, spending the decade not only trophyless, but also suffering the huge indignity of being forced into a name change, with the 'Croatian' in 'Croatian Football Club' forcibly replaced with 'Yugoslav'.

Zagreb's powerhouse HŠK Gradanski were the league's dominant force prior to World War II. Having beaten Ilirija of Ljubljana in the quarter finals, they progressed to the final of the 1923 Yugoslav championship in Zagreb thanks to a bye in the semi. The two-legged final pitted them against Hajduk's conquerors SAŠK, with a tight 1-1 draw in the first game followed the very next day by a 4-2 victory for Građanski in the second. By the time war broke out in 1939, Građanski had won the Kingdom of Yugoslavia Championship five times and the cup competition twice.

They were a team to be feared by western European giants. During a 1923 tour of Spain, they beat Barcelona 1-0, and thrashed Liverpool 5-1 in Zagreb a few years later. In between, they managed to draw 0-0 against a Brazilian national team that included luminaries such as Leônidas (credited with inventing the bicycle kick) and Waldemar de Brito, whose highly commendable record of 18 goals in as many appearances for his country is perhaps overshadowed by the fact that he was the man who first scouted Pele.

Teams from Croatia and Serbia dominated the Yugoslav league in the years immediately prior to World War II, with no team from any of the other republics getting so much as a look in. As in 1914, the outbreak of war in 1939 brought about a suspension of league competition, though it did not necessarily curtail football within Yugoslavia.

On April 6, 1941, the Axis forces invaded Yugoslavia along several fronts — the Germans attacked south from Austria, with Italian and Hungarian support from either side. The Royal Yugoslav Army capitulated quickly, with terms of surrender being sought as early as April 14 and an unconditional surrender coming into effect on April 18. Even prior to Yugoslavia's surrender, the Independent State of Croatia (NDH) was declared and covered much of Croatia, Bosnia and Slovenia, although it was in effect a German puppet state. The brutal leadership of Ante Pavelić's Ustaše regime enacted racist Nazi legislation against Jews and Roma, but also added their own persecution against Serbs living under their control. Mile Budak, who played a crucial role within the NDH and who was executed after a post-war trial, once claimed that "The movement of the Ustaše is based on faith. For the minorities we have three million bullets. We shall kill one part of the Serbs, expel the second part, and convert to Catholicism the third part of them."

Unbelievably, amid the genocide and brutality there was time for football. A league system was formed and the Independent State of Croatia also became a FIFA member for a short time. Despite only half the league fixtures being completed, HŠK Građanski were declared champions in 1941. The following season, HŠK Concordia Zagreb were champions, beating Građanski 7-5 on aggregate in a final following a multi-group league system. Ironically, for a country run by an ultra-nationalist regime, Concordia had quite a melting pot of players. Coach Bogdan Cuvaj was Croat of Albanian extraction, keeper Zvonko Jazbec was born in Ohio in the US and moved to Croatia when he was four, and striker Slavko Kodrnja's career had taken him to France, Switzerland and Portugal before his second stint at Concordia. Građanski regained the championship in 1943, while the 1944 championships were not completed due to the war — although HAŠK Zagreb were initially declared champions, that decision was revoked in January of 1945. The final season of the league, prior to the reformation of the national Yugoslav league, saw Hajduk break the Zagreb duopoly, triumphing on goal difference ahead of Dinamo, scoring an impressive 51 goals in only 14 games (although a thought must be spared for bottom place FD Jedinstvo Susak who gained only two points in their 14 games and conceded an eye-watering 49 times).

The story of the Split clubs — Hajduk and RNK — under Axis occupation in World War II is an extraordinary one. RNK lost more than 120 personnel throughout the war as they made up a significant proportion of what became known as the First Partisan Squad. They saw military action in August 1941 in the village of Kosuta, where 13 RNK members lost their lives and several more were captured and sentenced to death. Italian rule inside Split itself was equally harsh, with mass arrests and deportations taking place. Among those caught up in the deportations was RNK player Bogdan

Srdelić, who was taken to the island of Lipari, close to Sicily, where he died under torture in April 1942.

Hajduk, meanwhile, refused to play in the Italian league system under the name of AC Spalato following an invitation by Italy; they also refused to take part in the Independent State of Croatia Cup following the city's change of control after Italy's withdrawal from the region. In the spring of 1944, many of the club's players decamped to Josip Tito's headquarters on the island of Vis in the Adriatic Sea to become (according to the club's website at the time of writing) the official club of the anti-fascist movement. Tito was the towering and overarching figure in Yugoslav history. In 1939, he was appointed as the President of the League of Communists of Yugoslavia and following the Axis invasion of Yugoslavia in 1941, Tito led partisans in the resistance of Axis rule. Following the war's conclusion, he was first Prime Minister and then President of Yugoslavia until his death in May 1980. Hajduk played several allied teams, most notably suffering a 7-2 defeat to the British army in Bari in front of an estimated 40,000 people, a huge number given the circumstances of war. The British team featured Stan Cullis of Wolverhampton Wanderers, who had famously refused to participate in a Nazi salute prior to an England vs Germany fixture in 1938 and was dropped from the team, effectively ending his international career as a result.

Hajduk's reputation as a club of resistance was further enhanced internationally as they embarked on a mammoth tour of the Mediterranean, playing 90 games and taking in five countries under the name Hajduk JA ('Yugoslav Army'). Their international efforts were recognised by others and following a fixture in Lebanon, the club were presented with the title of 'Team of Honour of The French Free Republic', an accolade personally authorised by Charles De Gaulle.

World War II also saw the inception of the Croatian national team, who played their first fixture against Switzerland in April 1940, beating them 4-0 in Zagreb. Between Croatia's accession to membership of FIFA and the end of the war, they had played a series of games against Axis countries (as well as another fixture against neutral Switzerland) including a 4-0 win against an Italian team in 1942. Following the end of the war and Croatia's amalgamation into the now Federal People's Republic of Yugoslavia (FPRY), the Croatian football team became dormant until 1990, with the strange exception of a 5-2 win over a touring Indonesian team in 1956.

Although football had a distinctly amateurish feel in post-World War I Serbia, it was clear that the sport was gaining in popularity and required a framework to organise teams into a league system. The Belgrade Football Sub-association (BFS) was formed in March 1920 and included clubs from Serbia, Kosovo and North Macedonia (at the time called South Serbia). The league itself was tinkered with, redeveloped and renamed during the inter-war years, but survived in one format or another until Axis occupation.

SK competed in the Yugoslav First League until World War II. However, following the Axis invasion in 1941, they changed their name to SK 1913 and competed in the short-lived Serbian Football League, a decision which would come back to haunt them many years later. The league itself, which was established by the occupying Nazis, lasted until 1944.

In the aftermath of the war, several clubs suffered retribution at the hands of the victorious Prime Minister Tito for their actions during the conflict. HŠK Zrinjski Mostar, formed in 1905, had since inception been steeped in symbols of Croatian identity, initially wanting to call themselves Croatian Falcon. Eventually, they settled on the Zrinjski forename, taken from the Zrinjski noble family of Croat ethnicity. They fatefully decided to participate in the Independent State of Croatia league and after the end of the war, retribution by the Yugoslav government was swift. Zrinjski were banned outright, an exclusion which lasted until 1992. The actions of Zrinjski during the war were in stark contrast to their cross-town rivals FK Velež Mostar, who saw many former players and fans either lose their lives or be decorated for valour in the struggle to liberate Yugoslavia during the Axis occupation. Following the end of the war, the local municipal authority decided to build Velež a state-of-the-art stadium to replace the dilapidated old ground that they didn't even own. The message was clear and obvious: if you had nailed your colours to the wrong mast during the war, then you should expect no quarter in return.

SK Jugoslavija was another club quickly culled by the Tito regime for perceived collaboration. Jugoslavija's stadium, players and even their red-and-white kit were given to a club formed in early 1945 by a local Serbian United Anti-Fascist Youth League. The club was headed by Slobodan Penezić, who would go on to play a key part in Tito's Yugoslavia as Prime Minister of Serbia and also head of the secret police. Penezić later assisted in the capture of Draža Mihailović, the partisan but factional enemy of Tito. Mihailović was tried and executed by the Tito regime and Penezić was later killed in a car crash, though his wife always suspected foul play. The new club took some time to give themselves a name but after much debate and discussion commenced the 1946/47 season under their new name Red Star Belgrade, and a European football institution was born.

Nevertheless, lengthy wrangling over a name was probably the most straightforward job for the nascent Red Star, who still had to walk the tightrope of Tito's Brotherhood & Unity policy of federalisation (as opposed to a Yugoslav Republic with an emphasis on its own regionality. For example, their original choice of colours — red, white and blue with a star on a red background — had to be quickly dispensed as it bore too close a resemblance to the Republic of Serbia flag. Red and yellow were the colours on the first club crest, though from 1950, white was added too. A minor detail maybe, but even this change had to be handled sensitively as they were the colours of the defunct SK Jugsoslavija. Conflict was already taking its toll and meant that everything in the relatively young sport was imbued with meaning and symbolism, however subtle or accidental it may appear — Red Star, at least, were wise to this.

They were quickly promoted from the Serbian regional leagues into the Yugoslav First League, and by the late 1940s were progressing up the league. A third place finish in their debut 1946/47 season was followed by a fifth place finish. However, successive second places immediately afterwards led to a debut title in 1951, thanks largely to Kosta Tomašević's 16 goals. Tomašević finished his Red Star career three years later with an impressive 76 goals in 110 appearances and the manner of the club's first top-level title success was nothing short of spectacular too. With three games left, they were five points behind Dinamo Zagreb (with two points awarded for a win), yet by the final week Dinamo's lead was down to a single point. On the final weekend of the season, a choking Dinamo played a day earlier than Red Star and this pressure, with their Belgrade rivals not so much breathing as snarling down the back of their necks, saw them limp to a 2-2 draw with BSK Belgrade. To win the championship, Red Star had to beat their cross-city rivals, Partizan. Despite the relatively late formation of both clubs (Partizan were established in October 1945), the two teams had played each other nine times previously, the most recent result being a 6-1 victory for Partizan.

As the game got under way (with both goalkeepers wearing flat caps) it was Red Star who had the early pressure and scored through the tireless Tomašević. A second was added by Todor Živanović to put the game beyond doubt. The players hugged and celebrated their title win on the pitch while the crowd waved newspapers that had been set alight. By the end of the decade, Red Star had won the Yugoslav title a further four times and were the dominant force in Yugoslav football.

Much of this success was down to Aleksandar 'Aca' Obradović, known as Doktor O. Obradović had been a Chetnik resistance fighter in the war and had managed to escape from the notorious Banjica concentration camp. He joined Red Star initially as a physiotherapist, though he eventually rose to become a highly effective administrator for the club via several left-field methods, most notably working out of a local cafe rather than Red Star offices. He was responsible for bringing Vladimir Beara, one of the greatest goalkeepers of his generation from Hajduk Split to Belgrade (upon receiving his Ballon d'Or award in 1963, Soviet goalkeeper Lev Yashin refused to acknowledge himself as the best keeper in the world, stating that

Beara was instead). At this time, players had a seven-day cooling off period following a transfer in case they changed their mind — Obradović simply hid from Beara for that period in a contractual game of cat and mouse, just in case the goalkeeper reneged on the deal.

On another occasion, as he tried to steal a march on his rivals for the signature of a player from FK Spartak Subotica, Obradović drove to where the player was living, bundled him into the car and took him back to Belgrade. It was only on the drive to the capital that Obradović realised that there were two Spartak players living in the building he had driven to and this one, a goalkeeper, was the wrong one. A rather awkward and embarrassing car journey back to the building ensued, but the enduring myth ensures that Obradović is one of those few larger-than-life characters, transcending both pitch and dugout, to retain an honoured status among Red Star and their fans.

A short walk from the Red Star stadium that Obradović did so much to help rebuild, through the affluent, leafy Dedinje neighbourhood, lies the Autokomanda district. The area is dominated by a major road interchange, but it is also the location of the Partizan Stadium, home of Belgrade's other major football club. Partizan's original hierarchy was made up of officers from the Yugoslav People's Army (JNA), including Svetozar Vukmanović, a man who allegedly did nothing while his orthodox priest brother was captured and executed by partisans in May 1945.

Partizan participated in the 1946/47 league, with a team that relied upon the firepower of Stjepan Bobek, a Zagreb native who had previously played for Građanski. Bobek flourished in Belgrade, firing in 121 goals in 198 league matches between 1945 and 1959 and was later voted Partizan's greatest ever player. Partizan won the double in that first league season, finishing five points ahead of Dinamo Zagreb in the league and beating FK Naša Krila Zemun, a club formed by the Yugoslav Air Force, 2-0 in the cup final. The club was managed by Illés Spitz, a Jew from Budapest who had played in the Hungarian and Swiss leagues during a 20-year career. Following the outbreak of World War II, Spitz decided to stay in Yugoslavia where he had been coaching. It was a decision that almost cost him his life. When the country was invaded by Axis forces, the area of Macedonia in which Spitz was living was annexed by Bulgaria. Several clubs in the area, including Spitz's, were amalgamated to form Macedonia Skopje competing in the Bulgarian league system with Spitz staying on as a coach.

As a Jew, however, his position was constantly precarious, and in March 1943, Spitz was escorted to and placed on a train bound for Treblinka concentration camp. Fortunately, the train was stopped in South East Serbia and he was removed by two club officials, Dimitar Gyuzelov and Dimitar Chkatrov, both of whom were denounced after the war as fascists by the Yugoslav government and were shot in a remote location on the edge of Skopje.

The newly-formed leagues soon attracted a large amount of interest as entire populations yearned for a sense of normality to return to their lives following the horrors of the war years. The first post-war championship in Yugoslavia began in September 1945, however, there was little in the way of club representation. Instead, each republic had its own team, as did the army. The clubs began to participate in 1946, with 14 teams taking part including three from Belgrade: Red Star, Partizan and Metalac.

With Spitz in charge of Partizan, they were the initial force to be reckoned with, winning the league in 1947 and 1949. Bobek was particularly prolific for Partizan during this period, scoring 24 goals in 23 games in the 46/47 season, including nine in a 10-1 rout of 14 Oktobar — a feat that had not been beaten by the time the league broke up several decades later. Spitz left Partizan in 1955 after three managerial spells across nine incredible years. As well as the two league titles, he also secured three Yugoslav cups, the first of which, in 1947, was part of a historic double.

Spitz had made Partizan a team to be feared both inside and outside Yugoslavia. His successor, Aleksandar Tomašević, managed the team in the first ever European Cup in the 1955/56 season. Following an 8-5 aggregate victory over Sporting Lisbon, Partizan faced eventual winners Real Madrid in the quarter final. In a fixture that took place on Christmas Day, they were beaten 4-0 at the Santiago Bernabéu by a Madrid team that included the legendary Alfredo Di Stéfano. After a bright start, Partizan gave the ball away in midfield and a left wing cross by Francisco Gento was swept into the net at the near post by the flying Heliodoro Castaño Pedrosa. Castaño doubled the lead following more left-wing trickery by Gento, but Partizan were still in the game and showed touches of what made them so successful in Yugoslavia. A cross fumbled by Juan Alonso in the Madrid goal while under pressure was hoofed off the line just in time by Rafael Lesmes, before confusion in the Partizan defence, with two players going for the same ball allowed Gento to slot in a deserved goal in the bottom right corner. The final insult came in the 70th minute, Di Stéfano receiving the ball centrally, turning beautifully under pressure and rifling the ball past Slavko Stojanović in the Partizan goal.

Down but not out, Partizan nearly managed the impossible in the second leg in a snowy Belgrade the following month. Miloš Milutinović, who had scored four in the home leg of the previous round against Sporting Lisbon, contributed another two in an heroic but ultimately futile 3-0 win. However, this was just the beginning of Partizan's European story and they went on to reach the final of the 1965/66 European Cup. Having beaten Nantes, Werder Bremen and Sparta Prague, Partizan overcame a Manchester United side 2-1 on aggregate in the semi final. Despite their decimation following the Munich tragedy, United were rebuilding and were a formidable force once more and featured Bobby Charlton, Denis Law and Nobby Stiles. Partizan triumphed 2-0 in the first leg at the JNA Stadium with goals by Mustafa Hasanagić and Radoslav Bečejac, Despite Stiles pulling a goal back in the second leg at Old Trafford, it was not enough, and Partizan progressed to the final.

Despite their outstanding victory against the English champions, Partizan were the definite underdogs against five-time European

Cup winners Real Madrid in the final, played at Belgium's Heysel stadium. It was Partizan who went close initially; the rare sight of an indirect free kick inside the Madrid area deflected wide by the defensive wall. The Partizan pressure paid off eventually though; in the 55th minute a deep corner was headed back across the face of goal for an unmarked Velibor Vasović to power a header home. Partizan could dream, albeit for just 15 minutes. In the 70th minute, Madrid's outside-right Amancio was played through and, after turning the last defender left and right, he slotted calmly past Milutin Šoškić in the Partizan goal.

Madrid pressed for a winner and just six minutes later, Fernando Serena controlled a high ball with his head before turning and letting it bounce, unleashing a flying shot from distance into the Partizan net.

Defeat in the final was devastating for Partizan. Many of their star players left for Western Europe; Milutin Šoškić, the goalkeeper in the final, joined 1. FC Köln, full-back Fahrudin Jusufi joined Eintracht Frankfurt, striker Milan Galić joined Standard Liège and goalscorer Vasović was transferred to Ajax. A fallow and trophyless period ensued, and lasted for a decade until the 1975/76 league triumph. Worse still, their biggest rivals Red Star fared much better, winning the league four times.

Spitz was tempted back to Partizan for a fourth, less successful, spell between 1958 and 1960, before moving to newly-promoted FK Vardar, based in Skopje. There, he won the Yugoslav Cup in 1961, enabling the club to play in the 1961-62 European Cup Winners Cup. It was a short-lived venture as Vardar were knocked out in the first round by Dunfermline Athletic of Scotland, who were managed by Jock Stein, then a promising young coach having his first taste of senior management. Sadly, Spitz never saw his team play in Europe. He collapsed and died of a heart attack in the dressing room following a Vardar league game on October 1, 1961. He remained one of the defining figures in Yugoslav football until the break-up of the country, and his legacy lives on at Partizan.

In Bosnia, despite Zrinjski's cull, other teams continued. Velež had suffered heavily during the war and were lavishly rewarded — having lost nearly 80 of their members, nine received the Order of the People's Hero medal for gallantry. Some went the way of Zrinjski too, though — *Muslimanski omladinski športski klub* (Muslim Youth Sports Club — MOŠK) were disbanded for continuing to play during the war years, though ironically, they had several former Velež players in their squad.

In October 1946, SD Torpedo were formed following the amalgamation of two clubs Udarnik and Sloboda (meaning 'Vanguard' and 'Liberty', respectively). The original name was a nod to the Soviet club Torpedo Moscow, but it was soon changed to SDM Sarajevo, and then in 1949 it was changed again to the current name FK Sarajevo. By this time, the club had won the second division under player/manager Miroslav 'Meho' Brozović, a Mostar native who, somewhat surprisingly given this post-war period of nationalistic government clampdown, had represented Croatia during the Axis occupation and was a former Zrinjski player.

However, the post-war years and much of the 1950s were fallow years for both Bosnian teams. In the 1947/48 season, FK Sarajevo replaced their relegated city rivals *Fudbalski klub Željezničar Sarajevo* in the Yugoslav First League. Their own stay in the top flight lasted only a season, after which Bosnia had no top flight representation until the turn of the decade. Indeed, they didn't trouble the podium-makers for another 12 years when Željezničar managed a third-place finish in the 1962/63 season. As an indicator of Bosnia's steady if not spectacular improvement and influence, FK Sarajevo finished fourth the season after.

Despite their league struggles, FK Sarajevo had made tentative steps into European football by the early 1960s. They were one of the clubs representing Yugoslavia in the 1960 Mitropa Cup. That season, the competition was contested by five countries, each of which sent six club teams to compete against each other in two-legged ties. Two points were awarded for a win and one for a draw.

Overall, FK Sarajevo lost 4-2 over two legs to MTK Budapest of Hungary, however aggregate wins for Hajduk Split, Velez Mostar and FK Vojvodina helped along by a 4-4 draw by OFK Beograd ensured Yugoslavia finished second to Hungary. They also came third in their group in the 1962/63 Balkan Cup and second in their group in the Intertoto Cup held in the same year.

These European adventures served Sarajevo well domestically. In the autumn of the 1965/66 season, they defeated the Croatian powerhouses Hajduk and Dinamo at home 3-2 and 2-0, respectively, and by the halfway point of the season, were in second place on 18 points, only five behind Vojvodina at the top of the table. Victory over the leaders early in the second half of the season gave FK fans the hope that a first league title was within their grasp, but a woeful run of form, during which they picked up a measly 12 points in the second half of the season, meant they finished ninth with a negative goal difference.

The following season, there was a grim determination to right what had gone wrong the season before. Sarajevo started with two wins, as well as a draw against Partizan Belgrade, the previous season's European Cup finalists. A 4-0 victory against Romanija featured the 100th and last goal for club legend Asim 'Hase' Ferhatović, who was forced to retire shortly afterwards due to injury in a game against Olimpija. Ferhatović was a Sarajevo native and club legend who had played for FK Sarajevo for 12 years between 1951 and 1963, before moving to Fenerbahce. He immediately realised that he had made a mistake and after just seven games, moved back to FK Sarajevo, where he stayed until his retirement scoring 34 further goals in 84 games. He once declared of his time in Turkey and his sudden move back home: "I'm grateful to them, they were fair and didn't make an issue out of it. I told them I can only play for Sarajevo."

Towards the end of the season, a vital 3-1 away win over closest rivals Dinamo Zagreb meant that FK Sarajevo were in pole position in the title race. However, a defeat to Novi Sad, coupled with Dinamo's win over Radnički, meant that with three games to go, the two teams were tied at the top of the standings, with Partizan Belgrade not too far behind and ready to pounce on any slip. A brace in the next game by the league's eventual top scorer Vahidin Musemić gave FK Sarajevo a win over mid-table Vardar. It was made all the sweeter as both Dinamo and Partizan lost their games, meaning that a win at home against bottom club Čelik, who were already relegated, would make FK Sarajevo champions. Čelik duly obliged, surrendering 5-2 in a rain-soaked game attended by 30,000 fans ready to witness history. The title win was not only the first for FK Sarajevo, but also the first for a Bosnian team in the Yugoslav first division.

By 1967-68, FK Sarajevo were the Yugoslav representatives in the European Cup and were drawn against Manchester United in the second round. With Vojvodina reaching the quarter-final the previous year (losing 2-1 on aggregate to eventual winners Celtic, despite holding a 1-0 lead from the first leg) and Partizan losing in the final to Real Madrid the season before that, Yugoslav football teams were certainly not to be underestimated. Speaking later in his life, United midfielder Paddy Crerand described how in complete contrast to pre-match preparations today, the team flew by plane to Vienna and then had a gruelling five-hour bus journey to get to Sarajevo. Crerand described his opponents as tough and that United were lucky with decisions from officials that day, escaping with a 0-0 draw. The FK Sarajevo website describes the game with a bit more of a declared interest, stating that a goal scored by Musemić was "unjustly disallowed".

The return leg at Old Trafford saw FK Sarajevo facing a Manchester United team including Crerand, George Best, Bobby Charlton and Brian Kidd, underlining that United were not underestimating their opponents. An early reducer by David Sadler on Milenko Bajić set the tone of a physical contest (the pair settled matters with a handshake).

John Aston opened the scoring at the Stretford End in the 11th minute, but the game exploded in the 62nd minute when Best was scythed down by Fahrudin Prljača just outside FK's area. Prljača was sent off and some of his teammates were fortunate not to follow him for manhandling French referee Roger Machin. From the resulting free kick, Bill Foulkes' looping header hit the crossbar and an unmarked Best lashed home the rebound from six yards out.

Again, the FK Sarajevo players were apoplectic, feeling that keeper Svetozar Vujović had previously shepherded the ball out of play. Several of them ran over to the linesman and this time their jostling of officials brought the police and FK Sarajevo management onto the pitch. Commentator Brian Moore felt the game was close to being abandoned, but it continued and the visitors pulled a goal back in the closing moments via a Salih Delalić header. A second, which would have seen them advance on away goals, remained elusive.

At the start of the 1965/66 season, a match-fixing scandal threatened to undo all the positive progress that had been made in Yugoslav football since the war. Željezničar goalkeeper Ratko Planinić turned whistleblower when he revealed to journalist Alija Resulović from the *Večernje Novosti* newspaper that the club had deliberately lost games at the end of the 64/65 season against both Hajduk Split and NK Trešnjevka, so that the clubs could avoid relegation, Planinić had been in goal for both games. Prior to the article going to print, an understandably nervous Resulović wished to corroborate the story and contacted Željezničar President Nusret Mahić for confirmation. An incredulous Mahić claimed that the incident was fictitious and insisted Planinić was making the story up. Mahić went further and actively encouraged Resulović to print the article, stating that the whole story was revenge for Planinić due to him being fined for a previous unrelated breach of club discipline. The fallout was huge — Resulović was immediately contacted by legal bodies as well as being summoned to the headquarters of the Yugoslav FA.

The resulting investigation concluded that there had been collusion between the three clubs and that several club officials, including Mahić, were given lifetime bans from football. The three clubs were punished with relegation, later reduced to a points deduction and Planinić, despite continual accusations that his motivation for his whistleblowing was that he was frustrated by his ongoing contractual negotiations, received no punishment at all.

Arising from the post-war dissolution of HŠK Građanski, Dinamo Zagreb quickly established themselves among the Yugoslav footballing elite and in the period from the end of the war to the late 1950s, won the league three times (an identical record to rivals Hajduk Split) and the Yugoslav Cup once. Yet while they became a truly formidable cup team, winning the Yugoslav Cup four times in the 1960s, they failed to win another league title for almost a quarter of a century, finishing runners-up five times, the last of which was by three points to Red Star in 1969. Their 3-2 victory against Partizan in the 1960 Yugoslav Cup final came courtesy of two goals from Dražan Jerković, who scored a remarkable 96 goals in 142 games for the club. He later became the first manager of the reformed Croatian national team, overseeing a 2-1 win in their first game against the United States, in October 1990 at Dinamo's Maksimir Stadium.

The cup final win over Partizan qualified Dinamo for the following season's Cup Winners' Cup competition where they faced Czechoslovakian side Rudá Hvezda Brno, defeating them 2-0 on aggregate. They eventually reached the semi-final where they faced Italian side Fiorentina who had won Serie A in the 1955/56 season, before coming second in the following four campaigns, as well as losing the 1957 European Cup final 2-0 to Real Madrid. Following their recent Coppa Italia win, *La Viola* were determined to return to trophy-winning ways. They showed little mercy in the first leg in Florence, winning 3-0 thanks to goals from Dino Da Costa, Gianfranco Petris and Brazilian Antoninho. Dinamo knew that they needed a miracle in the return leg in Zagreb and although they were 2-0 up inside 18 minutes thanks to goals from Željko Matuš and Zlatko Haramincic, Fiorentina pulled one back through Petris. Despite the second-leg loss, Fiorentina qualified for the final, where they beat Scottish club Rangers 4-2 on aggregate.

In 1963, Dinamo did reach a final — beating Bayern Munich and Porto in the Inter-City Fairs Cup succumbing to Valencia 2-1 over two legs. Dinamo were learning, however, and in 1967 they made it to the Inter-City Fairs Cup final again, having registered an incredible 5-2 aggregate win against Italian giants Juventus in the quarter-final and an even more astounding 4-3 aggregate win over Eintracht Frankfurt in the semi-final. Despite being 3-0 down after the first leg in West Germany, Dinamo pulled the tie back to 3-3 in a breathtaking match, with Josip Gucmirtl's 87th-minute equaliser forcing the game into extra time. Rudolf Belin was the hero for Dinamo in the 102nd minute, giving them a second shot at European glory.

English giants Leeds United stood in their way. Managed by Don Revie, Leeds boasted an array of talent, including Jack Charlton, Norman Hunter, Billy Bremner and Eddie Gray. Yet Dinamo were playing the first leg of the final at home and a good start could set them up for victory. Marijan Čerček duly gave Dinamo the lead in the 39th minute following a hoofed ball into the Leeds penalty area. In the 59th minute, a right-wing cross from captain Slaven Zambata found the feet of the onrushing Krasnodar Rora who slotted perfectly to the left of Leeds keeper Gary Sprake's goal, leaving an apoplectic Charlton waving his hands in the box angrily at any Leeds player who was unfortunate enough to catch his eye. It was advantage Dinamo after the first leg, and they just needed to keep the score to a minimum in the return match a week later at Elland Road. Despite the introduction of Johnny Giles to the starting line-up, Leeds couldn't find their breakthrough and a goalless draw was enough to give Dinamo their first, and so far, only, major European trophy.

Despite the cup success of the 1960s, the 1970s were a nadir for Dinamo. They achieved two runners-up finishes in the league, firstly in the 1976/77 season to Red Star, followed by an agonising season in 1978/79 where they lost out on goal difference to Hajduk. In Europe, a third-round loss to FC Twente of the Netherlands in the 1970/71 Inter City Fairs Cup was as good as it got. The one bright spot was a 5-4 aggregate win in the Balkans Cup against FC Sportul Studenţesc of Romania in 1976, though this wasn't without drama either: following a 3-1 first leg win at home, they lost 3-2 in Bucharest and only just squeezed over the finishing line.

Not all the Croatian clubs suffered in the 1970s. Hajduk won the first division title four times and the Yugoslav Cup five (including an historic domestic double in the 1973/74 season). In Europe, they reached the semi-finals of the Cup Winners Cup in the 1972/73 season after a British tour of sorts, firstly beating Wrexham 3-3 on the away goals rule in the second round. In the quarter finals, they took on Hibernian and despite losing the first leg 4-2 at Easter Road in Edinburgh, the away goals gave Hajduk hope. Two up inside 23 minutes in the home leg, a second-half own goal by John Blackley gave them outright victory.

In the semi-final, Hajduk faced Leeds United, with some of the old faces from their encounter with Dinamo several years earlier, such as Giles and Hunter, still present. Revie, too, was still in charge. At the time, Hajduk were in something of a slump domestically, finding themselves a mere two points off the bottom of the Yugoslav First Division. As a result, they tried to frustrate Leeds and keep the score tight at Elland Road by employing Dragan Holcer as a sweeper to give them extra defensive cover (Revie later described him as "the best sweeper I've ever seen").

Despite this, Allan Clarke put Leeds ahead after 12 minutes, but thereafter the visitors' defensive approach and time wasting infuriated the home crowd and players. Clarke finally ran out of patience and retaliated against a Mario Baljat challenge. He later said of the incident "my marker had been kicking the hell out of me all night ... I had a rush of blood and kicked him where it hurts. When I got back into the dressing room, I knew I had let my teammates and myself down". Hungarian referee Gyula Emsberger saw things slightly differently: "I sent Clarke off because he kicked a Yugoslav player twice on the thigh."

Despite the first leg deficit, Hajduk were confident of overcoming Leeds back in Yugoslavia, with coach Branko Zebec going so far as to say that "as far as I am concerned, we are home and dry". Leeds however were committed, none more so than Terry Yorath who missed the birth of his daughter Gabby to play in Split. Leeds soaked up vast amounts of Hajduk pressure to go through to the final 1-0 on aggregate, and Johnny Giles was aware of the test they'd been through, saying: "I was happy enough to hear the final whistle. Hajduk are one of the best sides I have played against in Europe." Leeds would go on to lose in the final 1-0 to AC Milan, thanks to a Luciano Chiarugi goal. Hajduk wouldn't make the semi-final of a European competition for another 11 years.

The abundance of European club competitions at this time ensured that it wasn't just the elite Yugoslav clubs that succeeded. *Nogometni klub Čelik Zenica*, a club from Zenica in central Bosnia, won back-to-back Mitropa Cup titles in 1971 and 1972. The competition featured clubs from several Central European Eastern Bloc countries as well as Italy, Switzerland and Austria. Zenica beat Austria Salzburg 3-1 in their first final, before an even more impressive 1-0 aggregate win against Fiorentina in their second. They were also joint winners of the 1975 Intertoto Cup. The format of the competition was 10 groups of four, with no knockout phase, and the trophy was shared with the other teams who finished top of their group, a bizarre scenario, especially as Austrian side FC Linz finished on 12 points, more than any of the other teams.

For the big two in Serbia, the 1970s could not have been a more contrasting decade in European competition. Partizan's best showing was a third round 5-2 aggregate defeat to FC Köln in the 1974/75 UEFA Cup, while Red Star enjoyed a much more impressive few years. They reached the 1970/71 European Cup semi-final, only losing on away goals to Panathinaikos with the score 4-4 on aggregate. A Stevan Ostojić hat-trick in the first leg looked to have given Red Star an unassailable 4-1 lead before the second leg in Athens. The Greeks' only glimmer of hope from the first leg was a 56th-minute goal from Aristidis Kamaras.

Back at Panathinaikos' Apostolos Nikolaidis Stadium a fortnight later under the sun and on the most bobbly of pitches, Antonis Antoniadis put the home side ahead after only two minutes, slotting the ball underneath the onrushing Ratomir Dujković in goal. He doubled the lead from a header early in the second half and as the Greeks raced to retrieve the ball from the back of the net and ran back to the centre circle, the fans knew something special was happening. They didn't have long to wait as Kamaras grabbed a third and the home side held out for a famous victory.

Red Star enjoyed their own famous moment as they reached the quarter final of the European Cup in 1973/74 by beating a Liverpool team containing Ray Clemence, Tommy Smith, Emlyn Hughes, Kevin Keegan, John Toshack and Steve Heighway in the second round. A 2-1 win in Belgrade, thanks to two stunning goals from Slobodan Janković and Vladislav Bogićević, set up the return leg at Anfield.

Red Star began brightly, with Clemence forced into an early save and Jovan Aćimović narrowly missing the top left corner at the Anfield Road end. Keegan then went close with a turning volley that sailed over the Red Star bar and into the Kop. In the second half, Red Star survived some early Liverpool pressure before launching an attack of their own in the 60th minute. Janković picked up the loose ball and fed Vojin Lazarević on the right-hand edge of the area. His shot gave Clemence no chance as it flew into the top right corner of the goal with barely any bend on the shot.

A moment of controversy followed soon afterwards as a Liverpool corner was shanked by a defender high into the air and fell towards a group of players on the penalty spot. Larry Lloyd outjumped three Red Star players and his header fell to Keegan, who was certain he had fired home from six yards. However, the shot was adjudged to have been stopped on the line by Kiril Dojčinovski. Keegan was adamant the ball had crossed the line; replays suggest it didn't.

John Toshack missed several chances for Liverpool and there was at least another last-ditch goal line clearance, as the feeling dawned that it was going to be one of those nights for Liverpool. Lawler managed to lash home an equaliser with seven minutes left to give them hope, but in the 90th minute, Janković put the tie beyond doubt, rocketing a free kick from just outside the Liverpool area past both the wall and Clemence's despairing hands into the net. As the final whistle sounded, some Red Star fans who had been sat among the Liverpool fans ran onto the pitch to greet the players with various banners and flags, while the players themselves formed a line and ran to the Kop to soak up the applause and contemplate their huge achievement.

However, it wasn't to be in the quarter final against Atletico Madrid. Goals from José Eulogio Gárate and Luis Aragonés saw Red Star lose the first leg in Belgrade 2-0, and the second leg at the Vicente Calderón Stadium in Madrid was goalless. However, they were never underestimated by the major European powers, nor were they overawed by English opposition. They faced Arsenal in the third round of the UEFA Cup in the autumn of 1978, where a narrow 1-0 win at the Red Star Stadium was followed by a 1-1 draw at Highbury thanks to a crisp late finish by Dušan Savić in front of the North Bank three minutes from time. Savić became a cult figure in Serbia among fans of Red Star and other clubs alike, perhaps epitomised best in the 1997 Serbian film *The Wounds*, in which the two main protagonists scream his name repeatedly while engaged with a sex worker.

Red Star once again beat English opposition in the following round, in the form of Ron Atkinson's West Bromwich Albion. A Savić goal gave them a 1-0 win in the first leg in Belgrade, with the return in the West Midlands on the most agricultural of pitches. Just before the break, Cyrille Regis pounced on a loose ball some 10 yards away from the Yugoslavs' goal; his turn and volley gave keeper Stojanov no chance. The visitors left it even later than they had at Arsenal: two minutes from time, Miloš Šestić latched on to a bobbling through ball from Slavoljub Muslin, got a lucky ricochet off a despairing sliding defender, and smashed the ball past Tony Godden to book Red Star a place in the semi-finals.

There, they had three German teams for company: Hertha Berlin, MSV Duisburg and Borussia Mönchengladbach. Red Star duly dispatched Hertha on the away goals rule, the tie finishing 2-2 on aggregate. The final was also a two-legged affair with the first leg taking place in Belgrade in front of 90,000 noisy fans. Red Star struck first as defender Muslin collected the ball on the Yugoslavs' right and reached the Mönchengladbach byline before cutting back for Šestić to slot home from close range. The unfortunate Ivan Jurišić ensured that the game went back to Germany all square as his diving headed clearance found only the back of his own net.

The Germans won the second leg thanks to a moment of huge controversy early in the first half, when Jurišić was harshly adjudged to have brought down Mönchengladbach's Danish striker Allan Simonsen in the area. A corner on the Red Star left found Simonsen, who ran at Jurišić and, as he tried to move around the defender, let his trailing leg feel the contact. The penalty was given; to say it was soft is being kind at best. Either as a curse against what was about to happen or an act of derision at the awarding of the penalty, Savić spat on the ball as it sat on the penalty spot waiting to be hit. It made no difference as Simonsen, with incredible coolness in the circumstances, duly scored. Even if Aleksandar Stojanović in goal had gone the right way, he would never have reached the ball. Red Star had their chances, none more so than Muslin's turn and shot from the edge of the box, which floated onto the Mönchengladbach left-hand upright with Wolfgang Kneib nothing more than a spectator. It wasn't to be, however, and it was the German side that emerged victorious.

Speaking to *ESPN* many years later, Cvijetin Blagojevic, who played in the final, said that he felt that Red Star were not a team lacking in self-confidence: "We all had good technique and tactical knowledge ... at that time we played 'tiki-taka' football, the kind Barcelona plays now." Despite their ability, it seemed that Yugoslav football was forever going to be the bridesmaid on the European stage. However, a generation of players that were increasingly unwilling to come second was coming through the ranks.

CHAPTER TWO
FISSURES

Sunday afternoons in Yugoslavia often meant that television stations would broadcast a football match. On May 4, 1980, it was Hajduk Split vs Red Star Belgrade at Split's Stadion Poljud, a ground opened by Josip Tito only a few months before. Hajduk captain Dražen Mužinić later told the *BBC World Service* how he was part of the club delegation that was to meet Tito on the day the stadium opened. They were under instructions that they were to talk to Tito for no longer than 10 minutes, yet such was the leader's warmth and enthusiasm for all things football, and in particular Hajduk, he stayed chatting for three quarters of an hour.

Some 50,000 fans from the two huge clubs crammed into the stadium that Sunday. In the 43rd minute, with the score at 1-1, an official walked onto the pitch and spoke to the referee. The game was immediately stopped and players from both teams lined up in the middle of the pitch, perhaps symbolically intermingled.

Tito had been seriously ill for some time and had been staying at the University Medical Centre in Ljubljana following the amputation of a leg. It was clear that the end was near and many in the stadium would have had an inkling of what had happened to cause the game's stoppage. Hajduk Split President Ante Skataretiko then addressed the crowd and announced that Tito had died and that the match was to be abandoned (it would be replayed a few weeks later). Despite no one being entirely surprised by the news, the reaction was dramatic. Some players held their heads in their hands, others stood, hands on hips, looking dejectedly straight ahead. All Mužinić could hear as he stood in the centre of the pitch was the sound of fans crying and although many of the players felt at a loss as to what they should do next, it felt natural to console each other as most knew one another very well from international duty. Referee Husref Muharemagić was in tears and later recalled that as he looked at the empty presidential boxes, he instantly knew what had happened. Spontaneously, the crowd began to sing a popular Yugoslav oath: *"Druže Tito, mi ti se kunemo"* (Comrade Tito, To You We Give Our Oath.).

Mužinić left Hajduk that same year for an ill-fated spell at Norwich City. Signed by John Bond for what was at the time a club record £300,000, he made just 30 appearances in two years for the Canaries, leading his teammate Justin Fashanu to proclaim: "I don't think we got Mužinić, I reckon we got his milkman". Bond later admitted that he'd never actually seen Mužinić play himself and he was signed purely on the player's reputation.

Speaking in the documentary *Croatia: Defining A Nation*, football journalist Jonathan Wilson commented that after Tito's death, people knew that "Yugoslavia was over". It was his sheer force of personality that had held the country together and with him gone, "it was just a matter of time before things fell apart".

The sense of loss was manifest in the Yugoslav clubs' performances on the European stage — it seemed like Yugoslav clubs had hit a glass ceiling in the 1980s as they struggled to make any real impact. Only two clubs from the country reached the semi-final stage of any competition. The first of these, in 1984, saw Hajduk play Spurs in the UEFA Cup semi-final. Despite winning the first leg in Split 2-1, they lost the tie on away goals after Spurs won the second leg at White Hart Lane thanks to a Micky Hazard 25-yard free kick.

The other semi-final loss came the following year when Željezničar from Sarajevo lost to FC Videoton of Hungary. Videoton won the first leg in Hungary 3-1 thanks to some poor defending and goalkeeping by the visitors.

With a point to prove in the second leg, Željezničar started very well. After five minutes, Edin Bahtić capitalised on confusion in the Videoton defence to put Željezničar ahead. With 18 minutes left, they doubled their lead through another Edin, this time midfielder Ćurić, who pounced on a horrendous error by goalkeeper Péter Disztl to swivel and turn the ball into an empty net. The tie was level on aggregate, but Željezničar were ahead on away goals. Cries of "Yugoslavia" rang out around the stadium, but they were silenced in the 87th minute when the Željezničar left back Mirsad Baljić briefly lost both concentration and his man, allowing József Csuhay to meet a cross in the penalty area and squeeze the ball into the back of the Yugoslavs' net. Ivica Osim, in his first managerial position, simply stood in the dugout with his head in his hands. The only audible noise was the Videoton players, who celebrated as one by the corner flag.

Domestically, the Serbian clubs dominated the 1980s, winning eight titles between them — the big two in Belgrade accounted for seven, with Vojvodina being the other champions. FK Sarajevo and Dinamo Zagreb were the only clubs outside of Serbia to trouble the trophy engravers during this time.

The Yugoslav national team had stumbled following something of a heyday in the 1950s and 1960s. Two World Cup quarter-final appearances in 1954 and 1958 were surpassed in Chile in 1962, when Yugoslavia reached the semi-finals. Petar Radaković's late winner was enough to see them past the West Germans in the quarters but they came unstuck against Czechoslovakia in the semis, losing 3-1, before also slipping to defeat against Chile in the third-place playoff. However, Dražan Jerković's four goals made him the joint Golden Boot winner (with five other players).

The performance should not have been a huge surprise as they had finished runners up in the 1960 European Championships, losing 2-1 in extra time to the Soviet Union. They reached the final again in 1968, beating world champions England along the way, but lost again over two legs to Italy. That was as good as it got — despite reaching the second group stage of the 1974 World Cup, they came last in the 1976 Euros, a tournament they hosted (only four teams qualified at this time), blowing a two-goal lead in the semi-final against West Germany to lose 4-2 after extra time. Group stage losses at major competitions in the early 1980s showed the national team to be at its lowest ebb.

There was, however, a growing feeling that a special generation of younger players was developing at a time when it was desperately needed. In 1984, 16-year-old Davor Šuker made his debut for Nogometni klub Osijek and quickly established for himself a reputation as a formidable youth player. Two years later, Robert Prosinečki made his senior debut for Dinamo Zagreb aged just 17. Born in West Germany to a Croatian father and a Serbian mother, he joined Zagreb from Stuttgarter Kickers, but the Dinamo coach Miroslav Blažević did not believe he had what it took to be a professional and so Prosinečki made his way to Red Star Belgrade.

Young players hungry for their opportunity continued to break through. Macedonian Darko Pančev scored 19 goals in his second season for FK Vardar. Siniša Mihajlović, Igor Stimac and Predrag Mijatović all made professional debuts during this period, as did the player who was arguably the jewel in the crown of this new generation, Zvonimir Boban. He first appeared for Dinamo Zagreb at just 16 and became club captain at just 19. These young players came together at a time when Yugoslav football needed something positive to look towards. That opportunity came in October 1987 at the FIFA World Youth Championships in Chile. Sixteen teams took part including Brazil, East and West Germany, Colombia, Chile, Italy and Scotland. Youngsters hoping to make their mark on the tournament included Colombian keeper Óscar Córdoba and Bulgaria's Emil Kostadinov, as well as East Germany's Matthias Sammer and West Germany's Andreas Möller, who would play together for the united German team in the 1990s.

The Yugoslavia players had already demonstrated their ability in qualification, scoring 21 goals in six matches and topping a group that contained France and Spain. Looking back years later,

Prosinečki said: "We were a new generation who could really play, they really were special players, and this was a springboard." The squad enjoyed significant strength in depth, so much so that Siniša Mihajlović and fellow defender Slaven Bilić were not even picked.

Mihajlović was left behind on the assumption that he would gain more experience playing league football, and the same reasoning was applied to Alen Bokšić and Vladimir Jugović. FIFA's own technical report notes that 10 members of the squad that qualified were eligible for military service "and were not available to the association". The Yugoslav FA was open in its disregard for the tournament and freely stated that they were, according to Jonathan Wilson in Behind The Curtain, "sending a team only to fulfil their obligation to FIFA". They refused to fund any journalist travelling to the tournament to cover the team. Toma Mihajlović, the only one who did travel, did so because he wanted to explore the Yugoslav expatriate community within Chile, rather than cover the football. He felt that the three group games would be played without any expectation, and the players would jet home again. However, once in Chile, the players found a hedonistic cocktail of girls, hotels and a receptive expatriate Yugoslav community — reasons enough to stay. Mihajlović stated that while the players did not drink when socialising, they had a good time and were often out until the early hours of the morning.

Despite their unexpected social schedule, the players themselves certainly hadn't travelled just to make up numbers. They were well coached, knew their roles within the 4-3-3 line-up (though this changed to 4-4-2 in the final) and what positions to take up when not in possession. They could flit between zonal and man-to-man marking, and tactically, they revolved around transitions in play, with the defence breaking up opposition attacks before releasing the midfield (usually Igor Štimac, Boban and Zoran Mijucić) with short passes before they themselves progressed forwards to find the interchanging myriad of talent that they had up front, namely Predrag Mijatović, Šuker and Prosinečki.

Yugoslavia kicked off the tournament against their Chilean hosts on a day so wet that the opening ceremony had to be cancelled. In the 14th minute, Boban opened the scoring in the most bizarre circumstances. A Chilean defender trying to turn with the ball in his own area was robbed of possession. The ball fell to Boban who side-footed past the advancing goalkeeper only for a defender to clear it off the line. The ball fell kindly back to Boban who managed to head the ball past the prostrate defender and into the net. The home crowd was stunned into silence as Boban wheeled away and leapt into the air in celebration.

Chile equalised within three minutes, but Stimac grabbed a second for Yugoslavia just two minutes after that. A second-half brace from Šuker extended Yugoslavia's lead and they ran out 4-2 winners. Another four goals in each of their games against Australia and Togo saw them easily qualify as group winners. The team were beginning to enjoy themselves and the method of Yugoslavia's qualification meant that they had managed to stay in Santiago for the rest of the tournament. Good news for those who enjoyed the delights of the capital, particularly Štimac, who had met Miss Chile on a night out that threatened to derail the whole campaign.

Stimac had received an invitation to a party prior to the semi-final and had taken Boban with him, where they both met the beauty queen and a friend. Both players were enjoying themselves a little too much to return to the hotel. When they finally did make it back, it was 6am and a furious Mirko Jozić was waiting for them. The manager told both players that they were to be expelled from the squad and to pack their bags for the return trip to Yugoslavia. The other players, unhappy at the prospect of losing two star players and perhaps more importantly, their friends, told Jozić that if Boban and Štimac did not play in the semi-final, then neither would they. Faced with no alternative to quell the player rebellion, Jozić relented, reinstating his two wayward players.

The team's togetherness and unity continued to propel them through the tournament, in evidence again when Red Star tried to recall Prosinečki for a European fixture against Club Brugge. The players vehemently protested to FIFA President João Havelange and Prosinečki was allowed to stay. He rewarded his teammates' loyalty by scoring the winning goal against Brazil in the quarter finals. His last-minute free kick was later voted goal of the tournament, though whether Brazilian Havelange appreciated the irony, it's hard to say.

Štimac and Šuker scored the goals that saw Yugoslavia overcome East Germany 2-1 in the semi-final and set up a final against West Germany, with Boban the hero at the last. The squad stayed in Chile for the next two days to celebrate both the victory and Robert Jarni's birthday — among those invited was the dentist who treated Dubravko Pavličić after he had two teeth knocked out following a clash with Matthias Sammer in the semi-final.

In hindsight, it's perhaps no surprise that Yugoslavia won this competition, given the careers those in the squad went on to have. Prosinečki was also awarded the Golden Ball for best player and FIFA's post-tournament technical report stated that "their results truly reflect the tremendous technical skills of the Yugoslavian players". Speaking to Simon Kuper in 2021 on a Zoom call titled *Football and the Collapse of Yugoslavia* for the website *pandemoniumu.com*, Boban recalls the moment of triumph and the feeling of solidarity: "I would do everything for my teammates, for my friends, which we remained all our lives. Despite the political facts and historical tragedies, the war and everything."

Not everything about representing Yugoslavia was as triumphantly glorious as it may superficially appear. In the documentary *Croatia: Defining A Nation*, Slaven Bilić explained how because of his father, the young player's path to representing his country was blocked. Bilić's father Ivan was an academic in Split who fell foul of the Yugoslav authorities: "We were labelled as Croatian extremists," explained the former defender, who was unaware of the political situation at the time. While acknowledging that he was not the greatest defender, Bilić knew he was good, and had a chance, but waited for a call-up that sadly never came. One day, a manager spoke to the young Bilić to explain "your family is labelled". "It was proof," Bilić added, "you can't separate football from politics".

Just as Yugoslavia's fortunes were changing on the pitch, off-field tensions were increasing. The situation was not helped by Serbian President Slobodan Milošević and his hugely provocative Gazimestan speech, where he invoked a Serbian sense of "betrayal" which "led the Serbian people and Serbia into agony". Betrayal by whom was not clear, but maybe that was the point. All Milošević needed to do was to remind Serbs of the glorious defeat of the Battle of Kosovo and make them feel downtrodden to exploit their support.

By way of ultra groups, fans were becoming increasingly politically vocal too. The most infamous of these were Red Star Belgrade's Delije and Dinamo Zagreb's Bad Blue Boys, known respectively for their incredibly pro-Serb and pro-Croat sympathies, respectively. In February 1990, Dinamo were playing a game in Vojvodina when the local Red Firm ultras became involved in altercations with the Bad Blue Boys. Though this mainly amounted to stealing each other's flags and tifo, there was a lengthy delay during the game to wait for the effects of pyrotechnics to disperse away from the pitch. Hajduk Split fans were also said to have burnt the Yugoslav national flag in a game against Partizan, whose players had to flee from the pitch.

One leader of the Delije, speaking to The Observer in 2004, said that from as early as the 1970s, the group were both anti-Communist and pro-nationalist and drew on inspiration from fan groups of Italian and English teams. And although in those early days, fan violence was rare, it wasn't unheard of. In 1978, Partizan fans rioted at a railway station after their train was stopped by police; they later went on to ransack the town of Sid.

There was a by-now infamous clash between the Delije and the Bad Blue Boys in May 1990 at Dinamo's Maksimir stadium in Zagreb. The match came just after the first Croatian multi-party elections for a generation or more, where the Croatian

Democratic Union (HDZ), led by Franjo Tudman, won over half the seats available.

Prior to the game, fans of both sides in the stadium sang songs deriding each other, as well as various aspects of Croatia and Serbia: "Serbian gypsies" came the chant from the Dinamo fans, with "Serbia all the way to Zagreb" the retort from the Red Star end. There had also been reports of the Delije causing problems for the citizens of Zagreb prior to the match and there was an air of inevitability to the events that were about to unfold. Fans of both sides were interviewed by television crews, including one wearing a flat cap emblazoned with a Union Jack. Both sets of ultras faced each other across the pitch and there was also a heavy police presence. Some Red Star fans began pulling down the advertising hoardings behind them which were hung flimsily to railings; after several of these had been torn apart, they began making their way en masse to the tier above where they had previously been stood. Once there, they began tearing up seats and using them as missiles to hurl at Dinamo fans, who in turn threw them back. The Delije then advanced towards the Dinamo fans and badly beat any who were unable to escape.

By this point, Dinamo players had begun to congregate at that end of the pitch to both observe events as they were unfolding and appeal to the authorities to intervene, with Boban having to be led away to safety. As both sets of fans continued to throw seats at each other, Dinamo fans ran back along the terrace to try and come to the aid of their stricken colleagues. The flow of these attacks occurred in waves as one side went after the other and then vice versa, with any individuals lagging too far behind the retreat becoming isolated and then horrifically beaten by those they were trying to escape from.

Bad Blue Boys in the terraces opposite looked on, appalled. Some decided to scale the fencing and take to the running track that separated the pitch from the fans. They made their way to the opposite end of the ground and began stealing items of the Red Star tifo, either to take as trophies or maybe to distract the Delije enough to let other Dinamo fans escape. The baton-wielding police, however, noticed and were merciless in their treatment of any fans that they managed to catch. Other Dinamo supporters, kept on the terraces by police, occupied themselves by throwing flares at the running track. At this point, players and staff were still on the pitch and, in a surreal attempt at keeping the peace, the PA was pumping generic Euro pop music from the speakers.

By this time, Dinamo fans were on the pitch, desperately trying to make their way back to the home fans' section of the ground. The slowest were caught and then beaten by police. Remarkably, several players on the pitch tried to comfort or protect injured fans lying on the ground. It's at this point that possibly the most iconic moment of the whole riot occurs. Boban, who had been attending to a fan with a head injury, walked to another fan who was lying on the ground and was trying to stand up. The available footage briefly cuts away, then returns to Boban, who appears to be running away from a group of police, before turning around, leaping into the air and aiming a karate kick at one of them. He then aims a punch at another. Boban was immediately protected by a group of fans while police looked for him, and a teammate tried to intervene.

Police back-up arrived in the form of water cannon vehicles, which were driven onto the running track at the edge of the pitch. They quickly became a target for rock-throwing Dinamo fans, who now poured out from the terraces. One tried to smash the windscreen of one of the trucks with a pole. This was too much for the driver, who had been trying to slowly back away from the fans. Now he accelerated, scattering the Dinamo fans, who began to make their way back to the terraces. That left only a few fans on the pitch — mainly those helping injured friends — as well as some police acting as a barrier between the two groups.

Those police then became a target for Dinamo fans in the terracing by the halfway line who, in response to police aiming smoke bombs at the Dinamo fans behind the left-hand goal, threw flares in their direction. This was following a brief intervention by the one remaining water cannon towards the fans on the far side of the pitch, a lull seemed to envelope the stadium as fans in the terraces shielded their eyes from the sun while trying to make out what was happening — or might be about to happen — next. It didn't last long, as small groups of Dinamo fans waving either Croatian flags or Yugoslav flags with the star torn out, paraded onto the pitch. The police responded by firing smoke bombs onto the grass to try to disperse fans, a game of cat and mouse that continued for some time until the police finally made their way into the Dinamo terrace behind the goal to force out any straggling fans. At the opposite end of the ground, Red Star fans in the upper tier also began to make their way out of the stadium.

It was now early evening and while most fans had left the ground, some remained on the pitch. Some Dinamo fans managed to tie an enormous flag around either post of one goal while others threw objects at police sheltered behind a water cannon. Those who had left, were still gathered outside the stadium, throwing flares and creating more disturbances.

Some have claimed that the events of this day marked the start of Croatia's war for independence, and there is a plaque outside the Maksimir that reads: "to all the supporters of Dinamo, for whom the war began on the 13 May 1990 and ended with the laying down of their lives at the altar of the Croatian homeland". Some go further, christening Boban's kick as 'The Kick That Started the War'. However, this seems little more than nationalist romanticism and is something Croatian academic Dario Brentin dismissed as 'nonsense' when I spoke to him about the events. Brentin believes that to suggest that the war started that day is nothing more than a "mythologised narrative that has been established throughout the 1990s" and that it was more a symptom of Yugoslavia as a disintegrating state than a cause of something greater.

Boban himself, described by author Simon Kuper as a "romantic nationalist", later said of the events at the Maksimir stadium: "Here I was, a public face prepared to risk his life, career, and everything that fame could have brought, all because of one ideal, one cause;

the Croatian cause". A man proud of his heritage, he once stated that Croatia was the reason he lived and he was ready to die for the country.

Boban continued playing for Yugoslavia until 1991 — his seventh and final appearance coming against the Faroe Islands in May of that year, during which he scored his only goal for the country. While Brentin feels that Boban was the acceptable face of Croatian nationalism — a gifted footballer, intelligent, articulate and learned (Boban had written a thesis on Croatian history), he argues that his role has been "over exaggerated".

Talking to Kuper about his nascent nationalist beliefs, Boban recalls that in his childhood he was not asking himself particular questions about his nationality. However, by his adolescence, "certain questions came" regarding both freedom and freedom of expression, as well as those of Croatian self-determination. Boban stated that his family, as far back as his grandparents and maybe before, held these same views and were unable to express them either. With this background it's easy to see why Boban felt the way he did when he saw Dinamo fans being assaulted by the Yugoslav police.

That's not to say that Boban did not feel Yugoslav. He describes the under-20 win in Chile to Kuper as "one of the most beautiful moments in my career". And telling Kuper his version of events from that day at Maksimir, Boban acknowledges that he was in a position of privilege to be able to react the way he did; "I had the number ten on my back and I was a star", before stating that he was reacting to what he perceived to be the injustice being meted out to Dinamo fans by the police. Having made his way off the pitch, he found himself in the Red Star dressing room, many of whom he knew from representing Yugoslavia and were sympathetic to his actions. He was also at pains to state that his actions were not anti-Serb either, saying instead that "it was an act against the regime for freedom"

Boban was suspended by the Yugoslav FA for six months following the incident. Several years later, the policeman on the receiving end of perhaps the most famous karate kick in Yugoslav history was tracked down. He was a Bosniak called Refik Ahmetović. Ahmetović had been due a day off on the day in question, but his boss had telephoned him and asked him to work, giving him the specific task of looking after the Red Star keeper Stevan Stojanović. Speaking of the events many years later, Ahmetović recalled how he had dropped his helmet and was picking it up when he saw Boban approaching. The next thing he felt was a knee to his ribs. Urged by colleagues to use the loaded gun he was carrying, and thankfully refusing to do so, he instead met Boban a couple of days later in a cafe close to the stadium. Speaking to the *Mondo.ba* website, Ahmetović explained; "We went to look for him, again I was decisive that they didn't beat him. We went to Maksimir in a day or two and found him. There were five or six of us who were well armed and well prepared. They tell me ' whatever you say, we'll do'." Again encouraged by his seemingly ever-vengeful colleagues to "iron him out" a bit, Ahmetović instead had a coffee and a chat with Boban about what happened. Ahmetović returned to Bosnia to carry on his police work, before later retiring and becoming a driving instructor.

The other main protagonist of the riot cast a long shadow across the wars: Željko Ražnatović, better known as Arkan. Arkan was born in April 1952 in the Slovene town of Brežice, on the banks of the Sava river close to the border with Croatia. His father was Veljko Ražnatović, a colonel in the Yugoslav air force and a former partisan in World War II. The family moved across Yugoslavia before Željko finally settled in a job in Belgrade. When he failed to fulfil his early ambitions of becoming a pilot like his father, Arkan fell into petty crime as a teenager, spending time in juvenile custody for stealing purses. His father then sent him to the Montenegrin coast to join the navy, but Arkan had other ideas and aged just 15, he travelled to Paris in 1967. However, he was arrested there in 1969 and deported to Yugoslavia, where he was convicted of several burglaries and sentenced to three years in a detention centre.

Arkan moved to western Europe in the early 1970s and in the company of other Yugoslav career criminals committed robberies in several countries. He amassed warrants or convictions in seven European countries, from Italy to Scandinavia, and was jailed in Belgium and the Netherlands, escaping from prison in both. By his early 30s, he had returned to Yugoslavia and following a bank robbery in Zagreb, two policemen turned up at his mother's house to question Arkan. He wasn't home at the time but when he returned a short while later, he shot and injured both officers. Arkan was arrested, but released only a couple of days later, with many believing this indicative of the fact he was enjoying some sort of institutional protection. Living a visibly extravagant lifestyle of casinos and expensive cars, he had become a man to fear.

He ingratiated himself with the Delije too, organising tickets, travel and accommodation for its members. He also saw what they could become — a disciplined group of men who, if directed properly, could become feared on the terraces and, given the prevailing wind of Yugoslav politics, elsewhere too. "They're noisy, they like to joke about, I stopped all that in one go," he once said of the Delije, adding: "I made them cut their hair regularly, not drink. The way it should be".

However, Arkan shouldn't be thought of as an Ultra leader in the traditional sense, argues Dario Brentin. Rather he was used to some extent by Yugoslav security forces to try and get an insight into and an element of control over a group of men who were at this point unreachable to authorities. At games, Arkan was more often seen wearing a suit and sitting with club officials than mixing with the grass roots of Red Star support on the terraces.

Following the events at Maksimir, Arkan formed the Serb Volunteer Guard (SDG). More commonly known as the Tigers, they included large numbers of Red Star's Delije who had been present at the stadium and their role was to support other units and paramilitaries during the Yugoslav wars. However, Dr Richard Mills, Associate Professor in Modern European History at the University of East Anglia, told me that despite the Delije making up the majority of the membership, they were by no means the only ones. Arkan was a hugely powerful individual within the state at the time and his reach extended well beyond the terraces of Red Star, especially given its standing as a multi-sports club. Nor was the membership solely drawn from Red Star — the Tigers also counted Partizan fans among their ranks and other sections of Yugoslav society beyond sports fans were represented too.

I asked Red Star fan Uros Popovic how supporters of the club feel about Arkan now who replied: "I'm sure there are those who remember him fondly ... but I think for most they consider him a gangster, because he was a gangster."

The author James Montague also told me that Maksimir and Arkan are "not really" still eulogised by Red Star fans, despite there still being "a war mythology that they will give everything to their country if called upon and they're very proud of that". Those Montague has spoken to, many of whom are his close friends, are also at pains to stress that Red Star, the club and its fans are so much more than Arkan and the events of Maksimir. In fact, many older members of the Delije told Montague that they weren't at Maksimir the day of the riot, they were at the memorial for a World War II partisan elsewhere. In Belgrade and at many other clubs, they still have memorials for fans who fought and died in the Yugoslav wars.

Despite the claims that the riot at Maksimir kickstarted the Croatian war, it did not actually begin for another 10 months. In the intervening period, the football continued. That season, Dinamo finished in second place, nine points behind Red Star. Croatian and Slovene clubs competed in the Yugoslav league the following season as well, with Dinamo again coming second to Red Star. There were still more cases of crowd violence however, notably during the Hajduk Split's home game against Partizan Belgrade, when home fans invaded the pitch mid-game, forcing the players off (Partizan were winning 2-0 at the time). The Yugoslav flag flying on one of the stadium's three flagpoles was set alight, while a Croatian flag was raised next to it. Though there seemed to be less violence than at Maksimir, the point made by the fans was clear. Dr Richard Mills believes Maksimir has become "something it never really was at the time" and was one of several incidents such as the Split-Belgrade confrontation which accompanied multiple other low-level instances of hooliganism that were common in Yugoslavia at the time.

Just over a year after the riot at Maksimir, Dinamo hosted Red Star again, in what would be their last meeting in the Yugoslav league. It was something of a dead rubber — Red Star were already champions and Dinamo had qualified for the UEFA Cup -and so the game was played out a lot more peacefully than the previous season, despite there being sections of the ground where large šahovnica (Croatian) flags were noticeable. Despite a brace from the ever-prolific Darko Pančev. Dinamo ran out 3-2 winners.

Robert Prosinečki later said that Red Star let Dinamo win the game, a claim backed up by Ljupko Petrović, who was Red Star coach at the time. There was no pre-match agreement between the teams to throw the game, Red Star simply recognised that the developing political situation, coupled with the events of the previous meeting at the Maksimir and the fact that Croatian president Franjo Tuđman was in the crowd, meant they couldn't win.

Watching footage of the game, it's hard to tell. Petrović, who would be ejected from the dugout during the second half, complained that Dinamo's first goal came from a penalty awarded following a dive by Šuker. But it seems clear enough that, as the cross comes into the area from the left, the Croat is pushed in his back by his marker. While there isn't a huge amount of contact, it definitely comes under the "seen them given" category. Red Star are then sloppy in defence, giving away both free kicks and the ball and presenting Dinamo strikers with chances to score. What's more, for every sloppy mistake or misplaced pass there was a good save or well-timed tackle and so if there was a collective decision to throw the game by Red Star, it seemed not everyone had got the message.

The Yugoslavian national team failed to qualify for Euro 88, held in West Germany, losing twice to England in qualifying and coming second in a group in which only the winners were guaranteed a place at the finals. They did, however, make easy work of qualification for the 1990 World Cup, with only Spain outscoring them in UEFA qualifying. But the squad that headed to Italy that summer looked very different to the under-20 team that seemed to have the world at their feet in 1987 - Boban was banned from the tournament following the events at Maksimir, and only a handful of his teammates from that victorious team had progressed to the senior national squad. Bosnian Zlatko Vujović, who was a striker for Paris Saint-Germain, was the Yugoslavia captain, but the star player was undoubtedly the hugely talented midfielder Dragan Stojković, who that summer left Red Star for Marseille.

Yugoslavia were drawn in Group D and needed to be at their best if they were to qualify. They faced excellent opposition in West Germany and Colombia, with the United Arab Emirates making up the numbers. Yugoslavia faced eventual champions West Germany in their first game at the San Siro in Milan and were soundly beaten 4-1, with Lothar Matthäus scoring two beautiful goals on his home ground. Fellow Inter player Jürgen Klinsmann, and Rudi Völler scored the other two, with Davor Jozić replying for Yugoslavia.

The team's second game four days later was against a Colombia side who boasted Andrés Escobar, Freddy Rincón and Carlos Valderrama. The game was settled by a stunning chest, turn and volley from the edge of the area by Jozić. Four goals in the final group game against the UAE, including two for Pančev, saw Yugoslavia qualify in second place and into the knockout phase where they played Spain.

Although Spain were not yet the force they would become, they were still a team not to be taken lightly. They had topped Group E, which included Uruguay and Belgium, and both sides were full of confidence as they took to the field in Verona. Yugoslavia opened the scoring in the 78th minute when Stojković met a cross, but instead of choosing the obvious option of volleying the ball from about eight yards out, he instead killed the ball stone dead, taking the sliding defender trying to block the expected shot out of the game, before coolly finishing. Spain equalised just six minutes later, sending the game into extra time. The match was decided by another piece of Stojković skill when he whipped a 25-yard free kick past Míchel in the far left of the Spanish wall and into the corner of Andoni Zubizarreta's goal.

Yugoslavia were in the quarter-finals, where they met reigning champions Argentina, who despite their status had underwhelmed the tournament to that point. On a beautiful late afternoon in Florence, the two sides met on a fantastically striped pitch, but the game failed to live up to the setting and was goalless after extra time, which meant it headed to penalties.

José Serrizuela converted the first spot kick for Argentina before Stojković strode up for Yugoslavia. He had arguably been their player of the tournament and largely responsible for them getting so far. However, he smashed his penalty against the crossbar and Yugoslavia were already playing catch up. Jorge Burruchaga and Prosinečki then successfully converted their penalties, before of all people Diego Maradona had a tame side-footed attempt comfortably saved by Tomislav Ivković low to his right. Dejan Savićević easily converted his penalty to make the score 2-2 and when Pedro Troglio missed, Yugoslavia were on the brink of a World Cup semi-final. Dragoljub Brnović took the potential decider, but his run up appeared less confident with each step he took, and his tame shot was easily saved by Sergio Goycochea. Gustavo Dezotti then dispatched his effort to put Argentina 3-2 ahead, which meant Faruk Hadžibegić had to score. He struck the ball to goalkeeper's left at shoulder height, but had telegraphed his effort and Goycochea saved two-handed. Yugoslavia were out. One thing that was evident at Italia '90 was despite the nationalist sentiment at the time, there was significant Yugoslav support at the tournament as demonstrated by the number of Yugoslav flags flown by fans at matches.

Yugoslavia had arrived at the World Cup with Red Star Belgrade as league champions, finishing nine points clear of closest rivals Dinamo Zagreb and advancing to the following season's

European Cup. Once there, they beat Swiss side Grasshoppers in the first round — an excellent 4-1 win in Zürich, with a large number of fans, replete with both Serbian and Yugoslav flags, travelling from Belgrade for the game. In the second round, Red Star swatted Scottish champions Rangers aside with equal aplomb, winning 3-0 at a Marakana fantastically ordained with flares, fireworks and tifo.

Red Star were simply wonderful to watch against Rangers, spurred on by the huge noise created by the home fans and with Prosinečki at the centre of everything. He was instrumental in the first goal, playing in right-back Duško Radinović whose cross was sliced into the net by Rangers' John Brown. Red Star's second arrived in the 65th minute when Prosinečki managed to curl an audacious 20-yard free kick past the six-man wall and beyond Chris Woods' dive, when a cross was the more obvious choice. Pančev grabbed a third soon afterwards. Although the 3-0 doesn't look like a rout on paper, it is clear watching the game back that Red Star demolished their Scottish visitors. A 5-1 aggregate win over Dynamo Dresden led to a semi-final against European royalty Bayern Munich.

Bayern had won the *Bundesliga* the previous season by six points, but they were struggling and the two teams met in the midst of a dreadful run of results for the Germans. They had lost what would later prove to be a defining game against Kaiserslautern and then suffered another 1-0 defeat, this time to Fortuna Düsseldorf. This was, however, still a Bayern team packed with huge names such as Stefan Reuter, Jürgen Kohler, Brian Laudrup and top scorer Roland Wohlfarth.

In the first leg at the Olympiastadion, the Germans took the lead after 23 minutes through Wohlfarth, who latched on to a subtle backheel to loft the ball over the onrushing Stojanović. Just before the break, Pančev slid in at the far post to equalise for Red Star. With 20 minutes remaining Savićević made a lung-busting run, easily surging past Kohler before slotting the ball home past Raimond Aumann in the Bayern goal. Draws against Borussia Mönchengladbach and Werder Bremen in the league prior to the second leg showed that

Bayern were still out of form, something for Red Star to exploit in Belgrade.

The extraordinary scene of pyrotechnic mania prior to the game surprised even the Red Star players. Pančev later claimed that "it was like the Marakana was on fire"; Siniša Mihajlović too believed that the cauldron-like atmosphere had unnerved Bayern. The game started positively for Red Star. After 24 minutes, a Mihajlović free kick from distance found its way into the bottom corner of Aumann's goal putting the Yugoslavs 3-1 ahead on aggregate. However, the tie was turned on its head in five second-half minutes. With just under half an hour to play, a Bayern free kick squirmed its way awkwardly through the hands and underneath the body of a distraught Stojanović in goal. Worse followed as Red Star failed to deal with a cross and an unmarked Manfred Bender was able to knock the ball into the net.

Extra time beckoned. But, in the final minute, Prosinečki made a run into the left of Bayern's area before laying the ball back to Mihajlović who crossed. Klaus Augenthaler attempted to clear the ball but instead sliced it high in the air and backwards towards the Bayern goal. Aumann realised the danger but was flat-footed and could only dive in vain as the ball looped over his outstretched arm. Augenthaler sat disconsolately on the ground while the home players and fans celebrated wildly. Red Star, against a giant of an opponent and in a country that was tearing itself apart, were through to the European Cup final. It was a huge slice of fortune that brought Red Star the winning goal, but Mihajlović felt that the luck was deserved owing to the team's performance over the two legs, and it is hard to disagree with him.

Their opponents in the final in late May would be French champions Marseille, who were in the middle of a run of four consecutive domestic titles and whose striker Jean-Pierre Papin would lead the *Ligue 1* scoring charts for five straight seasons. Stopping Papin was only one part of the problem for Red Star, they also had to nullify the threat of Chris Waddle, Abedi Pele, and their own former protege Stojković. Once that was done, they then had to somehow find a way past Basile Boli in defence. Years later, Mihajlović spoke about the Red Star tactics, detailing how their coach Petrović told his team that owing to Marseille's superior attacking prowess, Red Star should never expose themselves by attacking or the game would be lost. In effect, the instruction from Petrović to his team was that should they get the ball from Marseille, they should give it straight back again.

The build up to the game wasn't smooth for Red Star. The squad were placed in a state of semi-isolation away from loved ones, yet there was somehow room for former players, staff and even celebrities to make an appearance — hardly ideal preparation.

On the evening of the game at the Stadio San Nicola in Bari, British commentator Barry Davies, maybe aware of the growing tensions in Yugoslavia, emphasised the diverse ethnic mix of the Red Star team, stating on the live BBC1 transmission that "in these days of problems for Yugoslavia, it is worth noting that the leading team from the capital of Serbia has four Serbs; two from Montenegro; two from Macedonia; one born in Serbia but brought up in Romania; one born in Germany of mixed Serb and Croat parentage and one Muslim from the border of Montenegro and Bosnia". Speaking about the game later, Prosinečki suggested that he felt cut off from events on the ground in Yugoslavia, that almost because he was a sportsman, he had to focus on what he did best, unable to control anything else. Siniša Mihajlović, who had suffered personally in the fighting in and around Vukovar, felt the strain of his time away from the war — a few snatched hours at training, as well as during matches, were the only times he could isolate himself from the outside world. Despite having Croatian Prosinečki and mixed-heritage Mihajlović on the pitch, any talk of Red Star being a melting pot of diverse ethnicities on the pitch wasn't reflected among the travelling support. At one point during the final, a huge Serb flag was unfurled by the Red Star fans, displaying an obvious message that would not have been missed by those of different ethnicities watching at home.

Red Star fan Uros Popovic was brought up in Montenegro, close to the Croatian border, but he cannot remember a time when he was not a supporter of the club, despite the attempts of some Croats to make him a Hajduk fan in his youth. In his neighbourhood at the time of the final, most people were Montenegrin and Serb, with a smattering of Croats. Despite the mixed ethnicities and footballing allegiances, many were cheering on Red Star. This would have been reflected in other parts of the country too — Yugoslavia was a huge melting pot of ethnicities and within Croatia and Bosnia there was a significant number of Serbs who would have been cheering on Red Star. Dr Richard Mills mentions in his paper *It All Ended In An Unsporting Way: Serbian Football And The Disintegration Of Yugoslavia, 1989-2006* that a Serbian newspaper based in Croatia stated that "For Serbs from Croatia, Red Star is practically a part of their national identity! Until recently they did not dare to say aloud what they were by nationality, but they could say who they supported — always!".

I spoke with Dr Mills about the impact of the 1991 European Cup triumph on those who would maybe not immediately consider themselves Red Star fans. He stated that the win was "in many respects an all-Yugoslav victory". The Red Star team itself was multi-ethnic. As well as the many Serb-born players, Robert Prosinečki was Croatian, Dejan Savićević was Montenegrin as well as some players, such as Mihajlović, being of multi-ethnic parentage. There was even room for Romanian Miodrag Belodedici. Dr Mills also told me that "for many at the time it was a victory for Yugoslav sport", but that it was also inevitable that the fixture was "hijacked for Serb nationalist ends as well" citing the large number of Serbian flags in the stadium which bore the names of Serb-populated towns within Bosnia, Croatia and Montenegro.

The game itself was a dire affair. Petrović's plan of rescinding the ball and killing the contest worked, and at the end of extra time, the game was goalless. It would be settled by penalties, and here Red Star felt they had the advantage as the Yugoslav league system saw drawn games similarly settled with a shootout.

Prosinečki was first to take a penalty and it may have been one of the easiest of his career. Pascal Olmeta in the Marseille goal was both advancing out of the goal and diving to his right before the Croat got to the ball, and he coolly struck it into the left corner. First up for Marseille was the full-back Manuel Amoros, whose run up began at the edge of the D. However, his shot was at a nice height and Stojanović made a comfortable save. Both teams successfully converted their next two penalties, meaning the score was 3-2 to Red Star when Mihajlović stepped up to take the team's fourth. He thumped the ball straight into the bottom left corner and ran back to the centre circle celebrating like Italy's Marco Tardelli in the 1982 World Cup final.

Marseille's Brazilian Carlos Mozer also converted his shot low and left, leaving Red Star on the brink. If Pančev converted his penalty, then Red Star would be European champions. Like most of the penalties prior to his, Pančev began his run up outside the area and hit the ball incredibly true. It arrowed into the top right corner — Olmeta had again moved far too early and was a couple of feet off his line as Pančev struck the ball, with no chance of saving the shot. The ball hit the back of the net so hard that it bounced back towards the desolate Marseille goalkeeper. Pančev ran, arms aloft, towards the edge of the area where he was leapt upon firstly by Stojanović and soon afterwards the rest of his teammates. Popovic described the celebrations in his apartment complex the moment Red Star won, which included his Croatian neighbours; "they were thumping on the floor to celebrate; we would then do the same to our other neighbours". The only exception was those who were Partizan fans, who could not begin to contemplate their most hated rivals going one better than the runners-up position they had achieved in the 1966 European Cup.

There were reports that in the immediate aftermath of the game, fans in the stadium celebrated by unfurling a banner with the Serb Orthodox two fingers and thumb salute (the salute is seen to be significantly aligned with being a Serb as much as anything else).

Several of the players also made the gesture in a group photograph with the European Cup, although Croatian Prosinečki did not.

By the time of Red Star's triumph in May 1991, hostilities had already broken out in the rapidly disintegrating Yugoslavia. The Battle of Borovo and an incident at Plitvice had already seen lives lost and the Serbian Autonomous Oblast of Krajina (SAO Krajina) had begun seeking its own autonomy away from Croatia. For Red Star-supporting Serbs living in Yugoslavia but outside of Serbia, the victory meant more than being champions of Europe, it was a confirmation of a Serb national identity. The Croatian Serb newspaper *Naša Riječ* declared that "Red Star is more than a football club; it is a symbol of the Serbian being". Serbian newspaper *Politika*'s headline was "Red Star as Serbian Star". Coincidentally, the Stadio San Nicola, where the final was played, was a ground bearing the name of St. Nicholas, a saint of particular significance to the Serb orthodox church. *Politika* then went on to describe the win as significant for Yugoslavia "but above all for Serbia".

In December 1991, Red Star flew to Tokyo to play in the Intercontinental Cup in a bid to become club world champions. Their opponents that day were Colo Colo of Chile, managed by Mirko Jozić, who had been manager of the Yugoslav youth side that had triumphed in Chile four years previously and who had done so much for so many Yugoslav players. The result was a 3-0 win for Red Star, despite a red card for Savićević late in the first half. Jugović bagged himself a brace, followed by a wonderful team goal which began on the edge of the Red Star six-yard box before Radinović in the right-back position fed Jugović in central midfield. His pass into space on the left found Mihajlović bursting forward from left-back, who beat his man and slid a pass across the face of goal for Pančev to slot in at the far post. The move was as beautiful as it was breathtaking — 18 seconds from central defence into the back of the Colo Colo net in a wonderful flowing movement.

I asked Popovic about the rivalry between Red Star and Partizan, which could only have intensified following the former's European

Cup glory. While not describing himself as an Ultra or a member of the Delije, he did for a while follow Red Star both home and away. But the baggage of nationalism and fighting kept him away from becoming ingratiated further into Red Star's ultra culture. His first time in the North Stand at the Marakana was a game between Red Star and Italian team Chievo Verona in 2002. Fighting broke out between two sets of Red Star fans, which led to police in full body armour entering the terraces ("we called them Ninja Turtles") and objects including chairs being thrown. Popovic's only thought was hoping to survive.

Popovic is a veteran of over 20 Red Star-Partizan games, and describes the overall quality of football taking place as "horrible". However, the atmosphere on the terraces is always intense, starting outside the ground in Belgrade itself some time before kick-off. The area of Belgrade in which Popovic lives is approximately an hour's bus ride away from the Red Star stadium, but he describes the intimidating journey: "you would see the cops in full armour all around the city and they would be on horses". Violence has reduced in recent years, due to this increased level of policing but there are still isolated incidents.

Fans are funnelled to the games separately by police and Popovic recalled a fixture where he and his girlfriend stopped off en route to the Partizan stadium at the Red Star club shop to buy a sweatshirt and a bag. On their way from the shop to the stadium they were directed by police down a narrow footpath and it was only at the end of the footpath that the pair realised that they were among Partizan fans, and she had to clutch her Red Star bag close to avoid being noticed. However, she was able to take some photos of the Partizan fans before they quickly made their way back to the area where the Red Star fans were located. While Popovic didn't feel that Partizan fans would have attacked his partner as she was female, he acknowledged he would have been seen as fair game; "they maybe would say something to her, but then they would kick my ass". Although not a fan of the Partizan stadium, due to the lack of roof over away fans and the Belgrade rain, Popovic has been so eager to watch Red Star play that he has also bought tickets among the home fans and spent the game speaking English to his partner as they pretended to be tourists to avoid detection.

James Montague, who was himself a Belgrade resident, describes it as "madness" for him to choose either Red Star or Partizan, as he has friends from both sides and as such couldn't swing one way or the other. However, he did tell me that Red Star "despise" him in the false belief that he is a FARE (Football Against Racism in Europe) representative — the group travel incognito to stadia in Europe and report on any racist behaviour, which may lead to a UEFA sanction.

The season after the Maksimir riot was the final season in which clubs from Slovenia and Croatia competed in the Yugoslav league, before breaking away and forming their own competitions following the two republics' declarations of independence. Red Star won this final season at a canter, 13 points ahead of Dinamo Zagreb and 20 clear of Partizan. The following league season (1991/92) only featured teams from Serbia, Bosnia, Montenegro and Macedonia and the drop in quality, with teams such as Dinamo and Hajduk Split no longer competing, was obvious. The Serbian teams dominated and finished in the top five positions, while three of the bottom five teams were Bosnian.

Cessation from the Yugoslav leagues was not easy for the Croatian and Slovenian teams. Having previously played the Belgrade giants, as well as Dinamo Zagreb and Hajduk Split on a regular basis in the Yugoslav league, NK Olimpija Ljubljana played a lower standard of opposition in the Slovenian league system and were champions in the first four seasons of the Slovenian Prva Liga. Despite this success, they struggled to make an impact in the Champions League, losing 7-0 on aggregate to Milan in the first qualifying round in the 1992/93 season and 11-10 on penalties to Latvian side Skonto FC in the preliminary round a year later. The club eventually amassed a significant amount of debt and were forced out of business at the end of the 2004/05 season.

Red Star's defence of the European Cup was thwarted by the new grouping system employed as a precursor to the Champions League which would be unveiled the following season. Placed in a tricky group with Anderlecht, Panathinaikos and a Sampdoria team boasting Roberto Mancini, Gianluca Vialli and Attilio Lombardo, Red Star lost twice to the Italians and once to Anderlecht to finish second in the group, from which the winner — Sampdoria — went on to the final.

Robert Prosinečki had left the previous season to join Real Madrid, but the Red Star team that had achieved so much began to break up much more comprehensively by the summer of 1992. Darko Pančev, Mihajlović and Dejan Savićević all headed to Serie A, and they were to never be the same European force again.

The Yugoslav league's 1992/93 season commenced with only one team from Bosnia, (Borac Banja Luka from the Republika Srpska), and no teams from Macedonia as they had formed their own league following Macedonian independence. Borac Banja Luka had to play their games in the Valjevo region of Western Serbia due to the ongoing Bosnian War. This time it was Partizan's turn to dominate domestic competition, beating Red Star to first place by 14 points. It was, however, a familiar tale of dominance followed by break up as Slaviša Jokanović, Zlatko Zahovič and Predrag Mijatović all left to further their careers. The best example of the weakening of the league following the dissolution of Yugoslavia is the dominance of Red Star and Partizan. Since 1992, Red Star have won the top flight 12 times and Partizan 16.

In Croatia, Hajduk won the inaugural top flight by three points and Dinamo, under their temporary guise of 'Croatia Zagreb', won the following season. Domestically Dinamo have dominated the league ever since with 22 titles in all, stretching way ahead of Hajduk who in comparison have a miserly six.

Players of a high calibre at prominent Balkan teams were increasingly being picked up at an earlier age by the Western European giants. Niko Kranjčar and Luka Modrić both left Croatia in their early twenties for the Premier League, and this haemorrhaging of talent has had an impact upon clubs' European aspirations. Dinamo Zagreb's best performance in the Champions League was finishing second in their group in the 1998/99 season, though a quarter-final appearance in the 2020/21 Europa League does offer some hope. For Red Star, the dream of another elite European triumph is likely to remain just that. They finished bottom of their group in both of their last two Champions League campaigns, although a famous 2-0 victory over Jurgen Klopp's Liverpool did bestow upon their fans some treasured memories. They were also unlucky to lose on away goals to Milan in the first knockout phase of the 2020/21 Europa League. Partizan Belgrade and Hajduk Split's record is even worse, with the former not having made it to the Champions League group stages since the 2010/11 season, the same season that Hajduk had their most recent success, making it to the group stages of the Europa League but finishing bottom.

With players able to make lucrative moves abroad to major European leagues at an earlier age than their predecessors, Balkan clubs have at least benefited from the increasing transfer fees. When Modrić left Dinamo Zagreb to join Tottenham Hotspur in the summer of 2008, the transfer fee was £16.20m. The *Transfermarkt* website at the commencement of the 2021/22 season values Dinamo Zagreb at £118.62m and records their net transfer spend since the 2010/11 season as £126.92m — over £97m of that total has been since the start of the 2016/17 season.

For smaller sides, however, the story is a little different. HNK Gorica finished one point and one place outside of the Europa Conference League places in the 2020/21 Croatian top flight. Transfermarkt values the club at £20.25m with a net spend of £7.62m in the period since the 2010/11 season, though nine of those seasons saw no transfer fee expenditure whatsoever. Teams who qualify for the group stage of the 2021/22 Europa Conference League receive €2,940,000, with €500,000 for a group stage win and €166,000 for a group stage draw. For teams like

Gorica, European competition could be life-changing given the small opportunities for financial income elsewhere. Gorica play their home matches at Gradski Stadion Velika Gorica which has a capacity of 5,200 (as a comparison, Dinamo Zagreb's Maksimir has a capacity of just over 35,000). In the season prior to the Covid19 pandemic the Croatian top flight had an average attendance of 2,837.

It is easy to see which Balkan clubs sit where within the European food chain. The small clubs battle their hardest to make ends meet, while the larger ones use transfer fees to maintain dominance of their domestic league. Meanwhile they endeavour, often without success, to make inroads into the Champions League.

Red Star Belgrade were champions of Europe and then the world 30 years ago. It is difficult to envisage a team from the former Yugoslavia managing a similar feat within an identical timescale now.

★

CHAPTER THREE
BREAKUP

On April 20, 1987, Slobodan Milošević, President of the League of Communists in Yugoslavia, addressed a crowd of Serbs in the town of Kosovo Polje, a few miles south west of Pristina, capital of the autonomous province of Kosovo. The town's name translates as 'Kosovo Field' after the Battle of Kosovo in 1389, an event seared into the minds of Serbs throughout the centuries. The general tone of Milošević's rhetoric was very much one of Yugoslav togetherness: "exclusive nationalism based on national hatreds can never be progressive", he declared, pointing his finger at the crowd for effect.

Milošević probably wasn't expecting to be shouted down by some below him, but the voices that interrupted him protested that the Serbian Communist Party had done little to help ethnic Serbs in Kosovo. The local Serb leader, Miroslav Šolević, explained to Milošević that Kosovan Serbs felt forgotten and wanted a dialogue with him, rather than the monologue that they felt they were constantly receiving. Milošević concurred and agreed to come back a few days later to listen to what people had to say.

He returned to a very different scene: the Serbs of Kosovo Polje had used the time to organise themselves (Šolević even claimed that he helpfully brought trucks filled with stones "just in case"). Milošević sat, in a very mundane building belonging to the House of Culture, and listened as local Serbs vented their feelings. It was obvious that they felt passionately both about their vulnerability as a group, but also about Kosovo itself: "I want to live here where my mother carried me, I want to be buried in this soil, they will not drive me out," one woman told him.

Outside, the crowd became restless and began pelting the police with the stones that Šolević had conveniently left for them. Šolević approached Milošević and told him that it was the police who were attacking the rioters and the situation needed dealing with quickly. Milošević went outside to assess the situation for himself and was immediately confronted by a man who claimed that the police attacked first, and that they had even attacked women and children. The exchange then took a pivotal turn, not just for the crowd and the people there, but for Milošević, Yugoslavia and a generation to come. The elderly man, now inches from Milošević's face, carried on his plea "the Albanians got in amongst us, we were beaten up". Jostled by the crowd and surrounded by journalists with dictaphones and television cameras, Milošević, chin up and staring into the distance, proclaimed: "you will not be beaten again". The images were beamed into televisions on the evening news across Yugoslavia, a rallying cry for Serbs and a warning for everyone else.

It wasn't always like this. Under Josip Tito, the President of Yugoslavia from 1953 to 1980, the country had adopted a policy known as Brotherhood and Unity. The term itself had taken on significance during World War II as Yugoslavian Communists fought off Nazi occupiers and it became a key part of post-War government policy as Tito ruled over the country's ethnic melting pot. He died on Sunday May 4, 1980, of complications following leg surgery. His funeral was a few days later on May 8 and representatives from 123 countries arrived to pay their respects and give their platitudes. Mahmut Bakalli, who at the time was President of the League of Communists in Kosovo, later stated that "we all cried, but we did not know we were burying Yugoslavia".

Almost immediately after Tito's death, pockets of protest and tension began to eat away at Yugoslavia. In 1981, an innocuous demonstration by students at the University of Pristina over the quality of food that was served to them quickly progressed to protests about the nature of the courses on offer. The courses tended to be cultural or arts-based and specific to Kosovo. Graduates then moved into the Yugoslav workplace with few practical qualifications and the result was a large number of unemployed or low-wage workers who had a high level of intelligence and education. Following these initial grievances, a growing element of nationalism appeared among the protesters too, underpinned by their fear of an increasingly centralised Yugoslavia and the reduction of Kosovo's status within it.

By early April that year, the protests had become increasingly violent, leading to the army protecting several key buildings and Bakalli calling for armed vehicles to be deployed. One demand, that Kosovo be given the status of the seventh republic of Yugoslavia, was considered to be unacceptable to many Serbs both in Kosovo and also the rest of Yugoslavia. This was, they felt, because any such status for Kosovo could be a precursor for a Greater Albania, which would mean Kosovo being annexed into a larger territory outside Yugoslavia with a majority ethnic Albanian population. The declaration of a state of emergency on April 2 and the deployment of troops to Kosovo seemed to quell the protesters, with the demonstrations coming to an end shortly afterwards.

There were immediate consequences for the students, with many spending time in prison as a result of their actions. In the University of Pristina, Albanian texts were replaced with those written in Serbo-Croat. The protests also increased polarisation within Kosovo as the League of Communists saw what they believed to be the unacceptable nationalist element of the protests as something that needed to be eradicated.

Sporadic incidents across Kosovo did little to dampen the demonisation of one side by the other. Đorđe Martinović was a Serb farmer from Giljan who in 1985 was taken to hospital with a bottle inserted into his anus. He initially claimed that he had been assaulted by two Albanian men while working in his field, but when interviewed later by a member of the army, Martinović admitted that he had in fact inserted the bottle as a means of what investigators called "self-satisfaction". Community leaders in Giljan later confirmed that from their point of view Martinović's injuries were "accidental consequences of a self-induced practice".

However, Martinović was transferred to Belgrade for what can only be assumed was a thoroughly degrading inspection by a trio of doctors assembled from different Yugoslav republics. They concluded that it was impossible to self-insert the wide end of a 500ml bottle and that it must have been forced inside Martinović by a third party. A further investigation, this time by Slovenian Janez Milčinski, President of the Slovenian Academy of Science and Arts, deemed it was possible for the bottle to have been inserted by Martinović himself who by now was recanting his confession of self-abuse. His son also stated that his father was attacked by Albanians who were looking for anyone to perform the act upon, and that Martinović just happened to be in the wrong place at the wrong time. Elements of the Serbian Press ran with the story, claiming that Martinović was attacked by local Albanians who wanted his land, and that he was refusing to sell. Many Serb intellectuals also took on the Martinović case as a means of promoting their narrative of Serb victimhood in support of Serbian nationalism.

In September 1986, just over a year after Martinović made his claims, a draft document produced by the Serbian Academy of Sciences & Arts known as the *SNAU Memorandum* was leaked to the newspaper *Večernje Novosti* which struck a chord with many Serbs in Yugoslavia. Essentially the document stated that as Tito was a Croat born in a village on the border with Slovenia, and was himself a mixture of Slovene-Croatian parentage, his policies always favoured those two republics. This left Serbia as the poorer neighbour, despite the number of Serbs who died fighting with the Yugoslav army during World War II. Furthermore, Serbs in Yugoslavia outside of Serbia faced a bleak future. The document claimed that "Serbs in Croatia have never been as endangered as they are today" and that Serbs living outside of Serbia were not able to "use their own language and alphabet, to organise politically and culturally, and to develop the unique culture of their nation".

The document was not well received among politicians or newspapers within Yugoslavia. Future President of Serbia Slobodan Milošević described it as "nothing else but the darkest nationalism". However, given that two of the document's authors, Mihailo Marković and Dobrica Ćosić both went on to hold senior political positions, Milošević's condemnation needs to be accepted warily. The document did resonate with some Serbs and as Laura Silber and Allan Little wrote in *The Death of Yugoslavia*, "the draft memorandum did not create nationalism, it simply tapped sentiments that ran deep among the Serbs".

The statuses of both Kosovo and the region of Vojvodina in northern Serbia were coming into question too. Under the 1974 constitution created during Tito's rule, these regions were given the title of Socially Autonomous Provinces, giving them some constitutional and legislative authority over themselves. However, Tito was gone, and the policy of Brotherhood and Unity was disappearing too.

The term had its origins in the Axis occupation of Yugoslavia during World War II. As the occupying forces sought to expose ethnic divisions for their own means, the League of Communists of Yugoslavia used the phrase as part of its partisan operations as it attempted to unite people of different ethnicities from across Yugoslavia in its bid to repel the foreign invaders. After Tito's accession, the term 'Brotherhood and Unity' came to symbolise the fact that the republics inside Yugoslavia, and the ethnic groups that made up its population, could peacefully coexist.

Some Serbs were beginning to want Kosovo and Vojvodinia to be fully integrated back into Serbia. On October 5, 1988, a crowd managed to remove the ruling Vojvodina administration with the phrase "Serbia, made of three parts, you will be whole once again" ringing in their ears. One of the chief organisers of the protest was Miroslav Šolević. The Vojvodina rulers had played their hand poorly, cutting off water and power to the protesters thus only enraging them further. An attempt at feeding the protesters also went awry as the yoghurts provided simply became handy missiles to throw at the parliament building.

In Kosovo the situation was a little more in the balance. In November, two high-ranking Albanian officials were forced to resign due to Milošević's continual ratcheting up of pressure, both through protesting Serbs and political manoeuvrings. Milošević replaced them with his own trusted people. Three months later, in February 1989, more than 1,000 miners began an underground hunger strike in protest at the political situation. Circumstances in the mine quickly deteriorated though and despite supplies being sent in, 180 of the miners were hospitalised.

An offshoot of the hunger strike was further demonstrations in Slovenia, which took Serbs by surprise. There were even suggestions that Slovenes were sending food to the miners in a bid to prolong the strike. Milošević wanted to send in troops to clear out the mines, but was told by the Slovene Communist Leader Milan Kučan that the protesters were demonstrating against the revised constitution that Milošević himself was behind. On February 27, Kučan spoke in Slovenia's capital Ljubljana, declaring that "the situation in Kosovo shows that people are no longer living together but increasingly against one another".

Something was stirring within Slovenia, in part due to Kučan's refusal to be cowed by Serbia, but there was a grassroots aspect too. A Socialist Youth magazine called *Mladina*, which had a reputation for pushing boundaries, criticised the Yugoslav People's Army (JNA) as an "undemocratic institution always ready to stage a military coup". The magazine was particularly scathing of Branko Mamula, an Admiral within the JNA, for selling arms to the Ethiopian government, calling him the "merchant of death". They also noted Mamula's use of JNA conscripts to build a villa for him on the Croatian coast. When the JNA complained to the Slovene hierarchy, they were told not to be so thin-skinned. At a meeting of the JNA Military Council, Mladina was deemed to be "counter revolutionary". A member of the JNA then approached Kučan to ask how Slovenes would react to Mladina employees being arrested. 'Not well', was the answer. Kučan then spoke to the Yugoslav Central Committee insisting that the "anti-Slovene campaign being waged in Serbia and elsewhere must stop". He went on to mention the growing anti-Yugoslav feeling stirring within Slovenia too.

Relations between the Slovenes and the rest of Yugoslavia (in particular the Serbs) had deteriorated so much that when a Slovene delegation was required to attend a meeting in Belgrade with representatives from the rest of Yugoslavia, they travelled on separate flights in case an assassination attempt was made upon the group. They drove back to Slovenia via Bulgaria, rather than the more direct route by Zagreb. Kučan declared that "first of all we are Slovenes and only then communists". Nevertheless, they had support. For the first time, the Croatian delegates sided with their northerly neighbours, and the winds of change began to blow through Yugoslavia.

In April 1990, Slovenia held multi-party elections, the first since World War II, with Kučan emerging victorious. A referendum on independence followed in December, with 88% of the electorate voting for independence (roughly 88% of Slovenia identified themselves as ethnic Slovenes at this time too) and a declaration of independence followed on June 25, 1991.

Slovenia notionally took control of its borders, ports and air traffic control. However, if they thought that Yugoslavia would let them walk away, they were very much mistaken. Yugoslavia's federal parliament refused to recognise the Slovene declaration, leading to a bizarre scenario in which the JNA perceived the events as an internal policing matter (and not as an all-out war), and thereby frequently updated their Slovene counterparts on the movements of its troops.

Over the next two days, almost 700 Yugoslav police and customs officers were transported to Cerklje air base in Slovenia, from where they were further deployed to various barracks across Slovenia and Croatia. On top of that, anti-aircraft vehicles were moving in the dead of night from Karlovac in western Croatia, with orders to be at the Slovenian border by daybreak on June 27, a move which enraged Kučan almost as much as when he contacted a JNA general for an explanation and was told not to worry. Kučan called a meeting of the Slovene leadership at 5am on the morning of June 27, at which defence minister Janez Janša stated that barricades had been made within Slovenia but there had been no further orders to defend them, so JNA tanks were at that moment moving through them. Janša suggested that armed resistance was the only option left open. The members of the meeting were becoming acutely aware of the inevitable and the room was enveloped in silence. Kučan then asked if anybody wanted to speak. When the room again remained quiet, he declared "then I will speak. I suggest we face the fact that we are at war".

Following this, Slovenian defence forces surrounded manned JNA bases within Slovenia, cutting off their utilities, and warned that any air relief to the sites would be met by force. The JNA underestimated the Slovenes and a helicopter was shot down with both occupants killed (though ironically, the pilot was Slovenian). The Slovenes were suddenly on the front foot, attacking JNA forces in central Slovenia and inflicting casualties. A tank column from Croatia was blocked at the border crossing at Ormož. Yet the JNA held other key border points connecting Slovenia to Croatia, as well as Italy and Austria. At various points within Slovenia, tanks were blocked by truck barricades, leading to several lorry drivers being killed.

On June 28, just three days after their declaration of independence, Slovene forces captured three JNA tanks and destroyed more in the town of Nova Gorica on the border with Italy. Four JNA soldiers were killed and dozens taken prisoner, with fighting taking place just yards from Italian houses. The JNA also began to lose both key positions and combatants as many of its Slovenian members deserted. And although the European Community was brokering talks in Zagreb between Slovenia and Yugoslavia in a bid to negotiate a ceasefire, the Slovenes, sensing their military advantage, were reluctant to back away.

Eventually Slovenian authorities agreed to cease hostilities, but only on the proviso that it would not jeopardise Slovenian independence. The JNA, perhaps inevitably, rejected the idea and the fighting carried on, during which they continued to lose border points, equipment and machinery to the Slovenes while Yugoslav politicians and military leaders bickered over whether or not to launch a full-scale invasion. Eventually, as JNA units pushing towards Slovenia suffered mechanical issues, a ceasefire was agreed and the JNA withdrew back to their barracks.

With the signing of the Brioni Accord on July 7, hostilities within Slovenia came to an end and a roadmap to independence — delayed by three months — was agreed. Slovenian police and armed forces were to be recognised as sovereign within Slovenia. All that was left was for JNA forces to withdraw from Slovenian soil, which they did by October 26. The first of Yugoslavia's six republics had seceded. It wouldn't be the last, nor, sadly, would it be the bloodiest.

***

The stone ruins of Prozor Fortress sit imposingly on the hillside above the town of Vrlika in Southern Croatia. The site has been occupied since the third century BC, though the fortress wasn't built until the 15th century as a means of defending the region from the Ottoman Empire. It is possible to stand among the ruins and take in the breathtaking scenery of the surrounding mountains. Less prominent is a track that traverses the road leading east out of Vrlika towards the village of Kukar and the birthplace of Milan Babić.

Babić, born in 1956 was a qualified dentist and a long-standing member of the League of Communists of Croatia. Yet he felt that

Croatia was changing and, as a Serb, that those changes were not for the better, especially with the formation of political groups such as the Croatian Democratic Union (HDZ) in June 1989 by Franjo Tuđman. Tuđman had a political childhood — his father was a member of the Croatian Peasant's Party (HSS) and President of the local HSS committee, as well as the Mayor of Veliko Trgovišće, Tuđman's birthplace in Northern Croatia. During World War II, he joined the Yugoslav partisans and in the years after the war, he rose quickly through the ranks so that by the time he was 38 he had become the youngest general in the Yugoslav army — no mean feat considering almost three quarters of generals at the time were Serbs or Montenegrins.

Tuđman had spent time in prison in the 1970s and 1980s and had also stated that the Communist regime had exaggerated the number of Serbs killed by the Ustaše, a Croatian fascist organisation, during World War II. Given Tuđman's rapid rise, Babić had good reason to be nervous for his fellow Krajina Serbs. At a general assembly of HDZ members in February 1990 (the numbers swelled by many Croats based abroad who backed the HDZ), Tuđman called for the creation of an independent Croatian state. The HDZ's claims that they were peacefully seeking self-determination for Croatia did not soothe the minds of many Croatian Serbs, not least because Tuđman later remarked "thank god my wife is not a Jew or a Serb".

Voting in the Croatian parliamentary elections (the first since 1913) took place in late April and early May of 1990 and Tuđman's HDZ were the most popular party. Following the results, the JNA commandeered a large number of weapons inside Croatia in a bid to reduce the likelihood of any armed uprising by emboldened Croats. Meanwhile, the HDZ focused on political changes; a new constitution was adopted, Croatia became the Republic of Croatia and its flag was amended, with the red star removed and replaced by the red-and-white chequered chessboard, known informally in Croatia as 'šahovnica'.

Recognising the danger ahead for Serbs, Babić was vying for control of the Serbian Democratic Party (SDP) with Jovan Rašković, its heavily-bearded founder. At the time, Rašković was trying to negotiate with Tudman, but the negotiations backfired when details of the meeting were leaked. Babić took control. However, he did not have things all his own way, finding that Serbs were willing to listen to Croatian politicians and try to work with them. In mid-August, a referendum that the Croatian Serbs were scheduled to hold on their future autonomy was declared illegal and Croatian forces moved on Knin, the town in Dalmatia where Babić was mayor. The raid ended in humiliation for Croatia, symbolised when a group of Croat Interior Ministry helicopters were intercepted by JNA jets, forcing them to back down.

Local radio in Knin reported that Babić had declared a "state of war" within the area (something Babić later denied) and with the helicopters, which were full of police reservists, unable to reach Knin for fear of being shot down, the police on the ground were also unable to reach the town. The incident became known as the 'Log Revolution' due to rudimentary roadblocks being created from trees felled by those wishing to block access to the Croatian police. In the aftermath, rumours and denials persisted. The JNA denied its troops were involved, and said that any soldiers seen on the streets of Knin that night were on leave at the train station awaiting a train that was delayed by two hours. The *New York Times* quoted a local Serb news agency, Večernje novosti, which stated that thousands of women and children had been evacuated from Knin and up to two million Serbs within Serbia were ready to take up arms and help the Krajina Serbs within Croatia. At this point war within Croatia was almost unavoidable.

Tensions increased at the beginning of March 1991. In the central Croatian town of Pakrac, intimidation in the form of threats and machine gun fire in the dead of night had occurred for weeks. Local Serbs took over the police station and jailed those who refused to bow to their authority. A night-time raid by Croatian special forces retook the police station, arresting any Serbs they caught. Other Serbs managed to escape and when the JNA came to relieve the situation they found themselves caught in crossfire between

Serbs in the hills and Croats in the captured buildings. At the end of the month, the stakes were raised further in what became known as the Plitvice Lake Incident when Croatian Serbs organised a rally at Plitvice Lakes, demanding that the stunningly beautiful UNESCO World Heritage site be annexed into Serb hands.

In the days following the rally, Croatian staff were removed from the area by Serbs, prompting the Croatian special police to send 180 men to the area from Zagreb. They quickly secured a key bridge, but on March 31, another Croatian force, on its way to the lakes, was ambushed by Serb forces. During the course of the fighting, Croat Josip Jović was shot and killed despite wearing supposedly bullet-proof armour. He is recognised by some as being the first fatality of the Croatian war of independence.

Serbia's response was immediate. The Milošević government formally recognised Babić's Serb Autonomous Province of Krajina and sent officials to Knin to assess what aid could be provided. In Sarajevo, a qualified psychiatrist who also had worked as a poet and an ecologist called for armed Serbs to protect all Serbian enclaves of Yugoslavia. His name was Radovan Karadžić.

Tensions continued to increase with Borovo Selo, a village in eastern Croatia sitting on the Serbian border formed by the river Danube, becoming a flashpoint. In mid-April, an HDZ member and advisor to Tudman wandered through a cornfield to the edge of the village and fired ordinance in its general direction, hitting a house and a potato field, though the latter rocket failed to explode and there were no casualties. On May 1, four Croatian policemen, maybe with nothing more than hijinks in mind, drove into Borovo to attempt to replace the Yugoslav flag which flew in the village with a Croatian one. The misadventure backfired and they came under attack. Two of the policemen managed to escape, but two were wounded and eventually captured. The Croats came back the next day intent on rescuing their colleagues, but came across a village that was ready for them - 12 were killed in the ensuing firefight.

The Croatian media reported that the 12 men killed had been tortured and mutilated beyond recognition, and portrayed the Serbs as anarchic terrorists. Speaking on May 3, Tudman declared: "We are facing, I may say, the beginning of open warfare against the republic of Croatia." Incidents such as Borovo, and the subsequent siege of the village of Kijevo by the JNA, became more than isolated affairs. Croatia was at the point of no return, and made its declaration of independence on the same date that Slovenia made theirs.

The city of Vukovar, an ethnically mixed conurbation where civilians of all sides suffered, was the first large-scale theatre of war inside Croatia. For weeks either side of Croatia's declaration of independence, ethnic tensions increased in and around the city. Rural Serbs blocked routes to the city and Croat militias intimidated those Serbs still inside. Stipe Mesić, Member of the Presidency of Yugoslavia for the Republic of Croatia, ominously called the situation in Vukovar "Croatia's Stalingrad". The urban setting of the fighting and the amount and intensity of ordinance fired at the city were both similar to the brutal World War II battle in Russia.

At first, the JNA struggled to manoeuvre their larger vehicles around the tight streets. They were also hampered by snipers, anti-tank mines and anti-tank weapons being fired at extremely close range. The pro-Croatian forces inside Vukovar proved a tougher test than many imagined. The Croatian National Guard attacked JNA barracks within the city, while fighting also took place between Serb paramilitaries, armed by the JNA, and Croats in the south west, leading to many civilian casualties. Records from a director at the local hospital show that at this stage of the battle they were receiving up to 80 wounded per day, three quarters of whom were civilians. The JNA, despite arming local paramilitaries, saw high levels of desertion among their own troops, with commanders complaining that conscripts refused to leave their armoured vehicles.

In time however, the tide began to turn and the JNA began making progress. As Serb forces had taken the last road into Vukovar, refugees began fleeing via a footpath leading out of the city, which was overlooked by merciless snipers. By November 10, the footpath had also been closed as JNA forces took the suburb of Borovo Naselje. Those who remained in Vukovar began to live in mass shelters and eight days later the city fell completely. Those Croat forces trapped inside faced a fearful dash through enemy lines to try to reach friendly territory. For civilians who couldn't leave, one can only imagine the fear they felt as the fighting subsided and knowing that the Serb victors were coming.

The JNA agreed terms of surrender with Croatian forces, which included the evacuation of civilians and patients at the local hospital, to be supervised by representatives from the European Community and the International Red Cross. However, to the horror of patients inside, unsupervised JNA units arrived at the hospital. Approximately 300 people were removed and taken to a nearby farm complex named Ovcara, south of the city. They were horribly beaten during the course of the afternoon, followed by a mass execution over a period of four hours in the evening.

Paramilitaries were left to wander the city's streets with impunity. Families were separated and many never saw their loved ones alive again. Those who survived were taken to a detention centre before being stripped, beaten and subject to repeated interrogations. They were finally freed in January the following year. Vukovar wasn't the only massacre of the Croatian war, nor, tragically, was it even the final one of 1991: the names of Bruška, Voćin and the Zec family have all also gone down in history.

At approximately the same time that Vukovar was falling, the JNA set its sights on the stunningly beautiful coastal resort of Dubrovnik. The bombardment of the town began in October and carried on remorselessly and relentlessly until December, with shelling coming from both the sea and the high ground overlooking the town. Hotels harbouring refugees, as well as the old town, were targeted with shells, artillery and sniper fire. On December 2, the Libertas Hotel was targeted twice, the second time with the aim of hitting firefighters putting out fires from a previous strike.

It's hard to see the JNA's justification for assaulting Dubrovnik. There was no significant Serb population to protect and no JNA barracks to support and regardless of their motives, the attacks hurt the reputation of the JNA and Serbs internationally. Dubrovnik was a well-known tourist attraction and the siege gained international attention as Stipe Mesić led a relief effort via sea which could have easily led to his flotilla being sunk by the Yugoslav navy. Another significant consequence of the Dubrovnik siege was that on January 15, 1992, the European Community agreed to recognise Croatia's independence. By May 1992, Croatia was also a member of the UN.

Croatia's war for independence continued until 1995. In May that year, the Croatian army launched Operation Flash against the Republic of Serbian Krajina (RSK) which resulted in the RSK's surrender and Croatia's capture of 215 square miles of territory. On August 4, Croatia began Operation Storm, which was to have ramifications for both them and Bosnia. Croatian forces numbered 130,000 and with air support they began their advance towards Knin, the Krajina Serb capital, at 5am. Krajina Serb forces quickly melted away and on the following morning, the Croats entered the town itself.

Despite not quelling the resistance entirely, the Croatian Defence Minister Gojko Šušak declared military operations over on the evening of August 7. Terms of surrender were finalised the following day. The immediate aftermath of the battle made the Serbs within Croatia and Bosnia feel very vulnerable, possibly pushing them closer to diplomatic negotiations.

***

In October 1991, when Tuđman was calling upon Croatia to rise up against Serb imperialism, the Bosnian Parliament passed a 'Memorandum on the Sovereignty of Bosnia-Herzegovina'. Bosnian Serbs were outraged, claiming the move unconstitutional. They boycotted the debate, which carried on anyway, and at the same time, Croatian communities in Bosnia began to organise themselves autonomously.

To show how far the Serbs felt disenfranchised, in January 1992 they declared the 'Republic of the Serbian People in Bosnia-

Herzegovina', which later became more commonly known as 'Republika Srpska'. Negotiations on partitioning Bosnia along ethnic lines, held in Lisbon the following month, failed to reach a consensus and a referendum on Bosnian independence held shortly afterwards saw over 90% voting in favour (although, significantly, many Serbs refused to participate). The Bosnian parliament declared its independence on March 3. The threat of violence was constant, though - during the referendum, a wedding in Sarajevo was attacked by a notorious Bosniak criminal, who shot and killed the groom's father and wounded the Serb orthodox priest. The justification for the attack was supposedly the fact that guests at the wedding were flying Serb flags; claims and counter-claims only inflamed the situation. The following day, Serb defence forces had set up roadblocks across Sarajevo.

On March 18, Bosniaks, Croats and Serbs, under the brokership of the European Community, met again in Lisbon. The sides agreed to recognise the existing external borders of Bosnia and governmental devolution inside Bosnia along ethnic lines. These represented compromises for all three sides, but with fighting and targeted civilian deaths already occurring, Bosnian President Alija Izetbegović withdrew his agreement to the plan just 10 days later.

Violence was rife. Croat forces were accused of the murder and rape of the Serb population in Sijekovac, an ethnically mixed village close to the Bosnian-Croat border. In north-eastern Bosnia, Serb paramilitaries committed an equally brutal, but far more widely-known massacre of the local Bosniak population in Bijeljina. Local Serbs had begun intimidating the Bosniak population and with few police to defend the town, Izetbegović asked the JNA to provide protection. However, infamous Serb paramilitaries the Tigers, led by Željko Ražnatović, who was known as Arkan, began arriving in the town seeking out non-Serbs.

The Tigers came to the attention of the rest of the world in the area of Bijeljina in the far east of Bosnia. Prior to the outbreak of the war, the ethnic make-up of the municipality surrounding Bijeljina was majority Serb, with the city itself having a Bosniak (Bosnian Muslim) majority. In April 1992, a year into the Croatian war, the SDG entered the city and began to terrorise its citizens, throwing grenades into Bosniak-owned businesses as the woefully outnumbered local police force looked on helplessly. Alija Izetbegović, the Bosnian President, optimistically called on the Yugoslav People's Army (JNA) to help manage the escalating situation, despite their brutal methods during the Croatian war. With the city being both shelled and overlooked by sniper positions, Serb forces began to occupy key buildings and ask local Serbs to identify non-Serbs who lived in the town. Those who cooperated were given advance notice to leave the area, with the homes of non-Serbs (plus also any Serbs who refused to denounce their neighbours) and those living inside being targeted.

Arkan and the SDG were deeply involved in this process and despite his claims that "we can guarantee to the Muslim population that they can live normally with us", his actions proved otherwise. Ron Haviv, an American photographer, was embedded with the SDG with the consent of Arkan, and recorded their actions. They took a non-uniformed, unarmed man into the street and after ordering Haviv to stop taking photographs, they shot him in front of his pleading wife. She tried in vain to stem the bleeding, at which point she too was shot. A second woman was also brought out and shot, followed a few minutes later by the appearance of an SDG member who, while holding a cigarette and wearing sunglasses on his head, proceeded to kick the bodies of the recently executed civilians.

Later that day the SDG also captured a man they claimed was a Muslim fundamentalist from Kosovo and had apparently been shooting at them. Presented two small weapons as evidence, they proceeded to take the supposed offender away for interrogation, after which he was thrown out of a window before being kicked by Serb forces.

How is it known that these events happened? Because Haviv, at great personal danger to himself, continued to take photographs. Speaking to TV host and journalist Charlie Rose, Haviv described how he managed to covertly take the photographs, with his overall aim being to capture the soldiers and executed victims in the same photo: "I thought this was incredibly important for evidence ... I went to the middle of the street just to get a clean shot of the soldiers walking past, that's all I wanted. I framed my shot and from my left came this soldier with the cigarette and sunglasses, he walked into my frame, he lifted his foot back and I knocked off a couple of frames as he kicked the bodies. I put my camera down, the soldier turned towards me, I kind of smiled at him and said 'let's go', and he smiled back at me and we ran up the street." Upon realising that Haviv's photos had been published, a furious Arkan stated that he wanted the American dead.

In early April, the city of Sarajevo was shelled by the JNA stationed in the surrounding hills. Izetbegović complained to Serbian President Slobodan Milošević and asked him to withdraw the troops. Milošević agreed to move only those armed personnel who were not from Bosnia — a minimal amount — leaving Sarajevo in a perilous position. By May, it was totally surrounded, and the situation continued to deteriorate. A JNA column was attacked as it tried to withdraw from the city as part of an agreed ceasefire, while Izetbegović himself was temporarily detained at Sarajevo airport by Yugoslav authorities. The siege became oppressive and relentless for those living inside Sarajevo and in particular those who had to traverse the aptly and ominously named Sniper Alley, the road connecting the airport region to the Old City. Residents couldn't just stay indoors as they needed food and water, not to mention fuel in the winter. Yet there was no guarantee that those going outside to find these essential items would return home.

In February 1994, 66 people were killed and almost 150 were wounded when a mortar shell landed in the crowded Markale market in the city. The quick arrival of the international press meant the immediate aftermath was broadcast for a horrified world to see. It looked like the Serbs had indiscriminately fired into a confined area full of civilians. There was however some ambiguity as to who fired the fatal round. General Michael Rose, the head of the UN peacekeeping force UNPROFOR, initially thought Bosnian forces were responsible, however at a later date the UN decided that neither side could be blamed outright.

Markale was attacked again on August 28, 1995. This time five rounds were fired and 43 people died, with 75 wounded. The scenes filmed in the immediate aftermath of the attack were no less devastating than the previous ones had been. On one street, the dead lay strewn across the pavements, a motorcycle on the ground with someone lying beside it and a trail of blood several feet long. The wounded were loaded onto anything that could transport them to hospital quickly, including into the boots of cars. Huge pools of blood mixed with shoes, shopping bags and discarded bits of food. Again, the Bosnian Serbs blamed the Bosnian forces for shelling their own civilians, however this time they weren't believed and following their own investigation, UNPROFOR stated that "all mortar rounds fired in the attack on the Markale Market were fired from Bosnian Serb territory". On June 1, 1993, 11 people, including four children, were killed and up to 100 wounded when a football match in a residential district close to Sarajevo airport was hit by two shells, within moments of each other.

Edin Dzeko, the talismanic Bosnian striker who won the Premier League with Manchester City, lived through the siege as a child and describes in graphic detail the conditions he and his family endured. Forced to move at an early age as Bosnian Serbs occupied the area where he lived, he stayed with his parents and sister in his grandmother's basement. The situation was far from ideal, but the family at least had some sanctuary as they were in the Bosnian government-controlled area of the city. He had many close calls, including one when his mother called him in from playing football outside, just moments before the spot on which he was playing was struck by a mortar round.

The second attack on the Markale market was too much for the UN, who now formally requested NATO air strikes in a bid to relieve the suffocating siege. NATO gave the Serbs ten days in which to move the heavy weapons surrounding Sarajevo to a cordon 20 kilometres away from the city centre. Radovan Karadžić, by now the leader of the Bosnian Serbs, declared that any aggressive NATO plane would be shot down and the Serbs began to dig their heels in, challenging the conditions of the ultimatum to the point that they were allowed to choose where to move their weapons, much to the anger of the incredulous Bosnians.

By May 1995, the Bosnian army was able to make a push on Bosnian Serb positions around Sarajevo. The Bosnian Serbs, perhaps unwisely, had stolen weapons from the UN, and used them, leading to UN commanders on the ground requesting NATO air support. NATO obliged, hitting an ammunition dump, but in response the Serbs kidnapped 377 UNPROFOR personnel to use as human shields. The situation was further exacerbated when Captain Scott O'Grady of the United States Air Force was shot down in his F-16 jet by a Serb-fired surface to air missile. O'Grady survived and spent several nights on the run in unfriendly territory surviving on a diet of bugs, foliage and the meagre amounts of rainwater he was able to collect. He was also intermittently using his radio to try and make contact so he could be located and saved.

On June 8th O'Grady was able to make contact and was ultimately rescued. While he remained undetected, however, tensions rapidly increased between NATO and the Bosnian Serbs with many Americans wanting retaliatory bombing against Serbs, whilst others urged caution given the 377 hostages that were still unaccounted for. In an effort to cool tensions, Serbs released 121 hostages and following the successful extraction of O'Grady, both sides relaxed and ultimately the remaining hostages were freed.

On January 9, 1996, 55-year-old Mirsada Durić became the final person to be killed in the siege as the tram in which she was travelling was struck by a grenade fired from a Serb-held position. The siege was finally lifted on February 29, 1996, two and a half months after the signing of the Dayton Agreement which had ended the war, as the Bosnian government retook control of the Sarajevo suburb of Ilijaš. In the aftermath, many Serbs left the city for Serb-held territory. Some burned down their own homes to stop them falling into Muslim hands, and some even exhumed relatives to be reburied close to their new homes.

Elsewhere in Bosnia, the situation was equally bleak, with Croats and Muslims fighting against each other despite officially being allies, most notably in the 1993 siege of Mostar.

The war intensified throughout 1995, with NATO continuing their air strikes and Serbs shelling the supposed "safe area" of Tuzla, from positions on the high ground outside the city, in response. It was one of several UN-designated safe areas in Bosnia, which some felt were doomed to fail from the start as there was a lack of political will to protect them. On the evening of May 25, a shell struck Tuzla, in the central Kapija district, killing 71 people and injuring 240. The average age of the casualties was 23, with the youngest being just two years old. The mayor of Tuzla appealed for direct intervention and in response to the incident NATO jets bombed Republika Srpska army (VRS) depots in Pale.

Of all the safe areas in Bosnia, arguably the most infamous is Srebrenica, in the eastern part of the country close to the Serb border. Immediately prior to the war, the town had a majority Muslim population and a significant Serb minority. The town had been besieged by Bosnian Serbs since April 1992, following a campaign by the combined forces of the JNA and the Serbian Volunteer Guard paramilitary unit.

The Bosnian Serbs were reluctant to let aid into Srebrenica or refugees out because of guerrilla attacks by Muslim forces in Serb villages which resulted in civilian deaths. This meant that many of those caught up in the town were not from Srebrenica itself, rather they had fled there from other nearby areas, exacerbating the unfolding humanitarian disaster in the town. Bosnian Serb general Ratko Mladić became increasingly agitated by the Bosniak incursions and finally lost patience towards the end of June 1995, contacting the UN in Sarajevo to tell them he was going to begin shelling Srebrenica.

In early July, the VRS launched 'Operation Krivaja' to try to retake Srebrenica and eliminate hostile forces within the town, including the Dutch peacekeepers DUTCHBAT, who came under fire. The remaining Bosniak fighters in the town could offer little in the way of resistance as the Dutch had seized many of their weapons. The situation within Srebrenica became increasingly desperate as DUTCHBAT were effectively held hostage as locals refused to let them leave town. NATO also refused to attack VRS positions. On July 11, VRS soldiers entered Srebrenica. Several thousand people fled to what they thought was the sanctuary of the UN headquarters, though Mladić showed his disregard for the UN by taking many of their personnel hostage. Thousands of other men, both Bosniak fighters and civilians, desperately escaped the town, fully aware of what their fate would be if they stayed. Mladić was in complete control. Having only managed to destroy a single VRS tank, NATO planes were called off after Mladić threatened to shell a UN base full of refugees in the nearby town of Potočari.

The next day it was a slightly different Mladić who met with representatives from the civilian population and Thom Karremans, the DUTCHBAT commander, casually asking the marital status of the only woman in the group, Camila Omanovic. He was amused that she was at school with one of his soldiers, asking if they were "old flames". She replied that they were simply friends and that they could never have foreseen that their situation would have come to this. Mladić simply, ominously replied "well, it has, it has come".

Gathered round the table over a constant stream of coffee and cigarettes, the meeting, while not informal, appeared to be progressive. Mladić seemed authoritative but compromising, promising Omanovic that he would personally oversee the safe removal of her family from Srebrenica and that "there is no need for your people to get killed". Yet there was still an aura of menace emanating from him.

The promises were hollow. According to later UN prosecutions, it had already been decided that "on that day the women and children would be evacuated but the men would be temporarily detained and then killed". On July 12, Serb soldiers began carrying out acts of violence and murders, as well as setting houses and haystacks on fire in a further bid to intimidate Muslim refugees. As night fell the horror continued as people were dragged away from their families; many would not return. Gunshots and screams were distressingly audible, the random nature of the attacks unbearable for those awaiting their fate. DUTCHBAT soldiers came across a young woman being brutally raped in full view of nearby refugees, who were helpless to stop it.

The following day witnesses came across corpses in a nearby stream they were trying to draw water from. Several buses arrived to take refugees to Bosniak areas, which provoked a crush as people tried to board to escape the horror. Attempts to escort the buses by DUTCHBAT were thwarted as Serbs removed the Dutch troops from their escorting vehicles at gunpoint, confiscating weapons and equipment. Speaking to *balkaninsight.com*, former DUTCHBAT members told how there was nothing that they could do to help. They were outnumbered by both Bosnian Serb soldiers and Bosnian Serb civilians, who turned up to loot whatever evacuated civilians could not take with them. At a later testimony to the Hague, DUTCHBAT Major Robert Franken speculated that this was "because they didn't want anybody to be around; that's obvious ... they didn't want us to witness whatever would happen". Tales of brutality, violence, murder and rape were later recounted to journalists and war crimes tribunals from those who lived through the events of those few days.

Several columns of Bosniak men, aware of what would happen to them if they stayed within Srebrenica, began leaving to try and find their way to Bosnian government territory through a series of forests. However, the sleep and water-deprived groups were harassed by Serb forces every step of the way, with survivors later describing how they had to tread on the same ground as the man in front to avoid accidentally stepping on a mine. Tanks and small arms fire raked the columns, with Serb soldiers calling upon those inside the treelines to surrender. Some did, with a cameraman asking one if he was afraid: "How could I not be?" was the bleak reply.

One column, estimated to be up to 15km long, was aiming to cross a road into Bosnian government territory in an attempt to reach Tuzla. It was intercepted by Serbs who appeared to use a chemical weapon which drove people in the column to hallucinate and start attacking each other. Serbs called upon those in the column to surrender, with reports that those who did were immediately killed. Many refugees wandered the Bosnian countryside for weeks afterwards trying to find safe territory. One group of seven men remained hidden for several months until they were found by American IFOR soldiers in May 1996. Inexplicably, the Americans decided the seven were to be handed over to Serb police and they were then held in prison, some until 1999.

The Srebrenica Massacre took place in Europe just five years before the end of the 20th century. This list of people killed or missing, compiled by the Bosnian Federal Commission of Missing Persons, contains 8,373 names at the time of writing. The aftermath has been drawn out. In 1995, Mladić and Karadžić were indicted by the Hague for war crimes including Srebrenica, and were finally imprisoned in 2016 and 2017 respectively. In 2002, the Dutch government resigned en masse following criticisms of the role DUTCHBAT played during the tragedy. In 2015, Serbian Prime minister Aleksander Vučić visited Srebrenica as part of the 20th anniversary of the massacre, where he was heckled and had objects thrown at him by relatives of victims in the crowd. Despite his declaration that "my hand remains outstretched to the Bosniak people", it appears that many are not willing to forgive nor forget.

As autumn fell, NATO air strikes, coupled with Bosnian government and Croatian advances against the Serbs continued, and it became clear that it was important to bring the three warring factions to the negotiating table to try and broker a peace.

American President Bill Clinton announced on October 5 that the protagonists had agreed to cease hostilities and over the course of several days at an air force base in Dayton, Ohio (deliberately chosen so that the negotiating parties had little else to do but work out an agreement), Tudman, Izetbegović and Milošević met to thrash out the terms of a permanent peace deal to end the war in Bosnia. Richard Holbrooke, one of the chief negotiators who had hoped that the conference would take 17 days, was frustrated that by day 16 they were still some way off settling on a suitable constitution and demarcation of communities.

Neither side wanted to be seen to blink first. This ridiculous situation was perhaps best exemplified by Holbrooke organising a face-to-face meeting between Milošević and Haris Silajdžić, the Bosnian Prime Minister. Milošević wanted to go and sit at Silajdžić's table, Silajdžić refused as he felt this would give Milošević the psychological upper hand. Instead Silajdžić went and sat at Milošević's table.

The main sticking point appeared to be the fate of the Goražde enclave, a Muslim area surrounded by Serbs. The Bosnians wanted it to be linked by a road to the rest of Bosnian territory. Using computer generated graphics of the Bosnian countryside and working until the early hours of the morning (and fuelled by a significant amount of alcohol, according to Holbrooke) a computer graphic of the road was constructed. Milošević didn't realise he was giving up 58% of the territory and when he did, he reneged on the agreement, leading to further talks.

After several more false starts they finally drank to an agreement which included ceding back to the Serbs land which had recently been captured by combined Muslim/Croat forces. However, nobody had told the Croats, who considered the deal unacceptable, to the point where Holbrooke described the usually mild-mannered Croatian Foreign Minister Mate Granić as turning into a "rhinoceros".

Negotiations had to restart again, with a by-now exhausted Holbrooke and US Secretary of State Warren Christopher becoming more assertive in their diplomacy and eliciting to a final concession from Milošević, who agreed to place the town of Brčko on the Bosnian/Croat border under international arbitration. At a packed news conference on November 21, 1995, Holbrooke announced that an agreement had been reached and it was signed by Milošević, Izetbegović and Tuđman at a ceremony in Paris in mid-December. Crucially, the issue of Kosovo's future was not discussed at Dayton. Its predominantly Albanian community were demanding greater autonomy, yet as a significant number of its population was also Serb, it was possibly kept out of the negotiations as a means of keeping Milošević onside.

Following Milošević's decision to revoke Kosovan Autonomy in 1989, the Democratic League of Kosovo (LDK) was created as an immediate response to both this and the Kosovan Parliament's acceptance of the matter. In 1992, it organised a referendum on Kosovan independence, in which Kosovo's Albanian population overwhelmingly voted in favour. Led by the charismatic Ibrahim Rugova in his distinctive silk scarf, there was an active policy of passive resistance, or in Rugova's own words: "It is easy to take to the streets and to head towards suicide, but wisdom lies in eluding a catastrophe". For some though, the policy of waiting for the international community to come to a resolution was not enough, particularly after Dayton, and they began to take a more assertive path. From early 1996, the Kosovo Liberation Army (KLA) began attacking government institutions and individuals within them, claiming retaliation for attacks on Albanians, but perhaps more cynically to provoke Serbia and therefore be seen as victims of Serbian aggression.

The KLA also amassed a huge quantity of overseas donations, some of it from questionable sources including suspected organised criminal drugs gangs. It also acquired weapons smuggled across the border from Albania, as well as training from countries such as Germany and the United States. Both NATO and the Organisation for Security and Co-operation in Europe (OSCE) stated that they believed the KLA were acting provocatively, and deliberately intimidating the non-Albanian population by both acts of violence and enforced evictions.

In February 1998 the KLA, under the leadership of its distinctively bearded leader Adem Jashari, carried out coordinated attacks resulting in the deaths of four Serb policemen in the village of Likošane. Following another KLA attack on police on the morning of March 5, the Serbs' patience finally broke. Police descended upon the house in Prekaz, some 30 miles north west of Pristina where Jashari, his brother Hamez, several fighters as well as women and children were encamped. After a stand-off, a firefight ensued. Two Serb police were killed as well as almost everyone inside the compound, the only survivor being Hamez's daughter, Besarta.

The incident created an international backlash with government criticism and street protests against Yugoslavia, which at this stage consisted of Serbia (incorporating both Kosovo and Vojvodina) and Montenegro. It became a rallying call for the KLA across Kosovo, and Jashari became the martyr figure used for propaganda purposes. If the KLA's policy was to provoke Yugoslavia into retaliation in a bid to make it look like they were the aggressor, they couldn't have played their hand better.

Clashes between Yugoslav and KLA forces continued during the early part of 1998 and despite the Albanians not wishing to negotiate directly with Serbia, they was willing to do so with Yugoslavia, On May 15, Milošević and Rugova met in Belgrade following an announcement by the tireless Richard Holbrooke, who had visited Milošević in Belgrade and also travelled to areas affected by the conflict. It was on this brief tour he was photographed sitting next to an armed KLA fighter. Being seen with such an esteemed American politician gave the KLA further legitimacy, making it seem as though it possibly had United States backing. A further intervention by Russian President Boris Yeltsin meant international observers were allowed into Kosovo to monitor the unfolding events.

The KLA continued to make advances in the late summer and Yugoslav attempts to remove them from Northern Kosovo were met with condemnation from abroad. KLA attacks on police continued, and on September 25, five policemen were killed by a roadside device between Likovac and Gornje Obrinje in central Kosovo. The retreating KLA then left civilians open to reprisals by the Yugoslav army.

This tactic of attacking and then retreating has been seen as a deliberate tactic by some. Fred Abrahams of Human Rights Watch stated in his book, *Modern Albania: From Dictatorship To Democracy In Europe,* that "the massacre revealed a disturbing side of the KLA. To get attention and Western support the group needed sympathy and civilian deaths helped their cause. The KLA frequently attacked Serbian forces and then retreated through a village, exposing the civilians to the predictably overaggressive response"

Following the September 25 incident, police entered Gornje Obrinje and executed 21 civilians, including 14 women and children, horrifically mutilating many of the bodies. The international condemnation came from the highest levels. Bill Clinton's Press Secretary Michael McCurry declared that: "It just underscores the ugliness and the brutality of the Serb presence in Kosovo and underscores the rationale for the efforts that we have been making both diplomatically and through NATO." Kofi Annan, the UN Secretary General, was particularly disgusted as he had been assured by Yugoslavia that such massacres hadn't taken place.

The humanitarian crisis was deepening. In scenes bleakly reminiscent of what had occurred in Bosnia and Croatia, groups of refugees fled their homes with little immediate chance of food, warmth or shelter. NATO was beginning to flex its muscles too, releasing a statement on September 24 warning that it had moved to "an increased level of military preparedness". The statement called on Milošević to cease hostilities against the Albanian population within Kosovo, alleviate the humanitarian crisis and be prepared for a political solution. This was backed up on October 13 by a further statement which said that authorisation for airstrikes to begin within 96 hours had been issued. The statement finished with a stark warning for Yugoslavia: "The responsibility is on President Milošević's shoulders. He knows what he has to do." Milošević must have realised that he had little other option than to sign a ceasefire agreement and having done so, Yugoslavia was given until October 27 to withdraw from Kosovo.

On January 15, 1999, the OSCE's Kosovo Verification Mission (KVM) received reports of an incident in Račak in central Kosovo. Upon arriving at the outskirts of the village, the KVM were denied access and had to make do with observing fighting from a nearby location. The following day the KVM, plus representatives from the European Union and several journalists did gain access and came across 40 bodies scattered around, with a further five apparently already moved by families. The presence of the journalists ensured the horror and the raw emotions of the victims' loved ones were captured for the world to see. Walking up a narrow path where many of the bodies lay, the chief of the KVM William Walker described the gruesome manner in which the victims had been executed, saying "this is about as horrendous an event as I have seen".

Yugoslav state news agency *Tanjug* described those killed as terrorists, claiming that they had fired automatic weapons and mortars at Serb policemen and that they were wearing KLA uniforms and insignia, something refuted by British journalists who filmed the aftermath. One later wrote in *The Independent* that what he witnessed were older men in civilian clothing with single bullet wounds to the head. The Serbs tried to refuse access to other foreign investigators and removed the bodies for post-mortem examination, with the chief pathologist claiming that "not a single body bears any sign of execution".

Following the Račak massacre, the threat of further NATO strikes was enough to bring Milošević to talks with the other warring factions at the Château de Rambouillet, some 30 miles south west of Paris. Talks scheduled to last a fortnight began on February 6.

Both sides knew that to be seen as the belligerent party would have significant consequences. For the Yugoslavs it would be airstrikes, for the Kosovans it would be the loss of international support. Yugoslavia felt that the demands made upon them were too high and they, along with the Russians, refused to sign the agreement. It appears that they may have had unreasonably high demands set upon them on purpose, with one senior American official declaring that they had "deliberately set the bar higher than the Serbs could accept." Maybe the Serbs could be bombed into seeing sense, or maybe the Americans were wary of becoming involved in yet another internal ethnic conflict within Europe, and wanted to end it quickly once and for all.

After the talks failed, military action became inevitable. On the evening of March 24, NATO enacted 'Operation Allied Force', firing Tomahawk missiles and carrying out sorties by plane over Belgrade. As well as targeting military facilities, NATO also hit factories, telecommunication towers and bridges, leading many Serbs to stand on them to act as human shields. NATO also made a series of high-profile blunders with their aerial bombardments. An Albanian refugee column, believed by NATO to be a Yugoslav military convoy, was bombed and 50 civilians were killed. On May 7, the Chinese embassy in Belgrade was hit, killing three Chinese journalists and enraging its government. A prison within Kosovo was also struck by NATO. The Yugoslavian government claimed that almost a hundred Albanian prisoners were killed. However, Human Rights Watch claimed that the figure was much lower and a number of prisoners were killed by government forces in the subsequent days in an attempt to pass them as further casualties of the NATO attack.

However, despite all the bombing by NATO, Yugoslavia maintained its resolve to the point that Tony Blair, the British Prime Minister, began to lobby other NATO members to use ground forces. Milošević however saw that Russia would not commit its own troops to defend Yugoslavia should a ground invasion by NATO forces take place and reluctantly agreed on June 3 to a UNheaded military presence, supported by a high NATO presence. On June 12, the first peacekeeping troops (known as KFOR) arrived in Kosovo, and on the same day British and Norwegian special forces managed to navigate their way to Pristina. In some Albanian areas, the sight of KFOR troops arriving brought cheering citizens onto the streets, showering tanks and those riding on them with flowers. In stark contrast, columns of Yugoslav tanks pounding their way home along highways in the oppressive haze of the summer heat became a familiar sight on TV. So did the sight of families of Serb refugees fleeing for sanctuary, fearful of reprisals from the KLA and other Kosovans. The lucky ones had cars or tractors to carry their belongings, the unlucky had to use horses and carts or even walk, again in fearful summer conditions.

NATO didn't have everything their own way, Russian troops found their way to Pristina Airport first, leading to a stand-off with KFOR. NATO Supreme Commander Wesley Clark, furious at the actions of the Russians, ordered KFOR Commander General Mike Jackson to block the runway with NATO vehicles so that the Russians were unable to be reinforced. Jackson refused the order, saying: "I'm not going to start World War Three for you." Jackson's view was endorsed by one of his lead subordinates on the ground, then a captain, but also a future musical artist, James Blunt.

KFOR maintained a presence in Kosovo in the aftermath of the war and was still there at the time of writing in Spring 2023. The country's ethnic mix of Serbs and Albanians has occasionally erupted into violence, in particular in the divided city of Mitrovica, in which harassment and threats by one community against the other have been a common occurrence since the war. Kosovo's present ethnic make-up is difficult to assess as Serbs boycotted the 2011 census, however large amounts of the population were displaced after the war and not all of those would have felt safe to return.

Kosovo itself felt empowered enough to declare its independence from Serbia in May 2008. Kosovar Albanians greeted the declaration with delight. However, their Serbian counterparts were less happy and attacked UN and KFOR buildings. The reaction within Serbia was also vehement. Slobodan Samardžić, Serbia's minister for Kosovo declared the region to be a "fake country". Within a week of the declaration, 17 countries had recognised Kosovo's independence, amongst them the USA, UK, Germany and France. To date, more than 100 nations have recognised Kosovo as an independent country.

So, what of the three other republics that made up Yugoslavia; Macedonia, Montenegro and Serbia? In September 1991, Macedonia held a referendum on independence from Yugoslavia which was approved by over 95% of those who voted. American soldiers were posted to the Macedonian-Serbian border following the vote, but there was little resistance from within Yugoslavia and they were allowed to peacefully leave and became a member of the UN in April 1993. It was known as the Former Yugoslav Republic of Macedonia until January 2019, when an amendment in the constitution saw the country change its name to North Macedonia following an agreement with its southern neighbour Greece, which also holds an area known as Macedonia within its territory.

Yugoslavia limped on with just Serbia and Montenegro until February 2003, when it became the State Union of Serbia & Montenegro. In May 2006, an independence referendum was held in Montenegro and 55.5% voted in favour, narrowly passing the required threshold of 55%. The country declared its independence on June 3 that year. Following this Serbia inherited the UN position of the State Union of Serbia & Montenegro and quietly, with a simple piece of administrative procedure, what was once Yugoslavia was no more.

★

CHAPTER FOUR
ALMOST

In 1991, the year that Red Star lifted the European Cup and were crowned world club champions, Yugoslavia were in the middle of a qualifying campaign for Euro '92, which was to be held in Sweden. In a group notable for one of the great surprises of European football, when the Faroe Islands beat Austria 1-0 in their first ever qualifying game, a home loss to Denmark was the only blemish in an otherwise perfect qualification process, and Ivica Osim's side finished top of their group with 14 points from eight games (only two points were awarded for a win at this stage). Having won all their away games by a 2-0 score line, they also scored more goals than anyone else in qualifying with only France, who won their group with a perfect record, accruing more points.

However, as the team were preparing for the tournament, events on the ground in Yugoslavia were about to catch up with them. Massacres in Bijeljina and Zvornik in Bosnia were being broadcast on news programmes outside of Yugoslavia and there was increased pressure from international organisations to act. Therefore in May 1992, the United Nations finally did just that, passing 'resolution 757' with the explicit aim of imposing a trade embargo on Yugoslavia. Section 8b of the resolution stated that all member states would: "Take the necessary steps to prevent the participation in sporting events on their territory of persons or groups representing the Federal Republic of Yugoslavia (Serbia and Montenegro)."

The resolution was passed just 11 days before Yugoslavia's scheduled opening Euro '92 game with England. UEFA felt that they had little option other than to expel Yugoslavia from the tournament. Denmark, who were drafted in as late replacements, famously won the tournament. According to Uros Popovic, who still has his Euro '92 sticker album at his parent's house in Montenegro, the reaction to Yugoslavia's expulsion was mixed. "People were pissed but they had other things to worry about", he told me, adding that the decision to expel Yugoslavia was not unexpected by the country's fans. However, when Denmark went on to win the tournament he remembers the feeling changing with many of his friends cheering on the Danes and "Eventually we were like 'woah, this is like Yugoslavia won the Euros!'"

The Yugoslav players, however, did not share Popovic's enthusiasm for their Scandinavian replacements. Speaking to *The Guardian* in 2020 Slaviša Jokanović, who made his debut for the national team in 1991, still feels a sense of bitterness. "We had the Euros taken away from us and never got it back", he said, "We had a much better side than Denmark."

The UN resolution also led to FIFA banning Yugoslavia from the 1994 World Cup in the USA, and although they had already been drawn in qualification Group 5, the process carried on without them. They were also banned from Euro '96 in England. However, following the conclusion of the war in Bosnia, and elections in September 1996, the United Nations passed Security Council Resolution 1074 the following month which lifted sanctions on Yugoslavia and they were invited back for the 1998 World Cup in France, managing to qualify from Group 6 ahead of Euro '96 runners up the Czech Republic.

Yugoslavia's squad for the 1998 World Cup featured Dragan Stojković, Dragoje Leković, and Dejan Savićević, all of whom had been in the squad for Yugoslavia's last appearance on the world stage in 1990. They won their first game, against Iran, 1-0 courtesy of a trademark Sinisa Mihajlović free kick. A week later they faced

Germany and although they took a 2-0 lead, a Mihajlović own goal and an Oliver Bierhoff header meant the game ended all square. A 1-0 win against the USA in their final game was enough for Yugoslavia to finish second behind Germany and advance to the last 16, where they came up against a Netherlands team who had finished top of their group. The Dutch took the lead when Dennis Bergkamp stole a march on Zoran Mirković before quickly turning and firing a low shot under Yugoslav keeper Ivica Kralj, who should have done better. Nevertheless, Slobodan Komljenović headed an equaliser and Yugoslavia had a chance to take the lead when Jaap Stam persistently pulled Jugović's shirt and gave away a penalty. However, the resulting spot kick was hammered against the bar by Predrag Mijatović. In the 92nd minute, the Dutch had a corner which was played along the ground to Edgar Davids who drove the ball through a crowd of players and into the bottom left corner of the net. Heartbreak was yet again Yugoslavia's on the game's biggest stage.

In qualifying for Euro 2000, Yugoslavia faced two of its former constituent parts in Croatia and Macedonia. Despite having to play their home game against Malta in Greece due to NATO's bombing campaign during the Kosovo War, Yugoslavia topped the group, losing just one game. Their time at Euro 2000 itself was ended by a 6-1 drubbing in the quarter finals at the hands of the Netherlands, however their final group game against Spain has gone down in European football folklore. Leading in the 93rd minute Yugoslavia, who had been reduced to 10 men, were on the brink of winning the game and topping the group. However, they conceded a penalty which Gaizka Mendieta converted and then in the 95th minute Alfonso Pérez volleyed in a winner to send Spain through at the top of the group, avoiding the Dutch in the next round in the process.

Yugoslavia failed to qualify for the World Cup in 2002. They finished third in qualifying, a point behind Slovenia, partly due to a draw between the two sides at the Bežigrad Stadium in Ljubljana. Savo Milošević had given the visitors the lead with a tap in, but in the 94th minute, Zlatko Zahovič slotted home a free kick from some 30 yards, meaning spoils were shared and that, ultimately, Slovenia would qualify at Yugoslavia's expense.

For Euro 2004 qualification, Yugoslavia became known as simply Serbia & Montenegro and they failed to qualify. Despite an encouraging start, only taking one point out of a possible six against whipping boys Azerbaijan saw them fail to progress to even the play-off stage for the finals.

A far more assured qualifying campaign for the 2006 World Cup in Germany saw Serbia & Montenegro concede just one goal in 10 games and qualify unbeaten, topping a group that included Spain. There were also two historic matches against Bosnia in the group. The teams played out a 0-0 draw in Sarajevo before the return game in Belgrade saw the hosts win thanks to a Mateja Kežman goal, which unfortunately led to violence off the pitch. The Bosnia game would go on to have significant ramifications for Serbia & Montenegro at the tournament itself. Nemanja Vidić was sent off with only a few minutes left to play for a cynical block in midfield. Uros Popovic, who attended the game, described the atmosphere at the match perhaps a little understatedly as "not pleasant, with chants an hour before the game".

At the tournament itself, Serbia & Montenegro found themselves in a group with Argentina, the Ivory Coast and their perennial bogey team, the Netherlands. Hopes were high following such a successful qualifying campaign, and the squad had a blend of experience with Milošević and Dejan Stanković as well as exciting youth prospects, such as new Manchester United signing Vidić who along with Mladen Krstajić, Ivica Dragutinović and Goran Gavrančić formed the nucleus of the incredibly stingy defence during qualifying. However, Vidić did not play the first game against the Netherlands owing to his suspension, and it took only 18 minutes for Arjen Robben to latch onto a lofted pass and outpace the defence to slide home underneath Dragoslav Jevrić in goal. It was the only goal in the game which was played in such hot conditions that Dutch Coach Marco Van Basten had to soak his face in the dugout with a sponge.

Vidić was still missing for the second game, against Argentina, picking up a knee ligament injury in training following the Netherlands defeat. The Argentina game would prove to be an even bigger test for the Serbia & Montenegro defence; their frightening attack featured Hernán Crespo and Javier Saviola, with Juan Román Riquelme playing in the hole behind as the puppet master. As if that wasn't enough, Argentina also had youth on their side, with Carlos Tevez and teenage Lionel Messi among the substitutes. Serbia & Montenegro's resistance lasted just six minutes, when neat trickery down the Argentinian left allowed Saviola to lay the ball back into the path of the onrushing Maxi Rodríguez, who fired the ball past Jevrić. A rampant and artistic Argentina weren't done, and they scored another five beautifully crafted goals.

Having lost their first two games. Serbia & Montenegro had nothing left to play for but pride in their final match. There they met Ivory Coast, who were making their World Cup debut and who had lost 2-1 against both Argentina and the Netherlands. Serbia and Montenegro didn't take any chances, switching from a 4-4-2 to a 4-5-1 formation. The Europeans quickly found themselves 2-0 up with two very similar goals from Nikola Žigić and Saša Ilić, both of which were the result of long balls causing confusion between Ivory Coast's defenders and goalkeeper. However, a complete breakdown in discipline from then on destroyed any hope of victory. A ridiculous handball led to a penalty for Ivory Coast, which was put away with precision by Aruna Dindane. Midfielder Albert Nađ was then sent off for a second bookable offence in first half injury time, a feat made all the more impressive given he had only been introduced as a substitute in the 16th minute. Dindane then snuck in between the two central defenders to head home an equaliser in the 67th minute, before another handball led to a second Ivory Coast penalty three minutes from time, which Bonaventure Kalou converted.

A campaign which had promised so much following qualifying never got going. Serbia and Montenegro had the worst record of any team in the competition and were at best abysmal. They were hardly presenting a united front, either — only two Montenegrin-born players, Dragoslav Jevrić and Mirko Vučinić, had been selected for the squad, with Vučinić injured before the World Cup and never even participating. Given the political situation at home at the time, it was perhaps inevitable that the two countries would soon go their separate ways.

Following the conclusion of the tournament in 2006, Montenegro applied for its own membership of UEFA, with Serbia taking Serbia & Montenegro's place both in European competition and with FIFA. Dejan Savićević, who was, and still is at the time of writing, President of the Montenegrin FA, claimed at the time that "Serbia is closest to my heart after my native Montenegro and down here we will all cheer for the unified team in Germany and for the Serbs in the Euro 2008 qualifiers". However, not everyone was so pleased with events. Savo Milošević, who was born in Bosnia but was of Montenegrin extraction, claimed that both he and Jevrić were unhappy with the outcome. Alluding to the wider political split between Serbia and Montenegro he said: "I wish I could congratulate the winning camp in Montenegro, but I just can't because I was an advocate of the unified state." Milošević's comments made no difference however; Serbia tried and failed to qualify for Euro 2008 and Montenegro played their first competitive game against Bulgaria in September 2008 as they attempted to qualify for the 2010 World Cup.

In the qualifying process for Euro 2016, Serbia and Albania were drawn together in Group I. Despite the obvious potential for clashes, UEFA claimed that they didn't feel that the two countries needed to be separated, as neither the Serbian nor the Albanian FA had made such a request, despite the fact that Armenia and Azerbaijan had to be kept apart due to the Nagorno-Karabakh War. UEFA optimistically stated that the same precautions need not be taken as Serbia and Albania had never actually been at war against each other. And so, despite the potential risks, both teams kicked off qualifying in September 2014. Zoran Tošić rescued a point for Serbia with last-minute goal in Armenia and Albania beat Portugal 1-0 away thanks to a beautiful volleyed goal from Bekim Balaj.

Those who had feared trouble between the two sides were proven right when they met on a dark October evening at the Partizan Stadium in Belgrade. Before the game, in a bid to reassure those who expected violence, the Deputy Chief of Police in Belgrade, Nikola Popovac, stated that extra security would be present. "We'll have a double security check, metal detectors and will react to any sign of trouble in the stands. We are prepared for everything," he said. Despite these measures, the Albanian FA claimed that on the way to the ground their team bus was targeted by Serb fans throwing rocks, and that inside the stadium their players were also pelted with objects, including lumps of concrete. As the Albanian team emerged from the players' tunnel in their tracksuits to take in their surroundings, the ground was by no means full - nevertheless they were met by an angry and vociferous group of Serb fans next to the tunnel, replete with flags and angry hand gestures.

The players stood in a group on the pitch looking unconcerned, with many filming on mobile phones the angry chanting of the home fans who had just greeted them. The mood lifted when the Serb players made their way onto the pitch to commence their warm-up, and they were in turn cheered back off it again when they finished.

There were more whistles and roars as the Albanian lineup was announced on the big screen with giant photos of each player, though applause for the hosts was the overriding sound as the players appeared onto the pitch. The game began brightly for Serbia as they went close early on, though some Albanian players seemed to be dropping on the ground quite easily and referee Martin Atkinson booked full back Ansi Agolli in the 34th minute for time wasting.

Trouble began in the 42nd minute when Atkinson suspended the game after flares were thrown onto the pitch. The game then took a far more sinister turn. A drone was flown into the stadium carrying a flag showing a map of Greater Albania (a geographical area covering Albania, Kosovo, the Preševo Valley region of Serbia and territory in neighbouring countries). Serb defender Stefan Mitrović pulled down the flag as the drone dropped towards the pitch, however he was then surrounded by Albanian players Andi Lila, Taulant Xhaka and Bekim Balaj who managed to snatch the flag from him. Uros Popovic was at the game and he recalled that when he saw the drone his first thought was "what the fuck is happening?". Like many others present, it took him some time to understand it, although in the days afterwards he and others he spoke to were relieved that all that the drone was carrying was a flag and that nobody was seriously injured. Looking back, he feels the whole incident was a "stupid provocation".

Once Balaj had the flag, he tried to make his way off the pitch, accompanied by Agolli, but he was attacked by a Serbian fan wielding a plastic chair. This led to a melee with the Albanian players coming to Balaj's defence. More Serbian fans streamed onto the pitch and the Serb players tried to break up the fracas. A semblance of calm was restored as the two groups of players talked, albeit rather animatedly, between themselves. Perhaps if the game had restarted at this point, then it could have reached its conclusion, especially with half-time being so close. However, it was decided to take the players off at this point, with the Albanian players leaving the pitch first down the players' tunnel, surrounded by the Serb fans. Objects and at least one flare were thrown from the stands and baton-wielding riot police stepped in to keep fans at bay and protect the players.

Further lines of riot police stood on the running track between the chanting fans and the pitch. Some moved into the stands to forcefully eject fans as, bizarrely, Cher's 'Believe' blasted out over the PA system in a bid to calm everyone down. After a delay, the Serbian starting XI and substitutes reappeared to a rapturous reception from the home fans. They formed a huddle in the centre of the pitch, then turned to applaud all corners of the ground before walking off the pitch one final time. The game was then abandoned, with Albania's players understandably unwilling to venture outside again.

The Albanian team arrived back at Rinas International Airport in the early hours of the following morning to be greeted by several thousand jubilant fans, proud of how the events of a few hours earlier had played out. The country's Deputy Prime Minister Niko Peleshi and Minister of Sport Lindita Nikolla were also there to welcome the players back. Fans had also gathered in several ethnic Albanian areas across the Balkans to celebrate the events of the night, and in particular the flying of the flag.

The reaction on the Serb side was somewhat different, with accusations being made that the drone had been piloted by Olsi Rama, the brother of the Albanian Prime Minister Edi. Serbian authorities suggested that Rama, who had attended the game in the VIP section, had been arrested and immediately taken back to Albania. Both Rama and the Albanian government denied this. Rama claimed that he was removed from the VIP section because of the deteriorating situation in the stadium and that because he also held an American passport, was therefore placed onto a waiting bus. Rama's innocence was verified by former Albanian captain and Lazio Sporting Director Igli Tare who said: "We are friends with Olsi. We were sitting next to each other in the stadium and he was holding a camera in his hand. The police came and took the camera from his hands and then returned it again. Then he quietly left for the airport."

Tare was also involved in an ongoing feud with Siniša Mihajlović. It began during the 2005/06 season when the pair were playing against each other for Lazio and Inter respectively. During the half-time break, Tare physically assaulted Mihajlović, who he claimed had repeatedly racially abused him during the first half. The Albanian got more revenge many years later in his role as Lazio's sporting director by vetoing Mihajlović's appointment as manager. Thus it was little surprise that Tare responded to the drone incident in an overtly patriotic manner saying "we Albanians are proud of our history, our roots and it seemed to us how proud our guys defended the flag last night". It wasn't exactly conciliatory language. Others responded in even more aggressive ways. In northern Serbia shops owned by ethnic Albanians were targeted, the Albanian embassy in Montenegro was attacked, and in Albania people took to the streets waving Albanian flags and attacking Serbs and ethnic Greeks. There were also incidents in Austria.

FIFA President Sepp Blatter and his UEFA counterpart Michel Platini condemned the scenes in Belgrade, with the former stating football "should never be used for political messages" and the latter releasing a statement through a UEFA spokesman saying "Football is supposed to bring people together and our game should not be mixed with politics of any kind. The scenes in Belgrade last night were inexcusable". UEFA also opened disciplinary procedures against both the Serbian and the Albanian FAs. The charges against Serbia related mainly to poor organisation and fan behaviour, while Albania were charged with refusing to play and the display of an illicit banner.

The inevitable finger pointing in the aftermath stretched right to the political summit of both countries. Serbian Prime Minister Aleksandar Vučić said that he had warned European Union officials several times that he felt it was inevitable that there would be some sort of Albanian provocation. "I warned our partners five times between 6pm and 6.50pm yesterday of a possible scenario of provocations by Albanian officials, and some of those officials wore KLA scarves so it was clear that they had come with an unambiguous intention to provoke the hosts".

His Albanian counterpart Edil Rama used the fallout from the game to try and appeal to Serbia to forge closer relations with both Albania and Europe, telling the Associated Press: "Serbia and Albania must try to end several decades of mutual hostility by focusing on important issues such as their shared desire to join the EU ... international politics cannot be driven by football games". However, in the aftermath of the game Rama's scheduled visit to Belgrade was postponed. He went on to try to allay any Serbian fears about a Greater Albania because "a Greater Albania is a Serbian nightmare, not an Albanian project, neither in Albania nor in Kosovo."

UEFA met on October 23 and ruled that the charges against Albania would stick, and that they were to forfeit the game by a score of 3-0 after they were charged with refusing to play and displaying an "illicit banner". Albania were outraged by the accusation of refusing to play, stating that their players were fearing for their lives and had been struck by missiles. Serbia were also deducted three points and ordered to play their next two home games behind closed doors. Both countries' football associations were fined €100,000, and both governing bodies appealed to UEFA, who upheld their original decision. The case then went to the Court of Arbitration for Sport (CAS). CAS rejected Serbia's appeal, and their points deduction stood. However, they partially upheld the Albanian appeal, awarding them the 3-0 win instead, the justification being that "the security lapses of the organisers and acts of violence exerted on the Albanian players by the Serbian fans" was the reason for players leaving the pitch and for the match to be abandoned. Albania still had to pay the €100,000 fine as CAS stated that "the FAA was responsible for the drone operated during the match, carrying a banner depicting Albanian nationalistic and patriotic symbols". Edil Rama wrote "That is European justice! 3 points for the Red-and-Black National Team in Belgrade!!!" with the Albanian coach Giovanni de Biasi believing that "Justice is in its place. I am very happy of course, because when justice triumphs everybody is happy."

The result left Serbia with just one point after two games in the group and their qualification hopes clinging by the tiniest of threads given the positive start made by their main group rivals. By contrast, Albania were now in a highly promising position. The return fixture was played under incredibly tight security in Elbasan, central Albania. The game was goalless until the 91st minute when Serbia's Aleksandar Kolarov slid the ball between the legs of Etrit Berisha in the Albanian goal. While the team celebrated, substitute Duško Tošić made a three-fingered salute. He was subsequently forced to apologise to the fans of the Turkish club Beşiktaş for whom he played. They did not take too kindly to the gesture due to its alleged links with Serb nationalism and use by soldiers during the Yugoslav wars. The game was sealed three minutes later by Adem Ljajić who broke from midfield before finishing with a delightful chip over Berisha and into the empty net. Whatever local bragging rights this may have temporarily given to Serbia it made no difference in the end as Albania's 3-0 win away in Armenia meant that they qualified for Euro 2016 in France, with Serbia finishing fourth in the group. While the deduction of points might have had a psychological impact upon the Serb players, it made no material difference as they finished eight points behind third-placed Denmark.

Two years later, Serbia did qualify for the 2018 World Cup in Russia and were placed in a group with Brazil, Costa Rica and Switzerland. Drawn to face Brazil in their final game, it was imperative that Serbia achieved positive results in their first two games. They got off to a perfect start against Costa Rica thanks to a beautiful left-footed free kick by Aleksandar Kolarov. However, their next test against Switzerland was about more than football. The Swiss squad was a melting pot of differing ethnicities, several of whom could trace their roots back to the Balkans, most notably Xherdan Shaqiri and Valon Behrami, who were both born in Kosovo. Shaqiri celebrated his split heritage by having the badges of Kosovo and Switzerland stitched into his boots, and then posting a picture of them on Instagram. The Serbian striker Aleksandar Mitrović asked "If he loves Kosovo so much and decides to flaunt the flag, why did he refuse a chance to play for their team?". To add to the tension, there were reports that Serb fans sang "*Kosovo je Srbija*" (Kosovo is Serbia) while celebrating their win against Costa Rica in the bars of Samara, where the game was held.

Switzerland's starting line-up included both Behrami and Shaqiri as well as Haris Seferović who was of Bosniak extraction and Granit Xhaka who was of Albanian descent and whose brother Taulant played for the Albanian national team (when the two sides met at Euro 2016, Xhaka's mother watched from the crowd with a jumper embroidered with half a Swiss and half an Albanian flag).

The author James Montague was inside the stadium watching the match from the press box while his Serbian friends watched from the terraces. He describes his friends' concern before the game about chants such as "kill the Albanians" and abuse aimed at Shaqiri in particular from some of their fellow Serbs. However, he was pleasantly surprised that outside the ground — apart from the odd chant of "Kosovo is Albania" — there was nothing of any particular venom.

Inside the ground, however, the atmosphere was different; "to me it was so obvious, you saw some war criminal-type posters", Swiss players of Albanian extraction were continually booed and the "kill the Albanians" chant was also heard. Following the game, Montague met up with his Serb friends who had been in the stands and where he had heard the anti-Albanian and other nationalistic rhetoric, they said that they had heard nothing.

There were many Serb and Russian fans in the Kaliningrad Stadium chanting songs of unity and there was even a banner declaring the two nationalities "brothers". It took less than five minutes for the deadlock to be broken as a Dušan Tadić cross from the right found Mitrović, whose header was never going to be saved by Yann Sommer in the Swiss goal. In the second half, Switzerland pressed forward. A Shaqiri left-footed curled effort was blocked by Filip Kostić and rebounded some distance but only to Xhaka who hammered a 25-yard shot through a penalty area crowded with bodies before Stojković in the Serb goal even had a chance to set himself. Xhaka wheeled away screaming in delight but with his hands interlocked at the thumbs, palms facing inwards and fingers wiggling, in a bird-like way. It was a deliberate act, a gesture known as '*duart e kryqëzuara*' (meaning the 'crossed hands') and is used to signify the eagle on the Albanian flag. There was some confusion however with a Brazilian commentator rather sweetly and naively describing Xhaka's celebration as a doves of peace gesture.

Switzerland had several more chances to score a second before in the final minute Shaqiri found himself free in the Serbian half and slotted the ball coolly underneath Stojković before performing the same celebration as Xhaka. The immediate reaction was as polarised as could be expected, Shaqiri tried to play the whole issue down, saying "I can't discuss the game I'm afraid … we are footballers not politicians". There was concern within the Swiss camp that their star players' gestures were provocative enough to earn an immediate ban, though when their punishment was announced, Shaqiri and Xhaka were merely fined 10,000 Swiss Francs each. Some Serb media outlets believed the amount to be so paltry that the country had been shamed. To rub salt into the wound, Serbia themselves were fined 54,000 Swiss Francs for their fans displaying provocative banners, with some fans going a step further by wearing clothing featuring an image of Ratko Mladic.

Only a few days after the incident, I spoke with Kirsten Schlewitz, a writer and editor of the *Unusual Efforts* website who is based in Belgrade. I asked her what the feeling towards Swiss players of Balkan extraction was among Serbian fans she knew. "It was mostly, let's just get this over with so that the media stops talking about it", she said. The fans she knew wanted to concentrate on the outcome of the match, rather than outside theatre. Although there was a general feeling of exasperation that the celebrations had occurred, those people in the bar where she watched the game felt that it had not been seen as a deliberately provocative act and felt that it had been blown out of proportion. She did however feel that if it had been a Serb player that had shown the three-fingered salute celebrating a goal, then the footballing authorities would have come down a lot harder.

As a further show of the politicisation of the celebrations, Albania's Prime Minister Edi Rama organised a fund to raise money to cover Shaqiri and Xhaka's fines called "Don't Be Afraid of The Eagle". In just two days it managed to raise $19,000 of its $25,000 target. Writing on Facebook, Rama said: "The eagle sign, like a high-five or a thumbs-up, is one of celebration among Albanians, a.k.a. from the Land of Eagles!" Uros Popovic also questioned whether the gesture is any worse than the Serb three-fingered salute. Although the aim was probably provocation, he felt the gesture itself wasn't too jarring for Serbs.

***

Less than a month after the Maksimir riot, Yugoslavia hosted an international friendly against the Netherlands at the same venue. If the Yugoslav FA felt that the best antidote to the previous events at Maksimir was to display national unity by playing a national team fixture with a smattering of Croat players, it horribly misjudged the situation. The Yugoslav national anthem was drowned out by whistles from Croatian locals, who were also there to cheer on the glittering Dutch team that included stars such as Ruud Gullit, Marco Van Basten and Frank Rijkaard. The whistles and boos were even picked up by the television commentator; "it was uncomfortable to hear the reaction of the minor part of our audience during the anthem, who greeted it by turning their backs and some even whistled at it". The commentator's assertion that this was the venting by a "minor part" of the crowd was perhaps a little optimistic. Watching the footage back now, it certainly seems like a significant number of fans.

Yet only a few months later those same fans returned to watch their own Croatian national team, albeit in an unofficial match against the United States. The game was paid for by a Croat businessman, who persuaded the American team to play the match as they were already in Poland for a game. While the visitors' side included stars such as John Harkes, Tony Meola and Marcelo Balboa, the more established Croatian players were competing at the under-21 Euros for Yugoslavia, where they finished runners up. However, the Croatian team was not cobbled together, it featured goalkeeper Dražen Ladić and Aljoša Asanović, who both featured prominently once the country was recognised by FIFA (the latter also played in the Premier League for a season with Derby County).

The day before the game, a statue of Croatian hero Josip Jelačić, which had previously been removed by the Communist regime, was unveiled in Zagreb Square. Prior to the match Jelačić's name was invoked in an address to the crowd; the statue also featured on the programme cover as did the chequered šahovnica. The programme notes, some of which were written by Croatian President Franjo

Tuđman, emphasised the fact that the game was a representation to the world of the Croatian state. Wearing the now famous Croatia shirt with the red-and white-chequers, it was Asanović who opened the scoring, firing high into the net from six yards out and earning a standing ovation from the dignitaries in the crowd. The hosts soon doubled the lead as Ivan Cvjetković latched onto a pass and slid the ball past Meola into an empty net. The United States pulled a goal back through Troy Dayak, but the hosts held on for a historic win. The following day, the Croatian newspapers celebrated the result and the event, labelling them as everything from a declaration of international recognition to a call to arms for the Croatian homeland. It was just the propaganda coup that the Croatian cause needed.

Tuđman, who clearly subscribed to George Orwell's ethos that sport was war minus the shooting, was well aware of the optics. The largest political and military power in the world was in Zagreb to play a fixture against a Croatian national team and the symbolism and perceived recognition of the Croatian state could not have been more obvious to the rest of the world, particularly, and more importantly, to Belgrade. In his quest for Croatian independence, Tuđman was keen to piggyback onto Croatian football fan culture and exploit it for his own ends. Many members of the Dinamo Zagreb ultra-group, the Bad Blue Boys, fought in the Croatian war of independence, some sewing Dinamo badges onto their army fatigues. Talking to Simon Kuper in his seminal book *Football Against the Enemy*, two Dinamo fans described sleeping in a house on the front line with a Dinamo flag protruding from the building. Every now and then as convoys of Croatian army vehicles passed, horns would sound as fellow Dinamo fans noticed.

Were the Bad Blue Boys integral in the fight for Croatia's independence? Speaking to me, Dario Brentin suggested that their role had been "exaggerated" and that many who fought on the Croatian side just happened to be Bad Blue Boys and Dinamo Zagreb fans, rather than being there because of their football allegiances. "Did they have a role to play? Yes," Brentin told me. "Was it of great significance? I don't think so." The Bad Blue Boys have happily cultivated the image of fighters battling against the odds, but the reality is there were fans of many other clubs who fought on all sides.

Croatian and Slovene teams ceded from the Yugoslav football system in the summer of 1991 with the first season of the Croatian league (Prva HNL) commencing the following year. What should have been a triumph for Tuđman quickly descended into acrimony and farce as he insisted that Dinamo change its name, first to HAŠK Građanski, and then Croatia Zagreb. He rejected the term 'Dinamo' because he saw it as a "Bolshevik" term, citing other teams from Eastern Europe with Dinamo in their name, and wanted to entwine a united Croatia around a sporting focal point at a time of war. It has also been suggested that the name change was designed to appeal to Croatian migrants living abroad in a bid to drum up support for the Croatian cause elsewhere.

The Bad Blue Boys may have loved and fought for an independent Croatia, but they loved their team more. Thus, the name change sent Tuđman on an unnecessary collision course with the ultras at a time when the two sides had more that united them than pulled them apart.

The President slandered the Bad Blue Boys as everything from foreign agents to drug addicts and alcoholics. Perhaps most damning of all, he condemned the group, of which so many members had spilled blood for the independence cause, as either 'Yugo-nostalgics' or 'anti-Croatian'. Graffiti appeared around Zagreb proclaiming that "if there was freedom and democracy it would be Dinamo and not Croatia". There were also terrace chants about the perceived Serbian spelling of Tuđman's grandson's name Dejan. Pips, Chips & Videoclips, a rock band from Zagreb recorded the song '*Dinamo Ja Volim*' ('Dinamo I Love You') which was adapted by the Bad Blue Boys on the terraces. The point made by the fans was clear: although Croatian independence may have been what both they and the President wanted, Dinamo was not the united front for the Croatian cause. It belonged to Zagreb and the Dinamo fans.

Outside and autocratic interference in their way of life was not welcome, whatever the motivation.

The irony of the whole situation was that Tudman should have seen it coming. He had attended Dinamo matches, personally congratulated players after key games and was good friends with Coach Miroslav 'Ćiro' Blažević, who was a member of the President's HDZ party. A club magazine even declared him a "true football expert". And it wasn't just the Bad Blue Boys who felt the name change unnecessary — Zagreb city council renamed the ground the Dinamov Stadion (Dinamo's Stadium).

Tudman passed away in December 1999, and the Dinamo name was restored in February of the following year. Whether the change would have happened eventually anyway will always be open to debate, but the point was clear, top-down changes were not welcome and would ultimately meet with strong resistance.

The Croatian national football team was readmitted to FIFA in 1992 and qualified for Euro '96 by finishing top of a group that included Italy. Indeed, Croatia took four points off the Azzurri including a 2-1 away win in Palermo. Prior to the tournament in England, they had attended a training camp in Ireland and received a letter from an Irish team who had touchingly written "you will not be at home in Zagreb or Split to hear the pulse of your own people. Therefore, let these words speak for them. Make your mark".

Croatia were pitted against Portugal, Turkey and holders Denmark in their group and they got off to a winning start as they beat the Turks 1-0 thanks to a bursting run and cool finish by Goran Vlaović. What was more remarkable was that Vlaović had recently undergone surgery to remove a blood clot from his brain. He later commented "when you go through the things that I have you grow ten years older ... words cannot express how emotional I feel".

This feeling was further emphasised by Davor Šuker in an interview during the tournament in which he discussed trying to get his family to join him in Seville during the war. They refused as they felt it unfair that they had a way out of the country, but their neighbours didn't. Šuker, with a burgeoning reputation, had just been transferred from Sevilla to Real Madrid and had scored a phenomenal 12 goals for Croatia in qualifying. Blažević had declared the striker as the greatest genius in football at the time. Against Denmark his moment came, his beautiful through ball deep from midfield found Mario Stanić who was clumsily brought down by Peter Schmeichel in the Denmark penalty area. Šuker made no mistake from the resulting penalty. He also got an assist for the second with a cross from the left of the penalty area which found Boban at the far post. In the last minute, Schmeichel found himself out of position in the Croatian penalty area and a cross-field pass found Šuker who lobbed the ball over the scrambling and stranded keeper to score one of the most iconic goals in Croatian football history. Croatia had reached the knockout phase of the competition with Tuđman, never one to miss an opportunity, sending his congratulations to the team and his old friend Blažević.

Croatia decided to rest players in the final group game against Portugal and were soundly beaten 3-0. Had they won then they would have topped the group and gone on to face the Czech Republic in the quarter finals. As it was, Croatia came up against a German team that had lost its air of invincibility after having been knocked out of the quarter finals of the previous World Cup by Bulgaria. Indeed, Blažević himself felt the Germans would be ideal opponents for the Croatians owing to both teams' styles of play. Furthermore, Germany had been one of the first countries to recognise the Croatian state and so it was fitting that the two sides should meet at such a high level. After 20 minutes Germany won a penalty when Matthias Sammer forced a handball from defender Nikola Jerkan which Jürgen Klinsmann put away. In the second half Nikola Jurčević robbed a dozing Steffen Freund before feeding Šuker who jinked around Andreas Köpke in the German goal before supplying a cool finish. However, it wasn't to be for Croatia, as a darting run by Sammer went unnoticed and he stole in ahead of Jerkan to score the winner.

Croatia's qualifying campaign for the 1998 World Cup began just a few months later. Despite the fact that their FIFA ranking of 39th meant they were seeded in pot three, it was clear from their victory over Italy a couple of years prior that they would be a stern test to any opponent. Their first match was against Bosnia and Herzegovina in a sparsely populated Stadio Renato Dall'Ara in Bologna where they managed a comfortable 4-1 victory, though the fixture is just as notable for Hasan Salihamidžić scoring Bosnia's first ever goal as an independent nation.

The return game at the Maksimir in September 1997 saw Croatia record a very lucky 3-2 win and they were grateful to captain Boban for a late winner as they battled with Greece for the second qualifying spot behind Denmark. In their penultimate games, Greece beat Slovenia 3-0 in Ljubljana, while the Danes gained a tiny piece of Euro '96 revenge by trouncing Croatia 3-1. This meant that going into the final round of matches, Greece had 13 points ahead of Croatia's 12. Greece however found the Danish goalkeeper Schmeichel in unbeatable form and the game finished goalless. Croatia for their part defeated Slovenia 3-1 and their World Cup dream had been realised.

In the tournament in France, they were paired in group H against Argentina, Japan and Jamaica, beginning their campaign against the latter. Mario Stanić had the honour of scoring Croatia's first ever World Cup goal, stabbing the ball home from close range. However, as so often it was Prosinečki who created the headlines when his left-wing cross wound its way into the back of the Jamaican net. Whether he meant it or not seems a moot point given how lovely the finish was. Šuker knocked in a third for a 3-1 victory. A 1-0 victory against Japan followed by a 1-0 reverse to Argentina gave Croatia a second-place finish in the group and a last-16 knockout match against Romania, who had famously bleached their hair as a team bonding exercise. The game hinged on a hugely debatable penalty as Gabriel Popescu was harshly seen to have fouled a turning Aljoša Asanović and Šuker scored with a retaken spot-kick.

Croatia's quarter-final pitted them against their Euro '96 vanquishers Germany who wanted to put their previous World Cup exit at the hands of Bulgaria in 1994 behind them. Thus, both sides had a point to prove. The match turned on the sending off of Germany's Christian Wörns towards the end of the first half for a clumsy body check on Šuker. Long-range efforts from Robert Jarni and Vlaović and a third goal from Šuker set up a semi-final against France.

The hosts had made their way to the semi-final with a golden goal win in extra time over Paraguay in the second round and a penalty shoot-out victory against Italy in the quarter finals. Like the Croatians, the French team were themselves a figurehead for their nation. The ethnic mix of players was set against the politics of National Front leader Jean-Marie Le Pen, who had polled over 4.5 million votes in the previous elections. Inevitably it was Šuker who opened the scoring at the start of the second half, but France equalised barely a minute later. Boban was robbed of possession and of all people it was the defender Lillian Thuram who was furthest forwards and able to score. In the 70th minute Thuram was again on hand to curl a left-footed effort into the Croatian goal. Thuram played 142 times for France over 14 stellar years; they were the only goals that he would ever score for Les Bleus. Despite missing out on a World Cup final in their debut appearance, Croatia managed to grab third place by beating the Netherlands 2-1 in the play-off with Šuker scoring his sixth goal and in the process claiming the Golden Boot.

Reflecting on the success of the 1998 World Cup, captain Zvonimir Boban in 2021 told journalist Simon Kuper that "our '98 was built a lot in '87 in Chile", in that there was no inferiority complex for Croatia. Players such as Boban, Robert Prosinečki and Davor Šuker had won the World Youth Championship in 1987 beating Brazil, West Germany and hosts Chile along the way. That experience, coupled with the responsibility that the players felt towards relieving the suffering that the Croatian population had suffered throughout the years of war — as well as a natural patriotism — fuelled the team in their bid for glory.

Back in Croatia there was obvious pride at how the national team had performed in their first World Cup. Inevitably there were comparisons to the Croatian War, with several newspapers making reference to the military operations Storm and Flash, which had taken place during the conflict, in their headlines. This invocation of military action had been noticeable a year earlier when the renamed Croatia Zagreb had played Partizan in a Champions League qualifier.

For the first game in Belgrade, a Dragan Isailović goal for the home team was the difference between the two sides. In the return leg, 40,000 fans crammed into a noisy Maksimir to see if Zagreb could turn the tie around. With Tuđman prominent in the stands, it took Zagreb just 12 minutes to open the scoring through Silvio Marić. Four goals later Zagreb had soundly put Partizan to the sword. With a jumping Maksimir, a giant Croatian flag adorning the scoreboard which had the score and the home team's new name 'Croatia' in huge neon letters underneath, and the camera pointing at Tuđman every time Zagreb scored a goal, the President could quite possibly have been the happiest man in the stadium.

Following the match, there was more invoking of war imagery and headlines involving the words 'flash' and 'storm' and Tuđman later suggested that "we have fought for our independence in spite of numerous enemies. Likewise, you have fought for the Champions League in spite of strong rivals". During the game itself home fans had chanted "Vukovar, Vukovar" and in the aftermath of the match, goalscorer Silvio Marić suggested that the "victory was for all of Croatia. Especially for the lads who were killed for its freedom".

The Croatian national team fell into a fallow period after its success at France '98. They failed to qualify for Euro 2000 and at the World Cup in 2002, a loss to Mexico was followed by another win against Italy, yet they lost to Ecuador in the final game and were eliminated at the group stage. At Euro 2004, they drew their first two games against Switzerland and France before coming up against England and a rampant Wayne Rooney, who for large parts of the game was unplayable. In fact, Croatia barely troubled anyone at tournament level until the 2018 World Cup in Russia.

They were however noticed by those who wanted Croatia to be a forward-thinking and progressive nation. The country achieved EU membership in 2013, a decade after making its initial application. Its membership was confirmed after it settled border disputes with neighbouring Slovenia and extradited several of its citizens accused of war crimes to The Hague to face trial. In November 2013, an unsavoury incident occurred in the immediate aftermath of a 2-0 win against Iceland, which secured Croatia's qualification for the 2014 World Cup. In front of 22,000 celebrating fans at the Maksimir, defender Josip Šimunić grabbed a microphone and shouted "*za dom*" (for the homeland) several times, to which the crowd repeatedly roared back "*spremni*" (ready). At face value, this might seem like the innocuous celebration of an important result, however, the background to the phrase provides a different context — it was commonly used during World War II by the Croatian Ustaše, an extreme right-wing Croat group responsible for numerous massacres of non-Croats in the region.

The phrase itself still had some recent use, notably by the Croatian rock group Thompson. No strangers to controversy themselves, the band and their singer Marko Perković, who is confusingly also known as Thompson, have been accused of having extreme views. They are also closely aligned to Croatian football. They have been known for performing (though not writing) the song '*Jasenovac i Gradiška Stara*', which refers to the names (Jasenovac and Gradiška Stara) of concentration camps established by the Ustaše inside which horrific crimes were committed. Youths in clothes with nationalist slogans have appeared at the group's concerts and they have been banned from performing in several European countries. Thompson himself, along with several media outlets and politicians, have robustly denied that he is a fascist, however the Jewish global human rights organisation the Simon Wiesenthal Center are vehement in their comments about him. In relation to Perkovic's invitation to travel with the squad from Zagreb airport to their homecoming in the city after the 2018 World Cup, the *Times of Israel* quoted Efraim Zuroff from the centre as saying "Marko Perkovic has never missed an opportunity to transmit his hateful messages". Zuroff also condemned the team's decision, stating "Luka Modric might indeed have deserved to be the World Cup's Most Valuable Player, but for inviting Thompson to sing he deserves a red card."

The group is also connected to Croatian football by its song '*Lijepa li si*' ('How Beautiful You Are'), which was played at half-time during national team games. In 2007, in a match against Israel the song mysteriously wasn't played, with some players feeling that its omission put them off. Josip Šimunić was one of those players upset by Thompson's absence: "Some strange things are happening. I don't understand why they didn't let Thompson go to us before the game and at half-time as they always do when they know it's upsetting us. I really have no words," Darijo Srna was also confused and refuted any suggestions that the Israeli camp had requested that Thompson's music be withdrawn as they were not even aware of the singer. Following Croatia's 3-2 win against England at Wembley Stadium to qualify for Euro 2008, both fans and players serenaded each other with the song.

I asked Croatian academic and researcher Dario Brentin whether Šimunić could have used the '*za dom*' phrase without appreciating its historical context. "It's a difficult debate," Brentin said, suggesting that the fact Šimunić's was brought up in Australia meant he could have used the phrase in a naive attempt at patriotism. However, Brentin also felt that the player should have seen the wider picture and the possible ramifications of the chant. Brentin said the event was a microcosm for how both Croatia and its diaspora dealt with both its past and '*za dom spremni*', that Šimunić's use of the phrase was just "the tip of the iceberg" and the debate had not gone away. I asked Brentin if perhaps Šimunić was trying too hard to be Croatian, but he refuted the suggestion "I think he was just an archetypal member of the Croatian diaspora in Australia", and that with Croatian diaspora communities in Australia, the Catholic church and football clubs are "two venues for the re-establishment of everyday Croatian identity".

This wasn't the first time Croatian football was the subject of accusations of racism. During Euro 2004, Croatian fans were accused of making monkey noises at France's Sylvain Wiltord. Football Against Racism in Europe (FARE) also asked for Croatian flags with Celtic crosses on, which can be seen as a symbol of white power, to be removed from terraces. The FARE website also reported that Croatian fans in Livorno, Italy, had organised themselves into a human swastika in the stands ahead of a Euro 2008 qualifier. The website also quoted one of its Austrian partners saying: "These kinds of actions are highly organised and illustrate that football must continue to intensify its work against racism". Livorno is a traditionally left-wing town and there were suggestions that Croatian fans were deliberately trying to provoke local AS Livorno ultras. There had also been chants of "*za dom spremni*" at a Croatian national team game against Andorra, though these had been condemned by then Prime Minister Ivo Sanader.

The response to the '*za dom*' incident at the Maksimir was perhaps not what Šimunić was expecting, both in the positive responses from the fans in the ground at the time, but also in light of the lack of sanctions imposed on previous incidents. In his post-match interview, Šimunić stated that if anyone took any offence for his actions then it was their issue and not his. But this time it was different. Željko Jovanović, the Croatian Sports Minister, suggested he would find Šimunić a history teacher to teach him what the phrase actually meant. Croatian State's Attorney Office fined Šimunić the equivalent of €3,000 for inciting racial hatred, and FIFA issued him with a 10-match stadium ban and fined him €24,000. Perhaps most painfully for Šimunić this meant that he would miss the upcoming World Cup in Brazil. Jovanović welcomed the punishment, yet many in the Croatian football community felt that the measures were incredibly harsh. Croatian national team manager Niko Kovač expressed shock at the length of the ban and the fact that Šimunić would miss the World Cup.

Šimunić appealed to the Court of Arbitration for Sport (CAS) requesting his sanctions be expunged or suspended, however the CAS arbitration panel unanimously rejected his appeal.

I emailed Šimunić asking him if he would do anything differently and how he felt the incident had been reported. "Looking back at it," he replied, "I would not do anything differently. Whatever I've done in my life I stand behind. Of course, I wish it was reported differently in the media, because it wasn't real or truthfully portrayed. There are still traces of communism unfortunately in today's independent Croatia and as a result the media isn't as transparent as it should be and therefore all of the reporting around the *za dom* incident was heavily biased and political."

However, speaking to the Croatian sport newspaper *Sportske Novosti* in early 2019 (and following a recent European Court of Human Rights ruling which went against him), Šimunić was still disappointed with how events had played out, saying that he felt that the case was never about anything other than him being unfairly represented and that his honour as a man was in question. For him the chant was simply about being pleased that Croatia had qualified for the World Cup; "I took the microphone because I felt the need to celebrate with our fans after our great success. I celebrated the victory, the victory of Croatia…I did not celebrate fascism, Nazism or any totalitarianism. I celebrated Croatia."

Croatia's ugly side reared its head yet again in November 2014, when they played Italy in a Euro 2016 qualifier at the Giuseppe Meazza Stadium in Milan. Ivan Perisic had just equalised for the visitors when jubilant Croatian fans threw flares onto the pitch from the upper tiers and the game was briefly stopped to clear them off. However, the flares kept coming and in the 70th minute, referee Bjorn Kuipers took the players off the pitch as police tried to restore order. Kovač said in the aftermath: "It's not the first time and it's not accidental. I hope the bodies in charge will find a way to solve the problem because it paints a bad picture of Croatia."

However, the issue would not go away and racist behaviour was once again reported following the home qualifier against Norway. The Croatian FA appeared more outraged by the origin of the accusation than the fan behaviour itself, coming as it did from an observer for FARE who was also a Croatian national, later referred to by the Chief Executive of the Croatian Football Union, Damir Vrbanovic as a "grass". Croatia were ordered to play their upcoming home game against Italy behind closed doors and it seemed that Vrbanovic was still vexed about the issue. "We are shocked by this draconian punishment for five firecrackers and two racist chants," he said. The criticisms of the FARE official, Zoran Stevanovic, by the Croatian Football Federation (CFF) continued as they wrote an open letter to him accusing FARE of being an organisation which made a living from informing UEFA about the behaviour of Croatian fans. In another open letter to Stefanović, the official national team supporters' group said that they believed that he had "denounced Croatia supporters and the Croatian people as a whole". In the end, FARE released a statement of its own insisting that two of its observers were at the fixture and that any punitive measures taken by UEFA had nothing to do with FARE.

Despite the game against Italy taking place being closed doors, there were still problems: somehow, a swastika had been scored onto the pitch. From there, Croatia really only had one path to forge following the latest transgression — a damage limitation exercise of apologies; "This is sabotage and a felony," said Tomislav Pacak, a spokesperson for the Croatian Football Federation, who added, "We apologise to all fans watching the game on television, to both teams and to our guests from Italy for the Nazi symbol."

If the Croatian FA hoped that a quick condemnation and show of contrition would act as mitigation for any future punishment, they were very much mistaken. UEFA imposed a €100,000 fine and banned the country from playing any future Euro 2016 qualifying matches at the Stadion Poljud in Split where the incident took place. Furthermore, the country's next two fixtures were to be played behind closed doors and perhaps more importantly, they were deducted a point. It made little difference in the end as Croatia qualified for Euro 2016, but this was not the popular, fresh new team of France '98, it was a team tainted by an unsavoury element to its support.

The souring of the team's public image was not helped in the build-up to the 2018 World Cup as midfield talisman Luka Modrić was charged by Croatian prosecutors with perjury. The investigation was launched in late 2017 after it was alleged that Modrić gave false testimony in the trial of Zdravko Mamić, a hugely controversial figure in the world of Croatian football. Mamić's conduct as director of Dinamo Zagreb was so poor (he was renowned for his hiring and firing of multiple managers) that he was at one point confronted by a group of Bad Blue Boys ultras. He was also successfully sued by former Arsenal striker Eduardo da Silva who had a clause in a contract with Mamić that for the entirety of his career he owed a significant proportion of his salary to the director.

Modrić suffered horribly during the Croatian war. His grandfather was executed by Serbs while driving his livestock up the street of the village of Modrići. The family fled, ultimately ending up at the Hotel Iž in the Croatian town of Zadar. During the height of the Mamić scandal Dinamo fans sang derogatory songs about the midfielder and graffiti was sprayed on the walls of the hotel where he and his family had sought refuge.

It was against this toxic background that Modrić was made national team captain, following the retirement of Darijo Srna, and he had the court case hanging over his head as Croatia began their 2018 World Cup campaign. In a tough group alongside Nigeria, Argentina and Iceland, Croatia got off to a winning start with a routine 2-0 win over the Super Eagles. Their next fixture came against Lionel Messi and Argentina five days later. The South Americans had drawn their first game with Iceland and needed a positive result and the pressure was telling. During the playing of the national anthems Messi was seen to be rubbing his forehead, acutely aware of the task ahead for his team. Argentina had the earliest chance; however, Enzo Perez was unable to take advantage of confusion between Croatian keeper Danijel Subašić and his defence, with his effort sliding wide. Next it was Croatia's turn to pass up a golden opportunity as Mario Mandžukić stole in behind the Argentine defence, but was unable to place his header on target. The breakthrough for Croatia came when Willy Caballero in the Argentine goal tried to chip the ball over the head of Ante Rebić to his full-back. The pass was horribly under hit and Rebić gleefully volleyed the ball over Caballero into the empty net. Argentina, finalists in 2014, were now facing a huge uphill battle to qualify for the knockout stage.

Argentina had a chance to equalise as a Gonzalo Higuain pull-back into the Croatian box found Messi, however his effort was stopped on the line by the outstretched leg of his Barcelona teammate Ivan Rakitić. With ten minutes left, Luka Modrić began his redemption with a shot from just beyond the edge of the area which curled beyond the despairing grasp of Caballero. Rakitić grabbed a third in injury time to confirm Croatia's place in the last 16 where they faced Denmark.

The match against the Danes was 1-1 after just four minutes. Mathias Jørgensen opened the scoring for Denmark before Mandžukić grabbed an equaliser. After that flurry, no more goals were scored and the game went to extra time. The tension around the stadium became increasingly palpable as the game inched its way towards penalties. Croatia were handed a golden opportunity to score towards the end of the second period of extra time when Jørgensen fouled Rebić as the striker was about to tap the ball into an empty net. This was a chance for Modrić to complete his reputational turnaround and slot the resulting penalty away to send Croatia through to the quarter finals, but Kasper Schmeichel in the Denmark goal easily smothered his effort. So, the game went to a shootout. Danijel Subašić in the Croatian goal saved three penalties and Rakitić slotted his away to send Croatia through to the quarter-finals, where they faced the tournament hosts, Russia.

They had to come from behind again, this time drawing 2-2, to take the game to penalties. Fyodor Smolov and Mario Fernandes missed their spot kicks for Russia and it was left to Rakitić to be the hero once more for the Croatians and send them through to their second World Cup semi-final. Now only England prevented the Croatian side from going one better than the generation 20 years before them. The Three Lions had been taken to penalties in the last 16 by a very physical Colombia side, but they had found Sweden in the quarter finals a far easier prospect and the perceived wisdom in some quarters was that this England team would be too much for Croatia. Even Croatia's coach Zlatko Dalić conceded: "We've played five difficult games; they've taken their toll" although he would not allow fatigue to be an excuse for his players.

England got off to a tremendous start, with an inch perfect free kick into the top left corner of the Croatian goal from Kieran Trippier opening the scoring. Subašić made a token attempt to try and get the ball but it was always going to be a vain effort. Gareth Southgate's team were dominant and had they taken some of the chances they had to increase their lead, it looked like they would have secured victory. Yet despite the best efforts of Harry Kane and Jesse Lingard, England could not grab a second goal. Then, in the 68th minute, Šime Vrsaljko picked the ball up on the right and crossed for Perišić whose left foot beat the head of Kyle Walker to the ball, slotting it past the fruitless dive of Jordan Pickford. England appealed for a high foot by Perišić on Walker but neither the on-pitch officials nor the video assistant referee were interested. Suddenly, Croatia were in the ascendency. Marcelo Brozović hammered the ball high over the England bar from the edge of the area. Then Perišić beat Pickford but not the post and the game went to extra time. England had time to regroup and to come again at Croatia, and in the 99th minute John Stones headed the ball goalward from a corner, but Vrsaljko was covering on the line to clear. Next it was Croatia's turn as a low cross found Mandžukić, but Pickford came off his line and bravely blocked at the striker's feet to keep the scores level.

In the 109th minute, England failed to deal with a cross from the Croatian left and the ball was headed backwards into the area by Perišić. Mandžukić reacted the quickest, knocking the ball with his right foot to Pickford's left and into the net. The Croatian players celebrated by collapsing into a huge heap next to the England goal on top of a fortunate photographer, who managed to take some extremely close up and unforgettable photographs of the celebrating Croatian players. England could find no way back and it was Croatia, 20 years after their first appearance in a World Cup when the country was recovering from a war, who had reached the final.

Fans had gathered in their thousands across Croatia in town and city squares to watch on big screens, and they celebrated among a sea of flares and red-and-white chequered flags and replica shirts. Captain Luka Modrić said the English press had provided the team's motivation: "People were talking ... English journalists, pundits from television ... They underestimated Croatia tonight and that was a huge mistake". Perišić was more patriotic in his outlook, talking about how as a boy in Split he had watched the 1998 semi-final in his Croatia shirt, dreaming of standing on the same stage himself one day: "We knew what was at stake and how important the semi-final is for a small country like Croatia".

Their final opponents were France, the team that had beaten them in the semi-final two decades before. FIFA estimated a global TV audience of 1.12 billion and in Croatia itself 88.6% of all television sets were tuned into the final. Those watching saw their team make the early running. Perišić couldn't quite latch onto a long ball over the top, and Domagoj Vida saw a header from a free kick sail over the bar. They were made to pay for squandering these early chances as after 18 minutes, Antoine Griezmann swung in a free kick from the French right. Mandžukić attempted to clear, but under pressure from Raphaël Varane the ball brushed the top of his head and flew into the net. The tall Croatian striker, who had already scored twice in the tournament, could have quickly made amends, but he mis-hit his first-time swipe at Perišić's left wing cross and the ball trundled its way slowly to Hugo Lloris in the French goal.

Croatia didn't have long to wait, however. In the 28th minute a knock-down to the edge of the area found Perišić, who controlled the ball with his right foot before unleashing a left-foot strike past a crowd of players and beyond a diving Lloris into the left corner of the goal. Croatia were level. Buoyed on by the raucous noise their fans were making inside the stadium, they pressed to take the lead.

A Mandžukić cross from the right found Rakitić striding into the penalty area but his left-foot volley, under pressure, went high and wide. Perhaps the key moment of the game came in the 38th minute when a cross from the French right was aimed at midfielder Blaise Matuidi. His mis-timed attempted header brushed his back, before hitting Perišić on the hand. The Croatian was barely inches away from the Frenchman and the decision to award the penalty seemed immensely harsh, despite Argentinian referee Néstor Pitana analysing the incident for some time using the pitch-side monitor. Griezmann converted from the spot to put France 2-1 ahead. Croatia still had chances before the end of the first half but neither Perišić nor defender Dejan Lovren could make Lloris work in the French goal.

Croatia started the second half as they ended the first. A long ball over the French defence forced Lloris out of his area to chest and clear, before Rebić forced the French keeper into a smart save, tipping over the crossbar at his near post. Once again they would rue these missed opportunities — in the 58th minute, France extended their lead as Paul Pogba finished clinically from the edge of the box in a manner similar to Perišić's goal in the first half. Six minutes later teenage striker Kylian Mbappé rifled the ball in from distance; Subašić in the Croatian goal could have claimed he was unsighted by Vida, but his effort to reach the ball was poor.

Mandžukić gave the scoreline the respectability it deserved in the 69th minute, the ball trickling into the French net after he closed down a Lloris clearance, but it wasn't to be for Croatia. Soon after the final whistle, the heavens opened, and the apocalyptic rainstorm was maybe divine recognition that Croatia should have done better. Indeed, it wouldn't be unreasonable for the Croats to think that given a fairer wind, the result could have been different. The ball barely skimmed Mandžukić's head for the first goal and the free kick conceded by Marcelo Brozović on Griezmann which led to his assist was also highly debatable, as was the handball by Perišić which led to the penalty. Croatian manager Zlatko Dalić disputed the award of the spot kick, but was respectful in defeat. "In the World Cup final you do not give such a penalty, but it in no way diminishes France's win," he said in the press conference following the match.

Lovren declared himself to be "proud of everyone and for the country". While this is something said a lot by sportspeople, considering the political journey Croatia as a nation had taken since declaring its independence in 1991, there was a true feeling of statehood for this group of players given what they and their country had been through to almost reach the summit.

Apart from Modrić and his past with his grandfather, there was Lovren, who was born in Bosnia and fled with his family to Munich as the war broke out in the region. Speaking to Liverpool FC's in-house television channel, he recalled how the family hid in the basement of his home when the air raid sirens sounded. Following this they drove for 17 hours through many frightening roadblocks until they reached Germany. However, wider family members remained in Bosnia and some of those who stayed were murdered during the conflict. Lovren wasn't the only Croatian squad member forced to flee Bosnia as a child, with full back Vedran Ćorluka going through a similar experience.

Despite the loss, fans still poured onto the streets of Zagreb to show their appreciation for their team's accomplishment. Thousands of fans honked the horns in their cars, sang and celebrated the achievement of their national team. Andrej Plenković, the Prime Minister of Croatia requested that companies give their employees leave so that they could welcome back the team, saying "this is something that will be in our memory for the rest of our lives".

These were players from a country that had to start from the absolute bottom and had come so close. Yet despite not coming back with the World Cup, they brought something back to a country that could not be measured in trophies or medals. On the side of the team bus was the slogan *"Mala zemlja, veliki snovi"*. It translates to "Little country, big dreams" and it could be truly argued that those Croatian dreams had come to fruition.

★

CHAPTER FIVE
CAIN & ABEL

Borovo Selo can be easily mistaken for an unremarkable place where little, if anything, has ever happened. Located just north of the region's major urban area of Vukovar, to one side is a linear patchwork of fields, and to the other is the River Danube and the border with Serbia. The local town website is full of hum-drum administrative announcements, such as asking that residents not place hot ashes in their plastic rubbish bins and detailing how local pest control teams will sweep the town for rats. It's easy to enter Borovo, not be able to find its centre and pass out the other side before realising you've actually left.

Borovo though holds a place deep within the Croatian psyche as the location of one of the first major skirmishes of its war for independence in 1991. Historically, the village itself has had a predominantly Serb population. According to the 2011 census, nearly 90% of the village population was Serb, although the Vukovar municipality in which it sits had at the time a far greater Serb/Croat ethnic split.

In the spring of 1990, in Croatia's first free elections since the late 1930s, Franjo Tuđman's HDZ Croatian Democratic Union party won 205 seats in the Croatian Parliament. Their nearest rivals, the Communist SKH party, took a total of 73 seats.

Tuđman's nationalist principles worried many ethnic Serbs within Croatia and they reacted within hours of the result. In the southern village of Srb, Serbs met and declared their sovereignty. In August of that year, they met again in the town of Knin to express their desire for a referendum on Serb autonomy in areas of Croatia that had majority Serb populations. They felt their identity was gradually being eroded, and it certainly seemed that way: school texts on Yugoslav history were rewritten, administrative correspondence in Cyrillic was phased out and Serbs that held public roles were forced to pledge their loyalty to the new Croatian government. Failure to do so would lead to dismissal and possible arrest.

Led by local Serb politicians Milan Babić and Milan Martić (the latter of whom was sentenced to 35 years in prison for war crimes in 2007) an autonomous Serb region — SAO Krajina — was declared and local Serbs began placing logs across roads, blocking access to and from the rest of Croatia, an incident that became known as 'the Log Revolution'. The *New York Times* quoted a Western diplomat who accused Serb media of "inflaming passions" and the Serb newspaper *Večernje novosti* duly declared that there were two million Serbs ready to go to Croatia to fight.

In late March 1991, local Serbs, backed up by Krajina police, removed the staff of the Plitvice National Park, a UNESCO World Heritage Site in eastern Croatia. Croatian police were dispatched to the area to bring the situation back under control. The buses that they were travelling in were attacked by Krajina police at approximately 07.00 on March 31 and, hampered further by snow and wounded men, the Croats struggled. After two hours, the Serbs withdrew their position to a local post office within the national park. The battle only ceased when the Croatian Interior Minister Josip Boljkovac telephoned the Head of the Yugoslav air force to evacuate casualties of both sides. The following day local Serbs at Borovo Selo began to assemble barricades and the local Yugoslav Army units in Vukovar began to increase their training exercises. An agreement was reached that Croatian police would not enter Borovo unless local Serb authorities gave permission. A rally was held in mid-April in Borovo, and Serb dignitaries upped their rhetoric, stating that there needed to be one united Serb state and a Greater Serbia needed to become a viable option. At approximately the same time, paramilitary units from the White Eagles and Dušan the Mighty groups began to arrive in Borovo too. It was the perfect storm.

Instead of entering the town, Croatian forces began firing Ambrust anti-tank missiles into Borovo, though there were no casualties. One missile landed in a field and failed to explode, and was later paraded on Serb television as an example of Croat aggression. During the evening of May 1, a small group of Croatian police tried to enter Borovo with the intention of replacing a Yugoslav flag flying in the village with a Croatian one. They were spotted and two of the group were taken prisoner while the remainder fled after being injured.

The next day, an agreement was reached that Croats could enter Borovo to retrieve their wounded. The group that entered Borovo numbered about 30, but they were intercepted by paramilitaries and a fire fight broke out until members of the Yugoslav Army arrived in armoured personnel carriers to disperse the protagonists. Twelve Croat police had been killed and more wounded. One Serb had been killed with a handful more injured. The two policemen who were to have been rescued were ferried across the Danube into Serbia and taken to prison before being released shortly afterwards. Allegedly, some of the dead had been horrifically mutilated in an attempt at provocation.

In the days after the battle, Tudman stressed that Croatia and Serbia were on the brink of war and called upon the international community to mediate and help resolve the escalating crisis. Following a meeting on May 9 between the presidents of the Yugoslav republics, the Croats allowed the Yugoslav army to deploy in areas of Croatia which had the potential to flare up along ethnic lines. It was also agreed that representatives of both Yugoslavia and Croatia would visit Vukovar to assess the situation in the locality too. While Yugoslav officials visited Borovo, their Croatian counterparts refused, believing that they would be liaising with terrorists.

The Yugoslav army also deployed to the area from Serbia, yet far from easing tensions, they continued to rise until the commencement of the Battle of Vukovar in August 1991.

***

Borovo is close to the birthplace of one of Serbia's most infamous and controversial footballers, Siniša Mihajlović. In an example of the complicated mix of ethnicities in Yugoslavia, Mihajlović was born in February 1969 to a Croat mother and a Serb father in nearby Borovo Naselje. Despite his football career, Mihajlović's split ethnicity, coupled with the fact he hailed from an area that was a flashpoint of the Yugoslav war for Croatia, meant he was unable to escape the clutches of the past.

Eventually, Mihajlović nailed his colours to the Serb mast, his 'what if' moment coming in the spring of 1987 while he was playing for the lower-league HNK Borovo. He was brought to the attention of the hierarchy at Dinamo Zagreb by the youth players Zvonimir Boban and Robert Prosinečki, who had seen Mihajlović while representing Croatia at an inter-republic youth tournament. On their recommendation, the Dinamo Head Coach, Miroslav Blažević, a Bosnian Croat, spent time watching Mihajlović before inviting him on a mid-season team break in Italy where Mihajlović played in a friendly for Dinamo against SEF Torres in Sardinia.

The flirtation with Dinamo continued and in September 1987, Mihajlović was invited to represent them at a youth tournament in West Germany. He excelled, leading Dinamo's youth coach Zdenko Kobeščak to recommend him to Blažević. Having just signed three other players — Haris Škoro, Marko Mlinarić (who made more than 600 club appearances for Dinamo) and Stjepan Deverić — Blažević stalled on offering Mihajlović a professional deal and instead offered him a scholarship. Mihajlović decided to turn his back on the club and returned home. There were also rumours that Blažević insisted Mihajlović cut his hair if he was to play for Dinamo, something the ever-impetuous Mihajlović refused to do. Mihajlović's rotten run of dealings with coaches continued when the coach of the under-20 Yugoslav team Mirko Jozić refused to take him to the World Cup in Chile, which they won.

Mihajlović has since claimed that he was blackmailed by Jozić to sign for Dinamo — threatened with losing his place in the under-20 squad if he refused — and his decision to reject them cannot be understated. He has often been portrayed as being overtly pro-Serb at a time when the Serbian nation was a European pariah. Yet with a Croat mother, a possible position in Croatia's fledgling national team and the opportunity to play for Dinamo, Mihajlović's public image could have been significantly different. Mihajlović's brother was studying in Zagreb at the time, and it was said that Mihajlović himself was a Hajduk Split fan, so it was truly a sliding doors moment when he decided to leave Dinamo and return to Borovo. If he was being blackmailed, the decision to return to Borovo seems more in line with Mihajlović's robust character than simply his refusal to play for a Croatian club.

Robert Prosinečki's life and career followed a similar trajectory. Born in Schwenningen, West Germany, to a Croat father and a Serb mother, Prosinečki also represented Yugoslavia at national level and may have had a similar crisis of identity. He played for both Dinamo (including during the 1990s when the club was known as Croatia Zagreb) and Red Star Belgrade, as well as the Croatian national team.

***

The Croatian border town of Metković straddles the Neretva River, nestled in the far south of the country between Split and Dubrovnik and sitting on the border with Bosnia and Herzegovina. On the Neretva's northern bank, Metković blends across the border into Bosnia and its frontier village of Gabele Polje, which forms part of the Čapljina municipality. The 1991 census puts Čapljina's ethnic breakdown at 53% Croat and 13% Serb, whereas the 2013 census shows Croats dominating with 78% of the population and Serbs a mere 2%. Back across the border in Croatia, 96% of the population identified themselves as Croats in the 2011 census.

The warmer climate encourages participation in sports, in particular handball and football. Darijo Srna was born in Metković to a Croatian mother and a Bosniak father, and until recently was the country's most capped footballer, having represented them at two World Cups and four European Championships.

Srna's story begins with his father, Uzeir, who was orphaned during World War II as the Germans and local Serb Chetnik paramilitaries battled over the frontline village of Gornji Stopići in eastern Bosnia. Having already fled the village, the Srnas decided it was safe to return in mid-1941. They were gravely mistaken. The Serbs returned under the cover of darkness and razed the village to the ground, with Uzeir fleeing to the cover of a nearby forest with his brother and father. His pregnant mother and sister weren't so lucky and were killed during the raid.

Along with other refugees, the surviving Srna males made their way to northern Bosnia, where Uzeir was separated from his father and brother and ended up making his way to Slovenia. His father stayed in the border town of Bosanski Šamac, where he was killed in a firefight. Uzeir's brother never gave up the search for his younger brother and eventually found that he had been adopted by a sympathetic family.

The two brothers eventually found themselves back in Bosanski Šamac, before Uzeir made his way to Sarajevo. A goalkeeper, he played for FK Sarajevo and later Metković, and once his career was over, stayed in Metković and married before starting a family. Dario's stellar career has surpassed that of his father. Having won the league with Hajduk Split in 2001 and the Croatian Cup twice, Dario joined Ukrainian team Shakhtar Donetsk in 2003, where he stayed for 15 years. During his time there he won the league an incredible 10 times and the cup eight. Between 2002 and 2016, he represented the Croatian national side 134 times, a record only surpassed in March 2021 by Luka Modrić.

Metković is also home to one of Croatia's more well-known post-war footballers, Igor Štimac. Born in September 1967, Štimac has been one of Croatia's more outspoken and provocative players, feuding with Mihajlović for two decades. Štimac spent an early part of his Hajduk Split career on loan with Dinamo Vinkovci, located only a short distance away from Vukovar and it was here that their paths first crossed. Despite associating with different peer groups and being encouraged by each not to mix, the two players did occasionally talk and bonded over their shared love of football.

Štimac was part of the victorious under-20 World Cup team, starting the tournament's first game and scoring in a 4-2 win over the hosts, a poacher's header from six yards out. He also scored in the semi-final win over East Germany with another clinical finish, lashing a loose ball home from 10 yards following a deflected free-kick.

Both players remained at their respective clubs within Croatia and Serbia during the start of the Croatian War of Independence, but in 1992, they both moved abroad: Mihajlović to Roma in Italy's Serie A, and Štimac to Cadiz in Spain's La Liga. For Štimac, the move may have been a saving grace after he experienced a few too many close encounters with the military. In October 1991, returning from a European Cup Winners Cup second leg defeat to England's Tottenham Hotspur, the Hajduk team had to travel back home to Croatia from an airport in Austria. This included a highly perilous trip close to the front line, where, Štimac later recalled, there was ordinance exploding around them and much of the surrounding area was on fire. A bridge that the team bus had to cross had been hit, meaning that the players and staff had to disembark the bus and jump over the hole in the road.

Štimac had other dangerous encounters during the war. The Hajduk training pitch was next to a Croatian military base and Štimac was easily distracted from his footballing pursuits. He was arrested on more than one occasion for possession of a weapon. The first time, he was caught with a machine gun and spent four nights in prison, though he insists that this was for his own protection, later saying: "Some teammates had brought guns to keep on the bus because we made the judgement that we might need them."

Only a few months later, Štimac found himself with some more explaining to do when he was caught up in a group of Croat vigilantes accused of committing arson against shops, cafes and cars belonging to ethnic Serbs. Štimac didn't deny knowledge or involvement with the group, indeed it included some of his family members and godparents to one of his children. Although he insisted that he wasn't involved with any crimes, it's clear he didn't find anything wrong with what the group were doing, saying: "My friends are part of an anti-terrorist group within the Croatian army. Their mission is to blow up certain buildings. During our conversations, they're always talking about how they will chase out the Serbs from Split since it's become impossible to live with them."

By this time, Štimac was in his first of three spells with Hajduk Split and captained the team as it progressed to the 1995 Champions League quarter-final. He had also already written his way into Yugoslav footballing folklore thanks to a now infamous clash with Mihajlović.

In the 1991 Yugoslav Cup Final, Hajduk Split played Red Star Belgrade. It would be the last time that the competition, also known as the Marshall Tito Cup, would feature Croatian and Slovenian teams. The game was played on May 8, 21 days before Red Star would achieve European Cup glory. The Hajduk team featured several players who would form the backbone of the independent Croatian national team: Alen Bokšić, Slaven Bilić, Robert Jarni, Goran Vučević and, of course, Štimac.

Set against the backdrop of growing ethnic tensions, the game was highly anticipated but not perhaps for footballing reasons. The match was to be played at Partizan Belgrade's ground, still colloquially known as the Stadion JNA. It wasn't full and the two teams lined up alongside each other happily waving to those that they recognised. There were misgivings from Hajduk about whether it was safe to travel to Belgrade at all, but they received assurances from Stjepan Mesić, then the Croatian Vice President of Yugoslavia, that the club could travel to Belgrade using military transport. Hajduk fans were encouraged not to travel, though three did make what could have only been a fraught journey from the Adriatic coast to Belgrade.

The two captains, Štimac for Hajduk, and the goalkeeper Stevan Stojanović for Red Star, exchanged handshakes, club pennants and bouquets of flowers before posing for photographs with the match officials. Hajduk players were wearing black armbands in honour of the 12 Croatian policemen killed in Borovo Selo a week earlier by Serb paramilitaries.

The game began with Red Star in the ascendancy and Robert Prosinečki twice went close, first with a long-range effort just missing the right-hand post and then seeing a free-kick comfortably saved by Vatroslav Mihačić in the Hajduk goal. As the first half progressed, Hajduk came into the game more — Bokšić cut in from the right flank only to curl a tame left-footed effort at the keeper, before Dragiša Binić turned in the Hajduk penalty area and blazed a glorious chance over the bar.

Hajduk's momentum began to build further in the second half, and Bokšić broke into the Red Star penalty area, but failed to beat Stojanović at his near post. Their winning goal came in the 65th minute, as Hajduk capitalised on confusion in the Red Star defence following a Grgica Kovač pass to Bokšić, who danced past three defenders and lashed the ball high into the net past an onrushing Stojanović. He wheeled away to celebrate as his teammates piled on top of him. Red Star attempted to restore the balance with a Dejan Savićević free-kick, and had to attack, though this left enormous holes at the back which Hajduk failed to capitalise on, at one point missing an open goal. Nevertheless they hung on for victory and after the referee blew his whistle, players and coaching staff celebrated on the pitch. The trophy was also presented pitch-side as the winning team posed with match officials and even some of the Red Star players.

However, the game is best remembered for a moment of infamy between Štimac and Mihajlović. Following a series of niggly fouls between the two players, there was a confrontation between players from both sides after a Mihajlović foul left a Hajduk player requiring treatment from the club physio. In the ensuing melee, Slaven Bilić and Ante Miše rush over to Mihajlović with the latter being seen holding the Red Star defender by the hair. It is then alleged that Štimac leaned towards Mihajlović and according to Mihajlović snarled "I hope that your whole family in Borovo gets murdered". The Red Star player was so enraged he claimed that "at that moment I could have killed him with my teeth". The insult from Štimac was poignant and personal coming just a week after the Battle of Borovo and at a time when Croatian President Tuđman was being pressed by his public to retaliate against the local Borovo Serbs with the same barbaric zeal that saw the bodies of the dead Croatian police at Borovo violated. Mihajlović's parents lived in Borovo, he hadn't heard from them for some time, and it was an obvious source of concern for him, one that Štimac fully exploited. The irony was that Štimac, alongside the rest of his Hajduk teammates, was wearing a black armband in honour of the dozen policemen who lost their lives at Borovo.

Both players were sent off for their indiscretion in the 70th minute and so began a two-decade long feud which encapsulated and polarised the two different sides in the Croat fight for self-determination. Štimac still believes that he shouldn't have been sent off on that wet May day, speaking to the author James Montague in 2013 for the writer's book, *Thirty-One Nil*: "In the mess caused by his tackle, I was staying in the middle keeping the players aside. The referee decided to send me off". Štimac also felt that people were sure that the end was coming for Yugoslavia and that war was inevitable: "It was knocking on the door."

Croatian academic Dario Brentin feels that Štimac and Mihajlović have contrasting political principles. Mihajlović's politics seemed to be "made up as he went along" with little in the way of political strategy behind it. However, Brentin feels that every expression or action of Štimac's was deliberate — he had enjoyed some publicity for making pro-Croatian comments and was adamant in his beliefs — with some sort of future political role in mind; everything was done for a reason.

Away from their politics, Mihajlović's and Štimac's flourishing careers abroad were in stark contrast to the war that was pulling Yugoslavia apart. In July 1992, Red Star accepted a £3.83m bid from AS Roma for Mihajlović. Štimac followed the same summer, leaving Hajduk for Cadiz in Spain. Štimac became one of the early pioneers for Yugoslav players in the Premier League, joining Derby County in October 1995. He played for the Midlands club for four years before transferring to West Ham United for a fee of £600,000. He attained cult status for Derby, and in 2009 he was voted into a greatest ever Derby County team by readers of the local newspaper the *Derby Evening Telegraph*.

Barely a month after Mihajlović departed Belgrade, UK-based journalist Penny Marshall gained access to the Omarska detention camp in northern Bosnia, in which over 3,000 Bosnian Croats and Bosniaks were held in appalling conditions by Serb forces. Beatings, rapes and summary executions were common, although following its exposure by Marshall, the camp was closed down and the prisoners transported elsewhere. A 2007 report by the International Court of Justice into genocide in Bosnia declared that Omarska was "perhaps the most notorious of the camps, where the most horrific conditions existed".

The reporting of detention camps such as Omarska was vital to exposing the atrocities that were taking place within Yugoslavia. Yet, the coverage also seemed to create a bias in the sporting arena against Yugoslavia and towards those it was fighting against. At the 1992 Summer Olympics in Barcelona, the Croatian athletes received a huge ovation as they were led out by arguably its most famous sportsman at the time, tennis player Goran Ivanišević.

Ivanišević himself was no stranger to courting the media with his thoughts on Serbia and its inhabitants. He became a popular figure at the All England Tennis Club during the Wimbledon championships and had competed in the final only a few weeks before the Olympics, narrowly losing in five sets to the flamboyant American Andre Agassi. Famous for his ferocious serve, which he claimed was down to him imagining that the ball was "a Serb", Ivanišević was warned during his final defeat to Agassi about swearing. He was adamant he knew where the complaint had come from: "Somebody called from Yugoslavia, probably some Serb, so [the umpire] told me, 'Don't swear'." Ivanišević then told the umpire that "I am a Croat, [the caller] is a Serb, so he hates me, so sure he's going to call". There was little condemnation of Ivanišević's comments and he became a popular figure at Wimbledon, losing a further final in 1994 before finally winning in 2001 as a wildcard outsider, beating the Australian Pat Rafter in an enthralling and emotionally sapping final.

James Montague believes that to this day the sense of Serb victimhood "runs very, very deep", having been mythologised by Slobodan Milošević since the 1980s when he would evoke the Battle of Kosovo. I asked Montague about why some people in Serbia still feel that during the war, Western media tended to focus mainly upon atrocities committed by Serbs and the Yugoslav army. He believes that while the Yugoslav army did commit a lot of violence upon civilians, there is "legitimate anger" among Serbs today that they were unfairly portrayed during the war and have been viewed as a European pariah since.

I also asked Montague whether Mihajlović's nationality played any part in his reputation. While he felt that the environment at the time would have been socially conditioned in a way that didn't help Mihajlović, "he didn't make it easy for anyone to like him either".

This polarised view can be summed up in two incidents surrounding Mihajlović during his time at Lazio, for whom he played from 1998-2004. The first came in October 2000 during a bad-tempered Champions League tie at the Stadio Olimpico against Arsenal, following which Patrick Vieira accused him of racist abuse. It was a fractious game which saw Arsenal's Gilles

Grimandi strike Lazio's Diego Simeone in an off-the-ball incident, forcing the Argentinian off the pitch to receive six stitches for a head wound (Simeone allegedly waited in the tunnel after the match for Grimandi to continue their confrontation). Martin Keown and Alessandro Nesta were also booked for their part in a subsequent coming together between both sets of players.

The Independent reported that Arsenal players had been pelted with missiles by Lazio fans and Grimandi accused Lazio players of "spitting in our faces". The *Daily Telegraph* suggested that Lazio fans were singling out Arsenal's black players for racial abuse, with Grimandi suggesting that Vieira had been deliberately targeted; "They said some awful things to Patrick. They were trying to upset him. It was a very strange atmosphere and very difficult." Vieira was adamant that Mihajlović had called him a "black bastard" and a "fucking black monkey" calling it "the worst abuse I have ever heard, it never stopped from the moment the teams were shaking hands at the start".

Vieira, who believed that the abuse was a hangover of the reverse fixture at Highbury which Arsenal had won 2-0, also claimed that Mihajlović's teammates apologised on his behalf saying, "they said that they were sorry and that he was stupid". However, in the immediate aftermath of the match, Mihajlović was unrepentant. In a press conference at Lazio's Formello training facility, he claimed that he was merely responding to Vieira's taunts: "He called me a gypsy shit, so I answered with black shit". Mihajlović was also upset that Vieira revealed the details of their bust-up after the game and claimed his reference to Vieira's skin colour was literal rather than racial: "I did call him a black bastard, but I didn't call him a monkey. He doesn't look like a monkey, but if he did, I would probably have called him that."

Mihajlović's own mitigations did not hold sway and he was banned by UEFA for two European matches. He made an on-pitch apology the next week following Lazio's 5-1 Champions League victory over Shakhtar Donetsk, after club President Sergio Cragnotti was placed under pressure by both Arsenal and the English FA. Mihajlović, standing at the side of the pitch holding a microphone addressed the Lazio supporters and stated: "I know I made a mistake, and I would like to take this opportunity to present my sincere apologies."

Within a few weeks, however, that apology was retracted — Mihajlović claimed in the Italian sports magazine *Guerin Sportivo* that Vieira needed to "wipe the slate clean" with regards to his own involvement in the incident and that Mihajlović's personality and history was a good excuse to do so. He also believed that had the same situation arisen in England and Vieira been racially abused by an English player, then no punitive measures would have been taken. "It's just that I am Mihajlović, I am a Serb, I am a gypsy," he said. His lack of contrition was emphasised further when he stated that the on-pitch apology meant nothing and that it was Lazio who wrote it and not him.

Football fans and the media in England were vociferous in their condemnation of Mihajlović's comments. The Vieira incident was part of a tempestuous year for Mihajlović. It had begun with the Lazio Ultras declaring their 'honour to the Tiger Arkan' shortly after the assassination of the paramilitary leader. Mihajlović won the Scudetto with Lazio on the final day of the season, thanks to a 3-0 victory against Reggina at the Olimpico and defeat for their nearest challengers Juventus. The Old Lady had held a nine-point lead over their Roman rivals with just eight games to go, but saw their lead whittled away and lost their grip on the trophy on the final day due to a 1-0 loss to Perugia in near monsoon-like conditions. Mihajlović had scored six goals in 26 appearances, playing a definitive part in what was only the club's second ever title win.

Mihajlović's testiness would be publicised again only a few weeks later at Euro 2000 when Yugoslavia played Slovenia at the Stade du Pays de Charleroi, in Belgium. They were 3-0 down after 57 minutes thanks to two goals from Zlatko Zahovič, the second coming as the result of a Mihajlović' pass across his own back line straight to the Slovene, and another via Miran Pavlin. Mihajlović was booked in the

56th minute for a tussle, however, barely four minutes later he was shown a second yellow for needlessly getting involved in an off-the-ball argument that was in progress between his defensive colleague Albert Nađ and Slovenian centre forward Sašo Udovič. Mihajlović inexplicably pushed Udovič to the floor and was promptly sent off by referee Vitor Pereira. As he grinned at the decision and trudged off the pitch, looking behind him and mouthing back towards the Slovenes and the referee, the television commentator declared that Mihajlović had "the worst afternoon of his entire career".

That Yugoslavia managed to score three goals in six minutes against a shell-shocked Slovenian team, was down to the efforts of Mihajlović's teammates and in particular Savo Milošević, who scored two of them. Mihajlović was suspended for Yugoslavia's 1-0 win against Norway in the second game but was back for their infamous 4-3 loss to Spain, which meant they missed out on topping the group. Yugoslavia were then knocked out in the following round, mauled 6-1 at the hands of Holland, with Mihajlović again having a questionable performance.

There is no doubt that Mihajlović's own vilification was in part down to the reaction of the English media. The Vieira incident came barely a year after the Kosovo War where Serb atrocities had been rightfully exposed, but as Italian football journalist Gabriele Marcotti explained to me "at the time, Croatians were generally seen in the Western media as the 'good guys'". With specific reference to the Mihajlović-Vieira incident, Marcotti described the media reaction within the UK as "cartoonish", and although he was undoubtedly a dirty player, the fact that Mihajlović was a Serb "certainly did not help him".

Even without his own hot-headedness, Mihajlović may always have remained an enigma due to his nationality and the atrocities that were committed by Serbs during the Yugoslav wars, which were fresh in the minds of the British population. There was a distinct sense of 'otherness' about Serbia to Western eyes: while Croatia uses the Latin script and its religion is overwhelmingly Roman-Catholic, the Serbian language is mainly Cyrillic-based, and the 2011 Serbian census showed that 84% of the population were Eastern Orthodox. Serbia's traditional influences came from its East too. It was part of the Ottoman Empire, and its historical ally has always been Russia, who offered solidarity in the months leading up to World War I and also the Kosovo crisis of the late 1990s.

Following the conclusion of the Yugoslav wars and Croatia's third-place finish at their debut World Cup at France '98, there was little sign of either the cooling of relations between Mihajlović and Štimac, nor a willingness or the opportunity for them to escape a past shrouded with alleged criminals and indicted characters from those wars.

In 2001, Štimac and several other prominent Croatian sportsmen, including Goran Ivanišević, and several members of Croatia's 1998 World Cup squad, signed a joint letter expressing dismay at the Croatian government's role in capturing two of its former generals upon the orders of the International Criminal Tribunal for the Former Yugoslavia (ICTY). The two men, Ante Gotovina and Rahim Ademi, were both later acquitted following a lengthy legal process, but the move provoked anger among Croatians. The signatories, who were in Split to welcome home Ivanišević following his 2001 Wimbledon triumph, wrote: "We were shocked to learn that the Croatian government has decided to extradite two Croatian generals to The Hague tribunal ... we are reasonable people hurt by injustice. Croatia was the victim [in the war] and its soldiers and generals were heroes." Following Gotovina's acquittal in November 2012, a jubilant Štimac declared he was one of the greatest heroes in Croatian history and wanted him to "take the kick off in the next qualifying match against Serbia". It was a comment that was at best naïve and at worst provocatively symbolic. To have a man such as Gotovina at a qualifying match against Serbia, at the Maksimir of all places, would always be an incendiary act.

Mihajlović too was having trouble escaping the ghosts of his past. In September 1997, Arkan was indicted by the ICTY for crimes against humanity and grave breaches of the Geneva Convention. There were 24 counts on the indictment which made for grim reading and showed the depths of depravity the former Delije member and those under his stewardship had allegedly resorted to. However, before he could face trial, Arkan was assassinated while drinking coffee with friends in the lobby of Belgrade's Intercontinental Hotel in January 2000.

Mihajlović may well have had a greater personal connection to Arkan too. Following the fall of Vukovar, his Croatian uncle had been taken prisoner. Arkan called Mihajlović and told him to come and collect his uncle before he was murdered by his men. In his book *Behind The Curtain*, Jonathan Wilson explains how in the hours prior to the Croatian recapture of Vukovar towards the end of the Croatian war, Serb residents were understandably scared for their future. Mihajlović's parents were acutely aware that they could become particular targets due to their son. They were smuggled out of the city and to safety just in time. It has never been confirmed who it was that did extract Mihajlović's parents but Wilson wrote that "the strong suspicion in Serbia is that it was Arkan".

Hence the Lazio banners — an uncomfortable reminder of the relationship between some Italian football fans and extreme political views that prompted the Italian government to promise to introduce increased security measures at football measures. Lazio Ultras had earned themselves a reputation and *The Washington Post* commented at the time that authorities may have acted because of the rise of the right-wing politician Jorge Haider in Austria, to Italy's immediate north.

So, was the banner for Mihajlović's benefit? Marcotti is unsure: "As I understand it, it was to honour Mihajlović, but had more to do with Arkan's role as an Ultras leader," he told me. "Lazio fans have honoured Ultras leaders at other clubs, including rival clubs and leaders associated with Ultras groups, including far-left Ultras groups." It was not an isolated incident. In the year before the Arkan tribute, Lazio Ultras had raised a banner telling Jews that

"Auschwitz is your country and the ovens are your homes" and as late as March 2017 they were condemned for their racial abuse of Roma's Antonio Rüdiger during a Coppa Italia tie. However, some Ultras travelled to Parma to petition for the black French defender Lilian Thuram to sign for them. They also raised a banner in 2001 to Carlo Giuliani who was shot and then ran over by police during a protest at a G8 summit in Genoa which proclaimed "Remember Giuliani. Different politics, same passion." However, as Lorenzo Tondo in the *South China Post* commented, this could have been due to Giuliani being seen as a victim of "state violence" and appealing to the Ultras' sense of being on the fringes of society.

***

In October 1999, Croatia hosted Yugoslavia in a vital Euro 2000 qualifying match at the Maksimir Stadium in Zagreb. It was the final round of qualification and Croatia needed a win to overhaul the Republic of Ireland and claim second place in Group 8, in turn giving them a play-off against Turkey to qualify for the main tournament. Prior to the fixture, Croatian coach Miroslav Blažević made it clear what he thought the final round of fixtures meant, saying: "we should not hide it; this is more than just sport ... every victory of the Croatian team is a victory for their people".

Blažević is an interesting case study into the mix of football and politics within the parameters of Croatian self-determination. He was a member of Franjo Tuđman's HDZ party and ran for the Croatian presidency in 2005 as an independent, polling 0.80% of the vote. He was also known to evoke a sense of Croatian consciousness during team talks to players.

Diagnosed with prostate cancer, he passed away in February 2023 and many paid tribute to his man-management techniques. From journalists to footballers, they state that he could make them feel that he believed anything was possible for them. In the documentary *Croatia: Defining A Nation*, Slaven Bilić warmly recalled an occasion at the 1998 World Cup in France where Blažević took the player to one side and told him "son, you are the best centre-back in this World Cup.' I know that's probably not true, he's not telling me the truth, but it doesn't matter". Jonathan Wilson described the motivation behind this technique for Blažević: "If you listened to him from one week to the next it'd be massive contradictions, but it just didn't matter. The whole thing was he knew it was bullshit. But it was bullshit to carry people forward". Football nearly missed out on Blažević; at 17 years old, his mother sent him to a monastery, however, he returned afterwards claiming that he could not be a priest as he had fallen in love with a nun.

Tudman himself had raised the stakes the year previously when he suggested that the Croats had "a team that knows that we are fighting for Croatia, against Yugoslavia, for one's homeland's reputation while the Yugoslav team will not be able to feature such homogeneity". With so much resting on the outcome of the match, there was already a febrile atmosphere heading into the fixture. The previous match at Red Star Belgrade's Marakana stadium had finished goalless, with both sets of goalposts leading charmed lives, in particular, the Yugoslav frame. After Pedrag Mijatovic struck the post early for Yugoslavia, Davor Šuker found the foot of the Yugoslav post and Mihajlović crashed a flying diving header against his own crossbar. At one point in the game, there was a power failure, and the stadium was plunged into darkness, leaving the Croatian players feeling particularly vulnerable with only the noise of hostile fans for company. When power was restored, the Yugoslav players had formed a circle around their Croat counterparts in a bid to protect them should violence have broken out.

In the immediate build up to the game in Zagreb, local retail stores were selling T-shirts with Croatian players' faces and the slogan "proud to be a Croat" emblazoned on the front. Fans with their faces painted in red-and-white checks and replica kits with Šuker and Boban imprinted on the back of them, sang in the streets of Zagreb in the hours before kick-off, as uniformed police with huge peaked hats watched on. Some Croatian fans in full kit even visited churches, lit candles and prayed, before one boldly predicted a 5-1 demolition.

The players in turn tried to downplay the emotions that were understandably high for a game that not only offered so much in background narrative, but also was a crucial fixture in terms of qualification. Croatian captain Zvonimir Boban acknowledged the importance of the fixture by stating that "it is undoubtedly the most important game to be played in Zagreb", but he also emphasised the importance of respect and improving the quality of life for both Serbs and Croats, saying: "We have to go on living side by side, we're neighbours."

However, it was sold by some as a continuation of war; a narrative that was bought by a lot of fans of both teams. "The game in Zagreb was built to be one of the biggest games in history," Red Star fan Uros Popovic told me.

The Bad Blue Boys sprayed graffiti around Zagreb telling people to "kill Serbs", thus making it a vain hope that Boban's words had been heeded. Speaking to *Transworld Sport* prior to the match, one leader of the Bad Blue Boys, a veteran of the Croatian war, sat calmly outside a café in a Zagreb square and explained what the fixture meant for someone like him: "I want this victory for everything that they did to us in the war ... for all those who were driven away, or were wounded, or killed. I want us to win this match to repay them on the playing field."

Fans covered one corner of the stadium with a huge Croatian flag and the Yugoslav national anthem was drowned out by a cacophony of whistles and jeers. Another giant flag was emblazoned with "Vukovar '91", and wounded veterans were paraded to the crowd prior to kick off. The Yugoslav players stood pensively during the anthem, their hands held awkwardly by their sides or behind backs. Savo Milošević looked particularly concerned. Barely any of the players sang along, the majority looked like men who did not want to be there, but who knew that there was a job to do and that only then could they leave Zagreb.

(It was not the first time Vukovar had been used as a symbol within football. In a 1992 game between Partizan and Red Star, both sets of fans began trading the usual insults at each other until abruptly, the chanting stopped. A group of Arkan's Tigers had appeared in full combat fatigues and began to hold up a series of road signs, '20 miles to Vukovar'; '10 miles to Vukovar'; until finally 'Welcome to Vukovar'. More Tigers began holding up different road signs of Croatian towns that had fallen to Serbs. Finally, Arkan, the orchestrator of this grim display appeared high up in the stands and received the adulation from both sets of fans. Both the Partizan and Red Star supporters may have loathed each other, but they were united in hatred of the common enemy of the Croats.)

In contrast, the Croatian team, obviously buoyed by the home atmosphere, sang their national anthem with their right hands over their hearts. Again, the Yugoslav players had the look of condemned men, with the odd one out being Mihajlović. He stood proud and upright during the Croatian anthem and even managed a smile and cheeky wink to someone he spotted in the crowd. It seemed to be that he relished scenarios like this when the world was against him.

With the game only a few minutes old, tensions threatened to spill over from the terraces onto the pitch. Yugoslavia's Zoran Mirković reacted to a challenge by Croatia's Aljoša Asanović in the Yugoslav right-back area and his teammates became involved in a bid to separate the two players. While this played out in front of a baying Croatian crowd, flares were thrown onto the pitch in the direction of the players which were hastily removed by officials.

Croatia opened the scoring in the 20th minute as a through ball from Davor Šuker wrong-footed Mihajlović, allowing Bokšić to calmly slot the ball past a rooted Ivica Kralj. The reception for the goal was rapturous from the Croatian fans lucky enough to be inside the stadium. Those who were watching the game on big screens outside released numerous flares in celebration.

Mijatović equalised five minutes later, beating the Croatian defence to a Mihajlović free kick and headed beyond the hapless

Ladić, who could have been forgiven for expecting a thunderous Mihajlović shot rather than a floating cross from the right-hand side of the pitch. The fans were stunned into silence and their shock was compounded after 31 minutes when Croatia conceded again. The second was almost a carbon copy of the first. A looping free kick was met by Dejan Stanković, who beat the Croatian offside trap to head the ball at Ladić, who allowed the ball to squirm through his arms and despite his desperate attempts to claw it back again, into the goal.

In the 41st minute, the game took a bizarre twist as Croatia's Robert Jarni was penalised for a foul on Mirković. Having shown his dissent to the referee, Jarni then berated the prostrate Mirković who responded by grabbing Jarni's testicles. Mirković was shown a straight red card by the referee and as he left the pitch, he gave the habitual three-fingered Serb salute to the outraged Croatian fans. Traditionally the salute was used in a religious Orthodox sense. The thumb, index and middle fingers are raised to symbolise the Holy Trinity, however it has come to be used to represent Serbs or Serbia. Yet, far from being seen as having put Yugoslavia's chances of winning the match in jeopardy, Mirković was hailed in his homeland for having salvaged his honour, a reaction that spoke to the priorities of the fans.

The game continued to be a physical contest as Croatian defender Igor Tudor was sent crashing over the advertising hoardings following an enthusiastic shoulder barge from Milošević. Then, following a Bokšić cross from the Croatian left, Mario Stanić grabbed an equaliser for Croatia with a header from six yards out. As a sign of how Mihajlović coped in such a hostile atmosphere, he thumped a trademark free kick from halfway inside the Croatian half onto the post via a deflection and on his way back to his defensive position, he shared a joke, smile and high five with Šuker.

When the referee blew for time, the jubilant Yugoslavs celebrated qualification on the pitch, while the Croatian fans and players were left to contemplate what might have been. The 2-2 draw was not good enough as Ireland had drawn with Macedonia despite a last-minute goal from Goran Stavrevski, who played his club football at the time for NK Zagreb. Thus, the Irish finished a point above Croatia, snatching second place from their grasp.

At the final whistle, Mihajlović walked towards the "Vukovar 91" banner. He knelt in front of it and crossed himself, provoking fury from the home fans. Mihajlović later said that he only wanted to commemorate the dead on both sides, yet his actions were seen by some as hugely provocative. Red Star fan Uros Popovic agreed, saying: "I think he simply just wanted to provoke." He added that he felt Mihajlović would have crossed himself in front of the flag "even if cameras were not there and even if he wasn't from Vukovar, he probably would have done it because he was just that sort of character".

However, Mihajlović, who described the match as "the most emotional game of my career", had a different view of his actions, saying: "When I entered the pitch to play Croatia in that qualifier, I saw the name of my hometown again. A huge flag was hung in the Croatian section behind the goal which read "Vukovar 91". I kneeled and made the cross sign in remembrance to all Serbs who had fallen there. The stadium felt like it would crumble to the ground from all the fury around me". Describing the atmosphere that night as a "volcano", Mihajlović continued: "Everybody still had the war in their bodies. There were many players from the old Yugoslavian team on the field, but this time we played against them."

The crowd did indeed howl their fury at Mihajlović, but again his actions can be seen in a number of ways. It might have been gesture made in good faith in the wrong place and wrong setting by a man who was, like so many others at the stadium, scarred by a recent brutal war which had ripped his family apart and destroyed the area he grew up in, or it could have been a premeditated act of provocation. Mihajlović believes it to be the former and has said so on many occasions, yet it's easy for the narrative to be misplaced and for his actions to be misconstrued into something more sinister.

Croatian academic Dario Brentin believes that Mihajlović has a provocative personality, though whether he was attempting to provoke in this instance is difficult to judge. Though as Mihajlović was photographed in front of the word "Vukovar" written in Cyrillic script as late as 2013, Brentin thinks that the provocation is always there; "he loves being provocative, so I think he knew exactly what he was doing. There's also pictures of him in 2013, somebody had written "Vukovar" in Cyrillic script and he was stood in front of it".

Igor Štimac did not play a part in the Zagreb match, though he did play in the first fixture in Belgrade. In August 1999, he had left Derby County for West Ham United but he continued to forge a reputation for himself in Croatia as a man with a definitive pro-Croat stance. In December 2002, he found himself embroiled in an ongoing dispute with a Split café owner, who accused Štimac of assaulting him after he refused to play songs which praised Ante Gotovina, the Croatian Lieutenant General.

His feud with Mihajlović simmered on too, despite the proffering of the occasional olive branch. Štimac appeared on a chat show and was played a pre-recorded clip of Mihajlović, who appeared to be suggesting that despite mistakes made by both parties, it was time to move on and maybe meet over a bottle of wine to discuss things. A disgusted Štimac reacted angrily, bringing up Mihajlović's threats of the past and his association with Arkan before giving a final unequivocal answer: "No, Mihajlović, I don't accept your offer. I can forgive him, but I'll never embrace him or drink wine with him."

By the early part of the millennium, Štimac's career was beginning to wind down and he finally retired in 2002 during his third stint at Hajduk Split. Mihajlović carried on and so too did the controversies, the most inexcusable again coming against English opposition. In November 2003, he was suspended by UEFA for eight matches and handed a £9,000 fine for spitting on Chelsea's Adrian Mutu in a Champions League fixture — he was also sent off in the game, but not for that particular offence. There were no mitigating circumstances for Mihajlović's actions and nor was it the first incident of its type: five years earlier at the France '98 World Cup, having squared up to Germany's Jens Jeremies, Mihajlović spat at his stunned German counterpart. Yugoslavia had been 2-0 up, yet they drew 2-2 thanks to a Mihajlović own goal and an equaliser from a trademark Oliver Bierhoff header.

Mihajlović later recalled another encounter with Bierhoff while the Kosovo War was taking place. Admitting he needed an "enemy" to motivate himself, he was once again undone by the prolific German. Prior to the game, Mihajlović was ready to say "anything and everything" to the striker, his opponent completely took the wind out of his sails by saying he was "very sorry for what was happening in my country, because my people did not deserve it. 'I am with you'." In the face of this unexpected empathy, and in a rare insight into his psyche, Mihajlović couldn't bring himself to be his usual combative and physical self, a situation that he described as "disappointing".

Despite all his on-pitch achievements for both Red Star and at international level, there are some Serbs who find their relationship with Mihajlović as complicated as the personality of the man himself. Red Star fan Uros Popovic is one: "I love him for what he did with Red Star, but ... I don't know". Popovic's voice trails off at the end of the sentence, as if contorting himself with how he should feel about a man so divisive. If it's not easy for those looking dispassionately from the outside to form an opinion about Mihajlović, it must be hugely difficult and complicated for those who have an emotional tie to him.

Mihajlović stayed in Italy for the rest of his career, finishing at Inter Milan, where he could count Patrick Vieira as one of his teammates (the Frenchman also made an appearance at Mihajlović's testimonial in 2007 at Novi Sad). In another bizarre twist of fate, Mihajlović also managed Mutu at Fiorentina. Speaking in late 2016 to Italian sports newspaper *Corriere Dello Sport*, Mihajlović defended his confrontational personality, yet was humble enough to acknowledge his own fallibility. "I always say things to your face by confronting issues like a man, not a coward," he said. "Mutu, who I spat at, was worried when I arrived at Fiorentina. I told him not to worry about it, that it was my fault and I apologised."

By 2012, Štimac and Mihajlović were in charge of their respective national teams and fate brought them together when Serbia and Croatia were drawn in the same qualifying group for the 2014 World Cup in Brazil (Macedonia were also in the same group). Both teams began positively, Croatia beat Macedonia 1-0 thanks to a neat close-range header by Nikica Jelavić in their first game and Serbia thumped Wales 6-1 in their second qualifying game, a match in which they showed some outstanding technical play.

Yet, as ever, Mihajlović couldn't help but court controversy. He had set out a code of conduct which players called up to the Serbian national team had to sign. One of its edicts was that the national anthem should be sung by each player. However, Adem Ljajić refused to do so before a friendly against Spain in May 2012. Ljajić is a Muslim from the southern Novi Pazar region of Serbia where the population is overwhelmingly Bosniak. The Ljajić anthem incident though, according to football writer and editor of the *Unusual Efforts* website Kirsten Schlewitz, is something that has been overstated in the Western media: "it was one right-wing politician and everyone else was 'we're over this'". Ljajić seems particularly unlucky with his brushes with management. During a Serie A match for Fiorentina against Novara earlier in the same month, Ljajić reacted to being substituted by sarcastically applauding his manager Delio Rossi. Rossi responded by physically striking the player and was fired after the match as a result.

Ljajić had decided not to sing the Serbian anthem for "personal reasons" and held a meeting with Mihajlović explaining what those reasons were. Schlewitz believes that there was nothing anti-Serb about Ljajić refusing to sing the anthem and if there had been, he wouldn't have been willing to play at all. Nevertheless, those reasons obviously cut no slack with Mihajlović and Ljajić was promptly sent home. A statement from the Serbian FA clarified that "the door has not been closed forever on the national team, but he needs to change his attitude and officially notify Mihajlović that he has done so ... when his form merits it, he can return." It's interesting that the door was left open for Ljajić — it hardly sits in tandem with Mihajlović having left him out due to purely nationalistic or ideological reasons. More likely, Mihajlović was wanting to instil a little self-discipline to a team that had failed so abysmally at the 2010 World Cup in South Africa. Serbia had finished bottom of their group and even a 1-0 victory over Germany, thanks to a close-range Milan Jovanović chest and volley, could not mask defeats to Ghana and Australia. Serbia had also failed to qualify for Euro 2008 and had lost all three group games at the 2006 World Cup while still called Serbia and Montenegro.

The Ljajić affair didn't seem to have hampered relations between the two initially, as in July 2016 Ljajić signed for Torino, managed by Mihajlović, and finished the season with a respectable 12 goals in 36 appearances. The following December though, Mihajlović's patience appeared to be wearing thin once again. He labelled the midfielder's performance in a 5-3 defeat to Napoli as a "disaster", saying: "Ljajić is the player who is supposed to make us step up in quality. If he plays like this, we'd be better off not having him in the squad at all. I hope he wakes up soon, otherwise we may as well use someone else." Mihajlović was true to his word — Ljajić was dropped to the substitute's bench for six consecutive games in January and February 2018, before spending the next season on loan at Beşiktaş.

Croatia and Serbia met in qualifying for the 2014 World Cup at the Maksimir Stadium in May 2013, and the anticipation of Štimac and Mihajlović finally meeting in the dugout after all the years of acrimony added extra spice to an already heightened atmosphere. The two men had met in a different setting in November of the previous year at a UEFA conference for Europe's national team managers, where they sat and drank coffee together for some time before parting amicably. It was the first time that they had spoken in 23 years and both felt that the meeting had cleared the air between them. Although they weren't the best of friends, the two understood and respected each other a little more.

Prior to the game, Mihajlović insisted that it should be played in "the right spirit" and that it was important for both teams to "offer the hand of friendship". However, in Vukovar, Serbs felt that they had to watch the match at home for fear of being attacked if they did so in public. Djordje Macut, President of the Vukovar Council of Serbian Minorities told *The Independent*: "We've had bad experiences in the past when we've tried to watch Serbia games and Croats have come and thrown stones at the cafés we're in."

The game was also played against the background of a deteriorating economic outlook for Croatia. Having ridden the storm in the immediate aftermath of the global financial crisis of 2008, unemployment had gradually risen, peaking at 22.4% just a few weeks after the decisive fixture. Thus, the match proved a distraction for those suffering economic hardship in Croatia at the time. "For a few hours it will allow people to forget that they can't pay their bills, that they aren't eating well. Instead they can focus all their attention on hating the Serbs," Croatian basketball coach Goran Gunjevic explained to *The Independent*.

Croatian security and police took no chances. Away fans were banned from attending both this match, and the fixture in Belgrade. Aside from football officials, the only other Serb representatives in the Maksimir were journalists who made their way into Zagreb under heavy security, though not without some reminders of their situation — a policeman boarded the journalists' bus and bellowed into a loudhailer that they should not respond to any provocation.

There were the usual banners in the stands and over railings, and despite little in the way of pyrotechnics before the match, the 35,000 fans packed into the stadium created a febrile atmosphere. The teams were led out onto the pitch with players on both sides holding the hands of mascots dressed in the replica kits of the opposition. As they did so, a banner was unfurled that said "Through the rough times and through the battles we defended our homes honourably. The ones who defended our land didn't die in vain. Our flag is flying and we don't hide it anymore".

The Serb national anthem was predictably drowned out by a chorus of boos, yet the players stuck to their written pledges and sang. It's here that Mihajlović's insistence that players sing the anthem appears to have paid dividends too. In singing along, unlike the previous visit in 1999 and whether willingly or otherwise, his players were concentrated and did not allow themselves to be distracted by the atmosphere. When it came to their anthem, the Croatian fans gave an impressive display of tifo, turning themselves into a mass of red-and-white checkers.

The pre-match exchange of handshakes and pennants between the opposing captains and officials took place in a calm and collected manner, perhaps because it was to the dugouts that the focus of the media was drawn. Fluorescent-bibbed photographers huddled together, vying for their chance to get the money shot of Mihajlović and Štimac's reactions when they finally met. As it was, both coaches walked towards each other, clasped hands and embraced in a professional and business-like manner, obviously aware that how they conducted themselves at that moment would dictate the behaviour of both sets of fans and players.

The game itself passed almost without incident. The first significant chance came in the 15th minute as Ivan Rakitić played a right-footed cross in from the Croatian left, which was flicked on by Ivica Olić and headed into the Serbian goal by Mario Mandžukić. The effort was disallowed, however, for a foul by Mandžukić on goalkeeper Željko Brkić. The tone was set though and Croatia only had to wait until the 23rd minute to find the net again. A poor Aleksander Kolarov free-kick from the Serbian left-back position went straight to Mandžukić, who found Rakitić to his right. He fed a perfect through ball to Olić, powering through the right side of the Serbian penalty area. Olić then played a square ball across the face of the six-yard box, past the onrushing Brkić, in turn completely wrong-footing defenders Matija Nastasić and Neven Subotić, and leaving Mandžukić to side-foot into the empty net. As the striker wheeled away, leaping over the advertising hoardings to celebrate in front of Croatian fans, Olić ran to the Croatian bench to do likewise. In response to taking the lead, the home fans chanted "Vukovar Vukovar" and "kill the Serbs", and while the action on the pitch remained fairly civilised, the game was punctuated by nationalist slogans from the stands.

There was one chance for a flare-up in the 36th minute as Kolarov leaned a little too much with his forearm into Mandžukić on the Croatian right and was correctly booked. While there were protests from the Croatian bench at Kolarov's foul, there were none of the histrionics that are often seen around such incidents. The Croatian players did not hound the referee and Kolarov himself put his hand to his chest in a conciliatory manner when explaining his actions to the referee. It would be interesting to see how this would have played out had the two managers not greeted each other in the manner that they did.

From the resulting free kick, the Croatian skipper Darijo Srna swung in a virtually undefendable ball from the right. Filip Đorđević looked unsure how to deal with it and appeared to leave it, distracting the already indecisive Brkić who let the ball bounce before it was bundled in at the far post by a grateful Olić to give Croatia a 2-0 lead.

Despite Croatia being in the ascendancy, Serbia grew into the game and had their chances too. At the start of the second half, following a run down the left wing, Kolarov forced a fine save from Croatian goalkeeper Stipe Pletikosa and Đorđević was unable to turn in the follow up. Pletikosa was on hand to deny Serbia again with a double save. The first came after a beautiful Dušan Tadić backheel set up Filip Đuričić, however, his low shot was too close to Pletikosa, who recovered to block the follow up from the luckless Đorđević as well. One member of the Serbian backroom staff was so upset by the miss that he knocked a layer of protective covering from the top of the dugout, having hit it so hard in anger. The 2-0 win placed Croatia in a dominant position for World Cup qualification, but effectively ended Serbia's dream for another campaign.

Both sets of players shook hands on the pitch following the final whistle and in an extraordinary moment of reconciliation, Štimac and Mihajlović met in the centre circle and embraced. The two foes, who had once embodied everything that the opposing sides had hated about each other so much and who had traded insults without directly speaking for two decades, were now displaying an example for all others to follow. Štimac and Mihajlović had their differences (to put it mildly), but by the end maybe they realised that they were both *too* similar in character. Both were hugely driven and proud individuals, ready to give all for their respective cause. In an article about their on-pitch rapprochement, the *New York Times* wrote: "They had promised peace for 90 minutes. But peace had spilled over its allotted time."

Following the meeting between the two men, their careers have taken a similarly nomadic route. Štimac briefly returned to Croatia to manage NK Zadar, before moving around Asia to Qatar and then Iran, before taking stewardship of the Indian national team in 2019. Under his tenure, India failed to qualify for the 2022 World Cup despite their best qualifying performance for 20 years and reaching the qualification stage of the 2023 AFC Asian Cup. Mihajlović, following his time with Serbia, spent most of his career managing in Italy, the one exception being a short stint managing Sporting Lisbon. In 2019, while managing Bologna, he was diagnosed with Leukaemia and began a course of treatment including chemotherapy and a bone marrow transplant operation. He continued to manage, often monitoring training sessions and administering team talks via video from his hospital bed.

Speaking to *La Gazzetta dello Sport* in early 2020, Mihajlović opened up about the effect that his diagnosis had on him and how it changed him as a person: "I used to go for morning runs with headphones to shake off the stress, but now I walk 7-10km per day to recharge the batteries instead. I look around, I listen, I breathe in fresh air, which after three months in a hospital bed with air conditioning is a wonderful sensation". He contemplated too how he had matured emotionally, crying a lot more at events and managing to control his infamous temper: "I've even become more patient!" he explained. "As a player, I couldn't even count to one before reacting, let alone 10. I've learned now to count to six or seven, I know I can get to eight, but counting to 10 is probably beyond me". He became a grandfather too, after his daughter gave birth to a girl in October 2021.

At a press conference in spring 2022, Mihajlović confirmed that his cancer had unfortunately returned: "These diseases are devious," he announced. He undertook treatment following the completion of the 2021/22 season, and returned to managing Bologna in time for the commencement of the following season. However, they failed to win any of their first five games: a 2-1 defeat on the opening day of the season against Lazio, who had goalkeeper Luís Maximiano sent off in only the sixth minute, was compounded by another defeat to champions AC Milan and draws with Hellas Verona, Salernitana and Spezia, leaving Bologna in 16th place. Not the best of starts, but by no means the worst either given their undoubted disruption during pre-season for Mihajlović's medical treatment.

However, for Chair of the club Joey Saputo, the manager's position was untenable and on September 6, Mihajlović was relieved of his duties. Saputo was at pains when announcing his decision to point out that it was a difficult conclusion that he had reached but a necessary one: "the time has come for a change of technical leadership: a painful decision that we had to make for the good of the team and the club".

Unfortunately, Mihajlović continued to deteriorate and on Friday December 16, 2022, in a Rome hospital, he passed away, aged just 53. He was undoubtedly a complicated personality — like anybody, a product of his environment. Some of his actions were indefensible, others when seen in context can be understood more. He remains the record goalscorer from free kicks in *Serie A*, was a winner of multiple league and cup titles, as well as a European Cup winner with perhaps the greatest Yugoslav club team of all time. He was, unquestionably, unique.

★

CHAPTER SIX
DOWN UNDER

An anonymous industrial estate several kilometres west of Melbourne is not the place one would expect to find one of Australia's most historically important football clubs. But among the grim mesh fencing, unused lorry trailers and the discarded flotsam and jetsam of modern day industrial life is Knight's Stadium, home to Melbourne Knights Football Club. Built on the site of a former drive-in cinema, it has been the Knights' home since it was constructed in the late 1980s, funded by donations from its members. Its continued presence is testament to the communal ethos that runs through the club and its core beliefs.

The Knights' website says the club has been "wholly owned by its body of members since its inception in 1953". Members get to vote on key decisions on a one-member-one-vote system, with any profits being reinvested into the club for the benefit of members and their communities. The club's constitution is structured in such a way that it can never be bought out by either an individual person or company. This community ethos is best shown by the 15,000-capacity stadium, which has an adjoining Croatian social club and large car park.

The Knights were founded in April 1953 by Croatian immigrants, a scenario repeated many times across Australia with Mediterranean migrants looking for familiarity and community as they sought a new beginning away from the bloody aftermath of World War

II Europe. The house where the club was founded in Footscray, a suburb only a few miles to the west of central Melbourne, is no longer there. In its place stands a small collection of shops; a sign of a latter wave of migration to the area from the Far East.

The southern European migrants were not its first case of mass migration to the country. Human presence has been detected in Australia for at least 40,000 years, though there is evidence of habitation on Rottnest Island, off the Perth coast, as long as 70,000 years ago. These early humans could have arrived in Australia via the land bridge known as Sahul, which connected Australia to New Guinea. Indigenous Australians had their own sports, and an 1857 sketch shows members of the Nyeri Nyeri people in northern Victoria playing something resembling Aussie Rules Football.

During an expedition to the Murray River, scientist William Blandowski noted: "The ball is made out of Typha roots: it is not thrown or hit with a bat, but it is kicked in the air with the foot ... the aim of the game: never let the ball touch the ground." The game itself was known as 'Marn Grook' by the indigenous Gunditjmara people of Victoria, though there is some debate as to whether the game itself was a direct influence on the growth of Aussie Rules.

Sport was receiving an injection of enthusiasm back in Australia's mother country in the late 18th century. The Marylebone Cricket Club was established in London in the year before the first fleet arrived in Australia; horse racing had also begun to grow with the St Ledger, Oaks and Derby also all taking place in the years prior to 1788. And though initially more concerned with their immediate survival, the first British settlers included individuals who were interested in sports participation, such as Lieutenant George Johnson, who briefly commanded the New South Wales Corps and became an early breeder of racehorses, as did Captain John Piper who arrived at the colony in 1792.

As free settlers began to arrive in Australia, sporting events began to become more commonplace in the areas they made their homes. Hyde Park in Sydney was the early venue for horse racing and cricketing events, and the first sports clubs were established by the 1820s. In 1829, *The Sydney Monitor* wrote about a football match taking place and not long afterwards, to celebrate the birthday of the young Queen Victoria, there was "a game of football which gave rise to sundry scuffles and broken shins to boot".

However, football was relatively slow to put down its roots Indeed the next mentions of the sport come nearly 50 years later in August 1875, when the Brisbane Australian Rules team played against inmates from a local asylum. Local newspaper *The Queenslander* described how the ball was neither "handled nor carried", though the main priority of the newspaper's coverage seems to be the "excellent spread" that was on offer for those playing to enjoy.

The game itself seemed a physical affair with clothing being ripped and at least one broken finger, however both teams were reported to be in good spirits as it finished. There was even time for a 10-minute smoking break. Unfortunately, there would be no rematch, as this would have meant the inmates leaving the asylum, which presented its own unique issues.

The pace of football's infrastructural development in Australia quickened and by 1880, the first match under its accepted rules took place in Sydney between the Wanderers and the King's School rugby team. Wanderers were founded in a Sydney hotel by Englishman John Walter Fletcher, a schoolmaster who had settled in Australia five years earlier, along with colleague J.A Todd. Fletcher, who has been described as 'the father of Australian soccer', appears to be typical of the Victorian pioneering spirit at the heart of Britain's 19th century expansion. He seems also to have been involved with the early development of Australian lawn tennis, and it was his wife Anne who apparently embroidered the velvet bag which contained the famous Ashes that winning captain Ivo Bligh returned to England with following their triumphant tour of 1883.

The match between Wanderers and Kings finished 5-0 to Wanderers in front of an estimated crowd of 1,000 at Parramatta Common. Fletcher's attempts to grow the sport in his adopted homeland saw him help organise a series of matches between teams from New South Wales and Victoria (one of which, according to the Sydney Morning Herald, was witnessed by 2,000 spectators, one of whom was unlucky enough to be struck by the ball mid-match) culminating in the formation of the Australian Soccer Association in 1921.

Following the end of World War I, football resumed in 1919 and a large crowd attended a cup match in Victoria in 1920 between Northumberland and Durhams & Melbourne Thistle. The Anglo-Scottish names bequeathed to the teams were unsurprising nods to the old country by the players, similar to the names later used by the newly-arrived European migrants.

An Australian side toured New Zealand soon afterwards, drawing crowds of several thousand. It was between these fixtures that football created its own Ashes urn. Following a banquet at the end of a tour in 1923, Australian and New Zealand captains George Campbell and Alex Gibbs shared cigars and a conversation. The ash from these cigars was collected in a cigarette case that the Australian team manager Mr W Fisher had used at the battle of Gallipoli and mounted into a case. At this point, both captains and the vast majority of players' names were still Anglo-Irish in origin — there is very little if any at all in the way of other surnames of European origin and certainly, nothing of Yugoslavian extraction.

The 1921 Australian census states that there were in total 829 people within Australia who were born in 'Jugo-Slavia', of which 524 were based in Western Australia. The United Kingdom still represented the overwhelming number of migrants, with over 570,000 respondents giving the UK as their birthplace (this figure includes the Isle of Man and the Channel Islands, though it discounts Ireland as there was no distinction on the survey between Northern Ireland and its southern neighbour). The 1921 edition was the first census in which any respondents gave their birthplace as Yugoslavia.

By 1933, this figure had increased to 3,969, with the overwhelming majority again living in Western Australia. By 1954, a total of 22,856 gave their birthplace as Yugoslavia. The significant difference from previous census returns was that for the first time Western Australia was no longer the destination of choice for Yugoslav migrants, instead they shifted towards New South Wales and Victoria. Furthermore, large numbers of respondents gave their birthplace as either Axis or occupied countries, suggesting their migration was prompted by World War II.

The world that these new arrivals encountered — a white Australian culture embedded with British roots — was far removed from the one that they had left. It was unfamiliar at best and hostile at worst. Football's early growth within Australia had stunted, largely due to competition from cricket, rugby in its various codes and Aussie Rules. For these new Yugoslav migrants struggling in Australia, even their beloved football was played with the wrong shaped ball. The early migrants found themselves feeling isolated in all aspects of their life. Wray Vamplew, Emeritus Professor in Sport at the University of Stirling, has written that "the low position of the European migrants on the Australian socioeconomic scale and their lack of power in politics and at work must have resulted in massive frustration, both individually and collectively".

Having arrived in Australia following a long and arduous journey from the other side of the world, new arrivals from Yugoslavia had to live very much on their wits. Food, accommodation and jobs were the immediate concern, as well as adapting to a new culture in a land where they may not have spoken the language. Understandably, football may not have been too high on the list of priorities for these new arrivals. On the plus side, there were jobs: multinational corporations such as Ford, International Harvesting and Shell had factories — and a labour shortage in the aftermath of the war — in Geelong and also Corio in Victoria.

Despite this relative security, many migrants felt that although their labour was welcome in their adopted homeland, their customs and cultures from the old countries were not. Roy Hay, Honorary Fellow at Deakin University in Victoria, stated in his paper *Our*

Wicked Foreign Game that "these migrants, arriving in a strange society which welcomed their labour but expected them to become assimilated Australians ... found very few institutions catering for them". Hay goes on to describe that football clubs became some of the few places where migrant groups could gather and essentially be themselves without the pretence of forced assimilation.

Josip Šimunić was born in Canberra, Australia's capital city, in February 1978. Grainy footage from the mid-1990s while he was playing for Melbourne Knights shows the young Šimunić in a quiet suburban street expounding the virtues of his mother's cooking, raspberry lemonade and his beloved Mazda 929, which seems far too small to hold his very tall frame. This confident but quietly spoken teenager, who spent the majority of his career playing his club football in Germany, never represented the Socceroos, instead playing 105 times for Croatia over a 12-year period. Known for his on-pitch assertiveness, Šimunić was until recently the coach of the Croatian under-19 team. I knew I had to speak to him for this book as his story is nothing if not fascinating, yet I was unsure as to whether he would be open to an interview about his Croatian roots, which would inevitably lead onto the thorny *za dom* subject discussed in a separate chapter.

I approached the Croatian FA, unsure if I would receive a response. Yet within 24 hours, I was given the green light to speak to him. I found him open, courteous and refreshingly honest.

His parents met and were married in Bosnia before emigrating to Australia in 1974. Like many first-generation immigrants, their time was devoted more to finding work and raising a family than to more leisurely pursuits (Šimunić admits he can't remember if his parents were football fans or not). Yet the young Šimunić, who appears to have been one of those annoyingly gifted pupils at school who excels at any sport they turn their hand to, enjoyed football from a very early age — more than any other game he participated in. From playing on the streets to his first club, Canberra Croatia, his peers were usually of a Croatian extraction too.

Canberra FC were formed in 1958 and the club's founders used football as a means of preserving an identity for the local Croatian community while equating success on the pitch with integration into wider Australian society off it. Having to comply with new regulations in 1960 which prohibited ethnic references in club names, the club renamed themselves Soccer Club Hope. Even here, the club administrators couldn't resist a subversive nod towards their roots, as 'Hope' referred to the Croatian Liberation Movement (*Hrvatski Oslobodilački Pokret*). The movement was created in Buenos Aires in Argentina in 1956 by Ante Pavelić, who had also founded the feared Ustaše and ruled the quasi-independent State of Croatia during the Second World War as an ally of Nazi Germany. Following several more name changes, the club came to be known as Canberra Croatia FC. The current kit is red, white and blue, and the club badge features the flagpole of Australia's Parliament House set against a background of Croatia's red-and-white checkers.

While he was growing up, Šimunić supported AC Milan, with his favourite players being Marco Van Basten and Fernando Redondo. In the old online clip of him as a teenager, he also states that he is a huge fan of Diego Maradona, an eclectic mix of players for such a combative centre half. He was fully aware of Dinamo Zagreb and Hajduk Split and was unable to choose between them as his favourite, a problem perhaps completely unique to him. In the pre-internet age, following clubs from the other side of the world had its issues: "typically I would find out the results a week after games were played through the newspaper or the TV," he told me via email. His family were however able to keep their fingers on the pulse and knew all about the disintegration of Croatia and its descent into war. "We definitely did pay close attention to what was going on in Croatia at the time; it was often reported on Australian media and there was a hotline based out of Melbourne where people could call and find out the latest news."

In 1995, despite having other options, Šimunić joined Melbourne Knights "because it was a Croatian club". He became National

Soccer League Youth Player of the Year and also won an NSL Championship medal. The club was ingrained in the local Croatian community — Šimunić remembers the squad spending much of their time promoting both the team and their Croatian identity within schools and clubs: "Everything was Croatian influenced, from the kit to the fans to the committee, and also a lot of players," he said.

His potential was obvious to see, and his career took him to Europe, where he enjoyed a 14-year career in Germany starting with Hamburger SV. Amongst his teammates were fellow Croat Andrej Panadić, Macedonian Saša Ilić and Bosnian Hasan Salihamidžić. I asked Šimunić if the issue of ethnicity or the war ever came up as a subject either with his colleagues or as a form of sledging with opponents. "Never", he replied unequivocally.

Following his acquisition of dual citizenship in 2001, Šimunić made his debut for Croatia in a friendly against South Korea in November of that year. For a boy who had grown up on the opposite side of the world to the country he represented, this was a moment of enormous pride for him. "As a child growing up one of my dreams was to play for the Croatian national team," he said. "But at the time, it wasn't possible, because Croatia wasn't independent yet, but after the war, the possibility arose and eventually my dream came true."

Šimunić represented Croatia at four international tournaments, most famously at the 2006 World Cup where, in a match against Australia, English referee Graham Poll showed him three yellow cards before finally sending him off. When booking Šimunić for the second time, Poll seemingly was thrown by the player's Australian accent and wrote down the name of Craig Moore, Australia's number three instead.

I asked Šimunić about this game in particular. I was intrigued to discover whether despite playing for Croatia, he felt split loyalties or if he felt like he was representing Croatians across Australia? "I felt like I was representing Croatians, not just in Croatia but all over the world," he replied. "Any team that I have ever played for — club or national team — I always wanted to win and for me that was like any other game." Šimunić is typical of those Australians who have a strong sense of loyalty to the Balkans, despite living or being born in a country on the other side of the world. Author James Montague believes that there is some correlation between being born within the diaspora, and having an over-inflated sense of nationalism, more so than those who were born within Croatia itself. Montague recounts a report for an American newspaper in which he reported from a square in Zagreb, with a big screen showing the 2018 World Cup final: "There were so many Aussies and they were the ones with the Ustaše flags ... they were the most hardcore nationalists."

As the numbers of Balkan immigrants to Australia increased after the war, they needed an expression of identity and football provided one of those very few outlets. They needed footballing success though to be able to give themselves greater affirmation. That success was to come via fair means or foul. While in the midst of a tight promotion title race in 1959, Croatia Geelong beat Brunswick-Latvia 29-1. Brunswick-Latvia seemed to have found their nadir in 1959 as they were also beaten 12-0 by West Melbourne Sicilia and 16-0 by Lions-Haydock. There does however seem to be a few issues with the Geelong fixture, to say the least. Allegedly, Brunswick were in dire financial straits at the time and Geelong were to pay the stricken club £2 per goal that they managed to score. It seems that not every Brunswick player received that memo however as they did manage to take the lead. With a 13-goal lead at half-time though, the Geelong president was at pains to ask his players to stop scoring so the fixture would at least retain the air of a normal game.

The referee, however, was convinced that Brunswick were trying and said as much to Stewart Beaton, the secretary of the football association. The Metropolitan First Division North was won that year by Croatia Geelong. Preston, the team who finished second in the league, successfully protested and were later awarded an extra two league points, leapfrogging Croatia Geelong to win the title by a single point.

In 1972, Geelong and Melbourne Croatia were expelled from the league following several on-field incidents. In the latter Croatia's case, it involved both a spectator pitch invasion and also an assault on Jimmy Brennan, the referee. Having already sent off Croatia full back Hugh Gunn, for a series of robust tackles, Brennan was pointing to the dressing room to warn another vociferous Croatia player that would be where he would be headed too should he continue with a similar tackling style. Croatian fans, mistakenly believing that Brennan was sending off another of their players, invaded the pitch and punched him. It was the final incident in a long line of transgressions committed by the club and its supporters, and a subsequent appeal was unsuccessful.

There are those who feel that Melbourne Croatia were unfairly treated. The fixture during which the referee was assaulted was against Hakoah, a traditionally Jewish club. In its pure and basic form, some felt that it was a case of Ustaše vs Jews (Jews had suffered terribly under the Ustaše during World War II), and that could not be tolerated. George Wallace of the Victorian Soccer Federation later claimed that this was not the case and due process had been followed in the case of Melbourne Croatia. The club made a comeback in an array of different guises before becoming the Melbourne Knights, the name they have retained to this day.

Violence within Australian football and the broad brush with which ethnic clubs and minorities were blamed is nothing new. In 1950 under the headline 'New Arrivals in Fisticuffs Soccer', journalist J.O Wilshaw in the *Sporting Globe* reported that the ethnically Maltese club George Cross had two men sent off in a match that saw the referee assaulted and the game abandoned. The article discusses "new Australians" and whether they should be allowed to form clubs revolving around their communities or should they be "assimilated into the ranks of teams mainly of British stock and thus become better mixers instead of keeping to themselves".

There was also a clash of footballing cultures at play. The traditional British game was based on covering ground on the pitch and on physical contact, with referees preferring to let the game flow rather than pull players up for niggly fouls. The game of the immigrants, meanwhile, revolved around little physical contact and an emphasis on technical skill. Articles like Wilshaw's did little to break down that cultural barrier or remove any of the scepticism one side had of the other. Wilshaw even went on to write another article for the *Sporting Globe* entitled 'Foreign Element Causing Trouble'.

This was the paradox that new Balkan arrivals, and others, found themselves in. On the one hand they were criticised for forming football clubs based around their own ethnic communities, yet on the other they were not made to feel welcome when they did try to integrate into already established clubs.

In July 1952, Wilshaw again played on these stereotypes in an article about a match between Melbourne-based clubs Brighton and Juventus headlined 'New Australians Attack Referee'. Juventus, chasing the league title, were leading when the referee awarded a contentious penalty from which Brighton equalised. Although the penalty was academic — Juventus won the league anyway — fans surrounded the referee as he walked off the pitch escorted by security and one tried to punch him, missed and hit another pitch invader. Although the incident did not involve fans from any Balkan clubs, Wilshaw's blanket condemnation tainted all fans of ethnic clubs: "Just when the New Australians had given some evidence of falling into line with the ethics of sportsmanship that has prevailed in Victorian soccer long before they came, there was another outburst by spectators.".

Wilshaw appears relentless in his attacks on football and the minorities who played it. Just a month later, he wrote another article entitled 'Will Soccer Incidents Never Cease?' detailing how Eric Dobric, a player for the White Eagles, was given a 12-month suspended sentence for assaulting a referee. While the incidents that Wilshaw reported on were obviously newsworthy, there does seem to be an uncomfortable undercurrent to his work. The Dobric incident followed an event the previous week in which a referee was assaulted after sending a player off. Wilshaw noted that "in each case a Jugoslav player was involved". Whether detailing the transgressors' ethnic origins was a deliberate attempt by Wilshaw to separate Anglo-Australian players from Balkan players or not, only he could properly explain.

Nevertheless, a profile of the Croatian community, written by the Department of Immigration and Multicultural Affairs, noted that it was football that helped many Croat migrants assimilate and go on to enjoy successful careers and livelihoods in Australian society. As academic Dario Brentin told me when we discussed Josip Simunic; football, alongside Catholicism, were two of the pillars on which Croatian immigrants could rebuild their identity in their new home.

By the 1970s, Australian national sports were having a fallow period. Its rugby union team hadn't won a Bledisloe Cup — a regular series of test matches against New Zealand — since 1949; with the exception of a draw in 1952, the All Blacks had triumphed on every occasion. Australia would have to wait till the very end of the decade until it tasted glory in the competition against its Kiwi neighbours again.

The team's record in its other test matches was little better. They lost all three home matches to a touring South African team in 1971, and in 1972 they lost three matches to New Zealand, were surprisingly defeated at home to Tonga and were beaten on tour by both England and Wales, failing to trouble the scoreboard at all during the latter match.

The rugby union team, however, must have felt smug when comparing themselves to the Australian cricket team of the same era. They didn't win a Test match at all in 1970, losing four games to South Africa and a home Ashes series to England 2-0. Indeed, during the entire decade, the Australian cricket team won only 30 tests out of 83 played.

They did, however, enjoy some success in football, qualifying for their first football World Cup in 1974 with a team made up of players born in such diverse locations as Scotland, England, Hungary and of course, Yugoslavia. The defender Dragan 'Doug' Utješenović was born in Belgrade, but made 61 appearances for the Socceroos. Ivo Rudic, who was an unused substitute throughout the tournament, was born in Split, as was striker Branko Buljevic who played 30 times for the national side.

Australia at this point were managed by Rale Rasic. Rasic, a Yugoslav, was born in Dole, Bosnia, close to the country's south western border with Croatia, and arrived in Australia in 1962. Rasic joined Footscray JUST and stayed with the club for seven years, interrupted only by an 18-month stint in the Yugoslav army for national service.

The Socceroos were unfortunate enough to come up against both East and West Germany in their group stage with Chile making up the numbers. Playing East Germany first, Australia put on a show of bravado which included a tub-thumping call to arms sung a bit too confidently in front of a camera crew while showering — "and if you are an Aussie then you know we cannot lose" was the cry. If this was the case, then unfortunately nobody had notified their opponents.

Australia started brightly and the score was 0-0 at half time. However, East Germany ran out winners thanks to two second-half goals, with the first an own goal by the Socceroos defender Colin Curran. A woefully-played offside trap allowed Jürgen Sparwasser to bear down on Jack Reilly in the Australian goal. As Reilly advanced toward the right corner of his area, Sparwasser slotted the ball underneath him and both watched as the ball trickled agonisingly towards either the goal or maybe the left hand post. Curran wasn't taking any chances though, and rushing back towards the goal line he attempted to smash the ball clear, but succeeded only in hoofing the ball into his own net.

Curran ends up in a rather undignified heap in the back of the goal, on his back, left leg in the air with his studs caught in the net. In a rather cruel attempt to further highlight his error, at the time of writing, Wikipedia denotes Curran as Australia's first ever goalscorer at a World Cup.

The second goal came from an attack down the German left. Eberhard Vogel crossed and despite Peter Wilson's despairing diving header, the ball arrived at the feet of East Germany's record goalscorer and appearance-maker Joachim Streich, who managed to meet the cross with his left foot as the ball reached the ground and caught it on the half volley, rifling in into the top corner.

If Australia's first game was tough, their second was even more intimidating as they took on hosts and eventual winners West Germany. The Germans imposed themselves from the start and soon enough an attack down their right led to intricate passing in the Australian area with four defenders and the goalkeeper wrong footed, though somehow Gerd Müller's shot was deflected for a corner. However a goal was inevitable and Müller again was at the heart of it, a run from midfield and an exchange of passes with Jürgen Grabowski eventually seeing the ball break to Wolfgang Overath, who after a couple of touches, hammered the ball into the top left corner of Jack Reilly's goal.

Australia's goal began to lead something of a charmed life, particularly when Müller hit the crossbar from a flying header. But it couldn't hold out against the onslaught and Uli Hoeneß crossed for Bernhard Cullman to grab the second after 34 minutes. Australia's defeat was sealed in the 53rd minute when a Hoeneß corner found Gerd Müller at the near post to add a deserved third.

Australia's final game was a 0-0 draw against Chile at a sparsely populated Olympiastadion in West Berlin, played on a pitch resembling a paddy field. Despite Australia having chances, they couldn't make the breakthrough. The match had little in the way of incident other than midfielder Ray Richards being sent off for two bookable offences. And with that, Australia were out. They had acquitted themselves modestly in an extremely tough group, but it was to be more than three decades before the Socceroos would grace the World Cup again.

Whilst unsuccessfully trying to qualify for future World Cups, the national team did play friendlies at various times against Yugoslav clubs. In June 1979, Partizan Belgrade toured Australia, losing 1-0 to a select Melbourne XI, followed by a draw and a 1-0 win against the national team. The Partizan team included seasoned professionals such as Slobodan Santrač, all-time top scorer in the Yugoslav first division and manager of the Yugoslav national team at the 1998 World Cup. The first Partizan game against Australia almost led to a complete abandonment after Tommy Cumming was punched by a Partizan player. Following a pitch invasion by the Partizan substitutes and coaching staff, the referee Jim Reeves took the players off the pitch for 15 minutes to calm the situation down. It appears Reeves himself may have needed calming down as it took the intervention of Australian Soccer Federation officials to persuade him to continue the match.

Nearly a decade later, Australia also beat Dinamo Zagreb 1-0 and drew 1-1 in two friendlies in Sydney and Melbourne in 1988. The fixtures were seen as precursors to Australia playing Yugoslavia at the summer Olympics later that year in South Korea. Australia caused somewhat of an upset at the tournament, beating a Yugoslavia team managed by Ivica Osim and featuring Dragan Stojković 1-0, courtesy of a Frank Farina goal.

Hajduk Split toured Australia in June 1990, just a few weeks after the Maksimir riot in Croatia. They played the national team in Sydney, losing the first of two games 1-0 thanks to a Paul Trimboli rocket from distance after just 33 seconds. Behind the goal there was a large Croatian šahovnica chequered motif, and the tour was significant for Hajduk. Away from the rising ethnic tensions within Yugoslavia, they felt emboldened enough to show their nationalist pride. In his book *The Death And Life Of Australian Soccer*, Joe O'Gorman explains that, "Hajduk had become a potent symbol of the emergent Croatian state, and as players ran onto the field at Parramatta Stadium they literally tore the logo, which featured the socialist red star of Yugoslavia, off their shirts". The large Croatian contingent inside the stadium lapped it up.

By July 1992, just over a year after the Balkan conflict began, Croatia was readmitted into FIFA and its first official matches were as a touring team against Australia. The first of the three games was a 1-0 Australian victory watched by around 11,000 fans in Melbourne's Olympic Park (there are varying numbers of attendees for all matches on this tour, I have gone with those on the reliable *ozfootball.net*). Andrew Marth tapped in the vital goal from a yard out following confusion in the Croatian defence, who felt that goalkeeper Dražen Ladić had been fouled in the build-up. The ball had ricocheted off the left-hand post and while the bewildered defender on the line was looking around for the ball, Marth tapped home. But maybe it was the occasion rather than the result that mattered — despite the loss, Croatia were officially on the international football map.

Three days later, under evening skies at Adelaide's Hindmarsh Stadium, Croatia fared little better. They were two goals down inside 12 minutes, and their defending was at best uncoordinated. After just 10 minutes, a cut-back from the left of the Croatian box found Ernie Tapai, who from around ten yards out neatly side-footed home. Two minutes later the Croatian defence was carved open again as captain Paul Wade played an incisive through ball, which really should have been cut out, to Warren Spink, who neatly rounded the stricken Ladić in goal and slotted the ball away into the empty net. However, in the 31st minute a tiny piece of Croatian history was made, when Josip Weber scored the country's first goal following their readmission by FIFA. The hosts grabbed a third through Jason Van Blerk in the second half and the game ended 3-1. Weber's only three games for Croatia were during this tour before switching allegiances to Belgium thanks to his grandfather. He went on to play in all four of Belgium's games at the 1994 World Cup and passed away in November 2017 following a battle with cancer aged just 52.

The final game in front of 12,000 fans in the Sydney sunshine was a lively 0-0 draw, meaning Croatia finished their Australian tour with a record of played three, lost two and drawn one, but the fact that there was a team there at all was something of a triumph. During all three games there was a significant Croatian presence in the stands, particularly in the second game, and a number of the Croatian players such as Igor Štimac, Slaven Bilić and Nikola Jerkan would make up the nucleus of the squad in the golden generation years to come.

The Australian footballing authorities' attempts to de-ethnicise clubs had continued, trying in 1977 and twice in the 1990s to remove clubs' affiliations, which they held on to with a rigid pride. Sadly, though, change within the Australian football structure had to come if it was to move forwards and compete with other sports. Dwindling attendances showed that football in Australia was remaining a niche game, albeit one followed by an incredibly passionate set of supporters. This was also a period when Australian dominance of sport was reaching a peak. The rugby league team had retained the World Cup in 2000, they were rugby union world champions in 1999 and, the same year, its cricket team won the first of three consecutive World Cups. Even in individual sports, Australia was making an indelible impact. In tennis, Leyton Hewitt followed up his 2001 US Open victory by winning Wimbledon in the following year and Cathy Freeman was dominant on the athletics track, claiming an iconic victory in the 400m in front of an adoring home crowd at the Sydney Olympics in 2000. Australian sport was a juggernaut crashing over the rest of the sporting world and there was no appetite, or need, for many Australians to take interest in football whilst there were so many successes elsewhere.

Something had to change before the game risked being relegated to little more than a footnote or sporting backwater in Australian society. The *Report of the Independent Soccer Review Committee* (usually referred to as the Crawford Report after the report's chair David Crawford), published in 2003, made a raft of recommendations, one consequence of which was the creation in 2005 of the Hyundai A-League to replace the failing National Soccer League. Two key appointments helped push the reforms through. Firstly, businessman Frank Lowy (best known to some as the man who fell off the platform when handing the A-League Grand Final trophy over to Melbourne Victory's Mike Milligan in 2015), and secondly John O'Neill, who became chief executive officer.

Lowy had arrived in Australia from Czechoslovakia via a Budapest ghetto in World War II, a period of internment in Cyprus and some time spent fighting in the 1948 Arab-Israeli war. He noticed that as the use of the motor vehicle increased, people in the United States were inclined to travel to large, out-of-town shopping malls. He co-founded the Westfield Development Corporation which established malls in Australia, the United States and in the United Kingdom too (Westfield in East London for example), and in 2014 Forbes estimated his wealth to be US$4.6bn. O'Neill, new to football, had been the driving force behind the success of the 2003 rugby union World Cup in Australia, an event which he expected to reap up to AUS$90m to be split between the Australian Rugby Union and the International Rugby Board.

Under the tagline "It's football, but not as you know it", the inaugural season of the A-League began in 2005, with clubs bearing names such as Melbourne Victory and Newcastle Jets, which couldn't be identified with one particular ethnic group. Yet despite this new sanitised version of football, issues still remained in terms of fan violence. *Daily Telegraph* columnist Rebecca Wilson was a vociferous opponent of A-League fan culture, and in one column in August 2012, she wrote of violence by fans of the newly-formed Western Sydney Wanderers, accusing the authorities of only paying lip service when it came to tackling the issue. Wilson's attitude can be seen as snobbery from those who value the "traditional" sports of Australia to that of football. She signed off the column by discussing what she perceived to be a haemorrhaging of youth players away from the Australian footballing system abroad, something she put down to trifling arguments between clubs and the age-old ethnic tensions.

In January 2014, Wilson discussed the Western Sydney Wanderers Red and Black Bloc ultras and their behaviour at a match between Wanderers and Melbourne Victory in which seats were torn up and flares were thrown. Again, bringing a comparison with 'traditional' Australian sport into the equation, Wilson compared the behaviour of the Red and Black Bloc fans to those who would be watching the Australian cricket team. The attitude of Wilson and others in the Australian media were rebuffed by former professionals such as Mark Bosnich, and sports website *theroar.com*. The latter wondered if Wilson's outrage was due to her genuine disgust at fan behaviour, or because she just dislikes football in general. It must be said, however, that Wilson is unable to defend herself now from these accusations — she sadly passed away from breast cancer in October 2016 at the age of 54.

Below the top level of the A-League, the older Australian clubs still exist with their ethnic and community affiliations. Melbourne Knights compete in the National Premier Leagues Victoria along with Dandenong Thunder, a team formed by the Albanian community. It is reassuring and touching to see that as the A-League increases its membership (Macarthur FC were added to the league in the 2020/21 season), the ethnic teams which have formed the backbone to many new arrivals within Australia are still holding their own.

★

CHAPTER SEVEN
THE FUTURE

In a quiet industrial park in the town of Brøndbyvester, some seven miles west of Denmark's capital city of Copenhagen, sits the office block containing the Cross Cultures Project Association (CCPA). The glass-fronted building is overshadowed by an imposing stadium with a modern grey frontage — the home of local football team Brøndby IF. As you approach the CCPA headquarters, you could be forgiven for thinking that you are at an out of-town industrial park anywhere in Europe. However, the work that is carried out there holds huge significance for those living within the borders of the former Yugoslavia several hundred miles to the south.

The CCPA avows that "Our mission is to use fun sports to bring people together to play and cooperate across ethnic, social and religious divides and contribute to peaceful co-existence, social cohesion and resilience". When discussing their mission, vision and strategic intentions the phrase "joyful games" is used, for if communities who struggle to communicate following bitter conflict are to interact once again, there has to be fun. If there is no fun, then there is nothing to attract children to participate and it is vital that if communities are to rebuild that children are at the epicentre of any interaction. Children are the future of any community and perhaps just as important, if they are interested and involved then their parents will be too.

CCPA is the brainchild of Anders Levinsen, who remains its Managing Director at the time of writing in 2023. He founded the CCPA in 1998, following a spell working for the United Nations High Commissioner for Refugees (UNHCR) and studying at Roskilde University. Recognition quickly followed and the organisation won the Michael Laudrup Award the same year and the Danish Peace Prize in 1999. Subsequently, the work of CCPA has given Levinsen wider recognition both within the former Yugoslavia and within UEFA too. However, personal recognition is not what motivates him. Speaking to the UEFA website about the CCPA's Open Fun Football Schools (OFFS) programme, he stated that "We also want our fun football activities to give participants a new story about friendship and cooperation, a story of positive experiences that counterbalance the old story of conflict, fuelled by mistrust and negative feelings."

A typical OFFS programme includes 200 boys and girls (a minimum of 40% of all participants must be female) along with 30 volunteers from different ethnic communities who come together for five days of sports programmes. The aim of the programme is not so much to teach children to become better footballers, but to enthuse them and to use football as a means of promoting exercise while also providing positive experiences of interaction between communities that have traditionally been divided. There is an emphasis on a bottom-up approach: a previous annual report made constant mention of the importance of the term "grassroots". There is a huge effort to try and involve members of the community and parents as coaches and volunteers. In 2014, CCPA employed 4,426 volunteers who offered their services for up to 100 hours; there were also 3,821 parents involved at almost 180 workshops. By 2021, CCPA had operated programmes in 21 countries in eastern Europe, Asia, the Middle East and Africa.

The programme's work has also been recognised at higher levels. An evaluation study in May 2011 for the Danish government by the Ministry of Foreign Affairs concluded that the "OFFS concept remains unique and impressive in the Balkans" and a 2004 joint evaluation by the Norwegian and Danish governments stated that "this is an exceptional project ... it has been highly relevant, particularly in its country of origin (Bosnia & Herzegovina)". The project has attracted external funding too from Scandinavian governments, as well as UEFA. The flexibility and methodology of the OFFS works to their advantage and in communities that have greater divisions along ethnic grounds, such as Bosnia and Kosovo, the OFFS provides an enormous local focus upon reconciliation.

However, there are those who feel that the work carried out by the OFFS has the potential to be undermined by local football federations. The 2011 Ministry of Danish Affairs evaluation study highlights an "elitist approach" by some football associations, who prefer to concentrate their finances and energies towards the higher ends of the spectrum, focusing instead on their national teams, club sides, players and the competitions that they play in. It's easy to see why there is this level of self-interest. The expansion of the Euro 2016 qualifying process saw Balkan countries qualify for the competition and progress into the knockout phase of the tournament. Should this format continue, then there is every reason to think that a Bosnian team with stars such as Miralem Pjanić and Edin Džeko could build on their World Cup 2014 success and aim to qualify more regularly for international tournaments. The estimated €14m prize money that Iceland earned for reaching the quarter finals of Euro 2016 cannot have gone unnoticed by various Balkan FAs. Such a sum could go far in financing future infrastructure projects. Croatia received $28m for reaching the final of the 2018 World Cup and with UEFA receiving three extra places as part of the expanded 2026 World Cup, Balkan FAs have every reason to think that they could achieve one of those coveted three positions.

There is no doubt that greater recognition within UEFA helps the Balkan regions too. In 2013, then UEFA President Michel Platini opened a state-of-the-art training complex in the Bosnian town of Zenica, which was to be used by the Bosnian national team. Costing €5m, of which UEFA and FIFA contributed a combined

€4.6m, the facilities boasted two full-size pitches, a 1,500-seat stand and a hotel as well. With football's governing bodies prepared to invest so heavily in local infrastructure and national teams, and the financial rewards for succeeding at tournaments at both club and international level, it is easy to see why the reconciliation of divided communities could slip down the order of priorities for national associations.

Another issue associated with the OFFS is that in some instances, the conflict resolution section of their programme is being forgotten or ignored by volunteers in favour of sports activities. The evaluation team for the 2011 Ministry of Foreign Affairs report noted that "generally, issues concerning peace and reconciliation appear quite low" on volunteers' lists of priorities. But despite some apparent differences between the stated aim of the OFFS and the volunteers on the ground, there can be no doubt that the OFFS have helped countless thousands of children not just in the Balkans, but also former scenes of conflict such as Iraq, Lebanon and Russia's North Caucasus region.

Levinsen is one of those people who inspires others to do better. It's still possible to see how his physical stature helped him become a defender in the late 1970s and early 1980s for Danish clubs AB and B93, before he entered into a coaching career at youth and senior levels. He then worked for the UNHCR in Iraq before moving onto Bosnia and co-ordinating the emergency effort with Colonel Bob Stewart in the early stages of the war. Before too long the pair gained a warranted reputation of being unphased by local armed protagonists. "He and I were outspoken. We did many things that were unusual, and we took some freedom in our mandates," Levinsen told me. His impeccable English and physical presence carry real weight and it's easy to see when I talk to him on a hot and sunny August afternoon how this is a man who would feel in control of any situation. He sits topless and barrel-chested in his house, talking and laughing with the air of someone who is entirely sure of themselves and their surroundings.

He builds up a picture of the war's psychological effects upon the local population. As a tense situation arose, roadblocks would be erected and services such as telephone communications would be cut, leaving people stuck in their homes and villages. This artificial inertia was what Levinsen had to overcome. "When you can't move or communicate, you end up in a war psychosis, driven by hatred, fear and nationalism," he told me. The most important role Levinsen had was to facilitate freedom of movement by negotiating with the different warring factions and to arrange ceasefires. Following his time in Bosnia, Levinsen returned to Denmark to regain a sense of domesticity, yet he couldn't get the country out of his mind.

He then recalls the moment that first planted the seed of the football schools in his mind: "my oldest son came home from a football school organised by the Danish FA. He said 'come and see what I can do' and he made the most wonderful bicycle kick and he was only nine years old at the time. I said 'wow, I've played in the best league and I've never been able to do this' and he said 'I learned this at my football school today'".

Curious by what went on at the school, Levinsen rang in sick at work the next day and went to see the football school in action for himself. "What I saw was the most wonderful sight. Boys and girls, black and white, playing together in a concept that was to promote football". The programme revolved around children purely enjoying themselves for the sake of participating in playing sport. The following day, Levinsen began to form the idea of taking football schools to Bosnia and other war-torn areas and he approached the Danish FA for help. He promised his wife that this would be his final Balkans trip, and that he would go for one year only. "I did it with my own money and savings," he told me. "I would close my Balkans book and get on with my life."

Levinsen has not been afraid to take risks in his efforts to reconcile differing groups within the Balkans through his football schools. One of the first schools was in Goražde, located in the southeast of Bosnia, a town that was besieged by Bosnian Serbs between 1992 and

1995. Before the war in 1991, just over a quarter of the population of the Goražde municipality was Serb, with 70% of the remainder being Muslims. Ten years after the end of the war in 2005, 94% of the population were Muslim. Open Fun Football Schools managed to take the first large group of Serb schoolchildren into the town in the years immediately following the end of the war. Following the programme, Levinsen wrote to one of his co-ordinators in Bosnia effectively handing over the running of the schools and putting as much distance between him and the project as possible. However, as much as Levinsen wanted to keep the promise he made to his wife, it was never going to be that easy. "My colleague in Bosnia rang me up crying, saying 'we need you here'. I said 'OK, but you have to assist me' and that's the beginning of the programme".

When Levinsen talks, it seems that he is a man given to nostalgia. At one point, I asked him whether he ever saw local people playing football during the war — "yeah, yeah" he responded immediately and enthusiastically, before recounting a story of how British peacekeeping battalions, deployed to Bosnia as part of the United Nations, sometimes organised matches with local forces. One game he refereed between British peacekeepers and a group of Bosniak troops descended into violence, while the bemused civilian population looked on.

I'm keen to know if in all the years that he has overseen the football schools, there is one event that makes Levinsen smile. After a few moments' thought he grinned and replied that when he was trying to start a programme in Mostar, some Serbs got wind of the football schools and wanted one for themselves in a Serb suburb of Sarajevo. After prolonged negotiations, a programme was set up and Levinsen went to see for himself the progress that was being made. What he found made him almost apoplectic with anger - nothing had been set up, no cones, and no goals, and the children were just running around after three footballs. The coaches were sitting lazily around drinking schnapps as all this was going on. "There was smoke coming out of my ears, I headed over to them to ask, 'what the fuck are you doing?'." It took the programme leader of the school to calm Levinsen down before he reached the coaches. The leader then explained that only four years previously, the same coaches had stood on the front line of the war but on opposing sides. Now the coaches were together in the same field and had recognised their former enemies from the sound of their voices. "During the war, they had been standing behind a container calling to each other 'come out you fucker or I will fuck your mother'. So they had to say hello to each other that morning with schnapps and we went in too and had schnapps whilst explaining what a football school was and how the children lined up. It was the first time that these people had been on the Serb side and they could breathe". Levinsen says that this was the moment that he realised that for the schools to work, they needed local coaches taking part as well as having local children.

I asked Levinsen whether the OFFS face cynicism either from local FAs or those members of the community who do not wish to ingratiate themselves with other ethnic groups. His answer was an unequivocal "never". He said that most parents who remove their children from the football schools on grounds of ethnicity tend to return them very quickly, while meekly apologising for their actions as the children get very upset. He added that local FAs are usually positive in their attitude towards the OFFS as well. Levinsen estimates that 70% of young footballers in Bosnia have passed through the OFFS system, including a young Edin Džeko. As post-war Balkan FAs tried to reorganise themselves into their regional entities, they concentrated their efforts on their national teams and improving their highest-performing clubs. There was little space for grassroots football. However, the OFFS provided a production line of young players with the raw street footballing talent and naivety that could be nurtured and honed. The quality of coaches began to improve too, including a former coach of the Yugoslav national team; a Serb who was married to a Muslim and decided to stay with her in besieged Sarajevo during the war. In the war's aftermath he found himself shunned by both sides and unable to find work until the OFFS offered him a position. He became one of seven former national team coaches to have worked with the OFFS.

This isn't to say Levinsen's experiences in the Balkans have always been positive. He was once taken hostage during the war in the eastern Bosniak village of Cerska and held with a gun pointing to his neck, something which he rather coolly plays down as "not a very pleasant situation". He was being held in the offices of a local football club in a room covered by memorabilia and grainy photographs of former players. After 10 minutes he began to engage his captors and asked if they ever played football. When they answered in the affirmative, Levinsen told them of his playing background and the gun was removed and they could talk in the international language of football. "'Football' was the key word that made them remove the gun from my neck," he said.

Towards the end of our interview, I told Levinsen that the word I have written down the most in my notes is "children". He didn't seem surprised by this. "I have two basic principles for the programme," he told me. "The first is we always put the child in the centre and the second is that the environment connects the children to football". I asked about the future for the OFFS. For an organisation that Levinsen names as one of the three reasons that peace exists in Bosnia today (the others being the removal of regional number plates on cars and the immediate role of women as the backbone of families, given the large numbers of men killed in the war) there is still a significant amount of work to be done. Having not quite succeeded with a crime prevention scheme in the Balkans, Levinsen hopes to move the football schools towards an anti-radicalisation programme. By focusing on reconciliation, people are brought together and realise that those they never mix with are not monsters at all. By focusing on children then situations are depoliticised: "It is child-centric and that is the key".

At around the same time I spoke to Levinsen, I also spoke to Vildana Delalic Elezovic, a Project Assistant in Sarajevo who has been involved with the OFFS for almost a decade. It is clear from our discussion that the enthusiasm and passion expressed by Levinsen is shared by Elezovic. "OFFS can provide a great platform for inclusion of different socially challenged groups," she said, "and it is growing to be just that — a tool to involve different social groups into common activity that is designed to address every child's abilities and needs". She explained that the "positive energy" that the OFFS gives off is felt by its participants. "We have many, many letters from parents saying that the OFFS has been the best thing for their kids." The lack of tournament and competitive focus means that the children taking part are able to mix with each other more freely, interact to a higher degree and are never paired up with those friends that they came with.

One regret that Levinsen does have is that maybe the events are focused too much on football, and not enough on the follow up to ensure that barriers have finally been overcome. For all the work that the football schools do, it is the kind of self-analysis that has made them such a success.

***

The Stadiumi Olimpik Adem Jashari is a landmark that combines football and political importance. It is here that Kosovo began its footballing journey, which led from exhibition matches against like-minded territories who were themselves seeking sporting self-determination, to recognition from both UEFA and FIFA in May 2016. In October of the same year, Kosovo made its competitive home debut in a World Cup qualifier against Croatia. It seems somewhat fitting that such a debut would be against a team that had also been successful in seeking their own self-determination.

The stadium itself is typical of many older eastern European and former Soviet grounds. It is a wide oval structure with three sides open to the elements, and a running track around the edge of the pitch pushing back the stands behind the goals. Its main stand faces east towards the city of Mitrovica. The stand is an amalgamation of green and grey plastic chairs in an upper tier connected by concrete steps to seats further down. The stadium also sits within one of Kosovo's more divided cities. There was an irony that a game of such historical importance for a country seeking wider independent recognition took place in an area close to ethnic Serb neighbourhoods. Somewhat more provocatively, the stadium is named after one of the founders of the Kosovo Liberation Army, who died in 1998 in a fire fight with Serb forces. The battle, in which 60 members of Jashari's immediate and extended family were killed, is known as the Attack on Prekaz, and has subsequently been condemned by Amnesty International as an attempt "to eliminate suspects and their families".

It was within these unassuming concrete confines, however, on an overcast and damp day in early March 2014 that history was made, and Kosovo played its first FIFA-recognised fixture against Haiti, despite yet not obtaining membership (They had played several non-recognised fixtures during the 1990s and early 2000s). Bound by strict guidelines outlined in a memo by FIFA Secretary General Jerome Valcke to other FIFA members in February 2013, there were to be no "national symbols" displayed pre-match and any matches to be played on Kosovan soil were subject to authorisation by the Serbian FA. This made little difference to the 17,000 spectators packed within the ground who witnessed the Kosovo players proudly take to the pitch. Once pennants were exchanged, dignitaries met and a joint team photo taken, the game began on a surface which could be best described as agricultural.

Most of the action appeared to take place in the stands. Despite the wet conditions, the fans generated a party atmosphere by jumping up and down and waving umbrellas in the air, Mexican waves and Poznans were heavily present. The match itself appeared to be impaired by the surface water resting on the pitch, yet there was no doubting either the enthusiasm of the Kosovar players, keen to make a positive first impression on the world of international football, or their obvious technical skill. The game itself ended

0-0 and the Haitian players generously left the pitch allowing the Kosovar players to lap up the adulation of the by now drenched fans who had witnessed their own little piece of history.

Three more official friendlies were played out before the end of the year. A 6-1 drubbing by Turkey featured a goal by Albert Bunjaku, which was the first Kosovan goal in a FIFA recognised fixture. It was followed by a 3-1 loss to Senegal and then, finally, a victory as they defeated Oman 1-0. The Senegal match in particular was important as it took place in Switzerland, a country with a high number of Kosovar émigrés. As kick off approached, an enormous Kosovo flag was unfurled, taking up a large proportion of one of the stands. Despite the ground only being half full, an extraordinary atmosphere was created by the Kosovo fans. Bunjaku gave the Kosovo fans hope by opening the scoring after he thumped a free kick into the top corner, but it was not to be as two quick goals by Oumar Niasse either side of half time followed by Diafra Sakho adding a third put paid to any Kosovan hopes of a victory.

Bunjaku is representative of one of the side effects of Kosovo receiving full FIFA and UEFA membership many years after it declared its independence. Born into the predominantly ethnic Albanian town of Gjilan, eastern Kosovo, Bunjaku emigrated to Switzerland with his mother and siblings to join his father who had already found employment there. A late developer in football terms, he didn't join his first club, FC Schlieren, until he was 13 in 1996, and his professional career has seen him flit between Switzerland and Germany. Beginning as a full back, Bunjaku finally made his impact as a striker by scoring two goals for Rot-Weiß Erfurt in the German DFB Cup against Jürgen Klinsmann's Bayern Munich in August 2008. A year later, he made his full Swiss debut in a 1-0 defeat to Norway, and earned six caps, the last of which came in 2010. At the time of writing, Bunjaku has now also played six times for Kosovo, scoring three goals. His career for Switzerland could hardly be described as stellar, even in the most generous of terms, yet he is a multi-ethnic vision for footballers torn between the country of their birth and the country of their family origins. Had he, Xherdan Shaqiri and others been able to play for a UEFA- and FIFA-recognised Kosovo following its declared independence in 2008, the country could have become a more established footballing force than it currently is.

Of the 23 players picked for Switzerland in the Euro 2016 tournament, six were eligible to play for Kosovo. To compound matters, those six were not so much fringe players, but players who are the heart of the team and can drive the Swiss forward to future success. Arguably the two biggest losses would be Chicago Fire's Xherdan Shaqiri and Bayer Leverkusen's Granit Xhaka. Shaqiri, the brightest star in this emerging golden generation of Swiss players was, like Bunjaku, born in the Kosovar town of Gjilan. Speaking in 2014 ahead of Switzerland's World Cup qualifier against Albania, Shaqiri seemed torn between his Swiss nationality and Kosovar heritage. He was at pains to state that despite the pride he felt having been born in Kosovo, Switzerland was his home. "My name says to all that my name is not from Switzerland but is from Kosovo ... but I made my school here, played my first football here. For me, it is always that I play for Switzerland. If I play, I play for Switzerland"

Now Kosovo has full recognition, Swiss players with Kosovan heritage could switch, despite having played competitive games for Switzerland. In late April 2016, Swiss newspaper *Blick* published an article on Granit Xhaka entitled 'The Kosovo Fear: could Xhaka and Shaqiri Leave our National Team Soon?'. Speaking to the *New York Times* in 2012, Xhaka stated that "for now we play for Switzerland, but later we will see what will happen".

Yet by the start of the 2016 Euros, Shaqiri seemed to have softened his stance at the prospect, although that might at least in part have been because he had been overlooked for the national team captaincy in favour of Stephan Lichsteiner. Speaking about the perceived snub, Shaqiri said: "what if the coach of Kosovo wants me as captain? Of course, I am thinking about it then". However, James Montague, who spoke with Shaqiri about this issue at the time for his book *Thirty-One Nil*, told me that he felt Shaqiri's loyalty to Switzerland was never in doubt, believing that he felt a huge amount of gratitude for the country that took him in, as well as raised and educated him. Montague did get the impression from speaking to some of the Kosovan Swiss players that while they were happy to keep their Swiss allegiance, they believed Kosovo should still have its own national team.

However, Montague went on to explain that immigration in Switzerland is an issue, just as it is elsewhere in Europe, and that some sections of the media were upset that the matter of Shaqiri switching teams was even up for debate, especially given he had stitched Kosovan and Swiss flags in his boots: "to a certain element within Switzerland that's almost seen as treasonous". He gave the analogy of what some sections of the British media would make if Raheem Sterling decided to play with English and Jamaican flags stitched onto his boots: "There would be a constituency that would be very upset by that".

Montague does feel though that the one player who could possibly have been swayed was Granit Xhaka who, despite being born in Switzerland, was still incredibly young when Kosovo received full recognition. While his family who migrated to the country may have felt grateful for their new Swiss home, Xhaka who was born in Switzerland and as a second generation migrant, possibly yearned for a nostalgic Kosovan ideal that may not have actually existed.

The acceptance of Kosovo by football's governing bodies was not an easy path to take. It has long been seen by Serbia as a spiritual heart and has a unique place in the country's psyche, due in a large part to the Battle of Kosovo in 1389 when a Serb-dominated force fought the Ottomans under Sultan Murad I. Both sides suffered heavy casualties and they fought each other to a virtual standstill. According to lore, the battle's defining moment came after a Serb knight, Miloš Obilić, supposedly deserted to the Ottomans and was granted an audience with Murad himself. There, Obilić produced a dagger which he thrust into Murad, killing him. Obilić was then set upon by the Sultan's bodyguards and was himself killed. However, it seems unlikely that these events actually took place. While Murad was definitely killed in the battle and Obilić was present too, there were no contemporary accounts of such a meeting. The earliest sources do not name Murad's killer and Obilić does not become part of the story until much later.

Yet the battle and the supposed actions of Obilić have struck a chord with Serbs down the centuries since the battle took place. In his book *Behind the Curtain*, Jonathan Wilson describes the alleged actions of Obilić and the battle as central to the Serb psyche, writing that "they are the wrongly oppressed but glorious losers". Indeed, when notorious football hooligan, international gangster and indicted war criminal Arkan was looking to purchase a football team, it wasn't his beloved Red Star that he bought, but Obilić. To own a club named after Serbia's national hero must have appealed to Arkan's vanity and national pride. They were forced to change their name in the Tito years, yet here they were, in their original guise and able to rise again from the Yugoslav regional leagues to recapture their glory years. Football writer and Serbian resident Kirsten Schlewitz believes that there is definitely a part of the Serbian psyche which identifies with the tag of glorious losers, and specifically mentions the Battle of Kosovo, saying "it's been over 500 years that they've been celebrating defeat".

Kosovo's parliament declared independence on February 17, 2008 in a session that was boycotted by all 10 Serbian MPs. Led by its own prime minister, Hacim Thaçi, the vote was carried and he declared Kosovo "proud, independent and free".

Protests immediately broke out in Serb areas of Kosovo, most notably in the divided Mitrovica which had provided ethnic flashpoints in previous years. Serbia's prime minister Vojislav Koštunica refused to recognise the vote and blamed the United States for using its military presence to give Kosovo the confidence to push ahead, saying: "Today the policy of force thinks it has triumphed by establishing a false state."

International reaction was mixed. Of the five permanent members of the UN Security Council, Britain, France and the United States recognised the declaration. China expressed concern. Russia, Serbia's traditional ally, also failed to endorse the vote, as did Cyprus, Romania and Slovakia, who feared that such recognition could provide hope to separatist movements in their own countries. China and Russia released a joint statement in May 2008 calling for a new set of negotiations between Serbia and Kosovo. In the week after the declaration, 17 nations had recognised Kosovo's independence.

Football's governing bodies had a difficult line to walk when it came to accepting Kosovo. FIFA's own statutes aim to promote friendly relations both between its members and also in society for "humanitarian objectives". Its own procedures for admitting a new member are set out in Article 10 of its constitution. An applying member must have been a "provisional member of a confederation for at least two years", but Kosovo gained acceptance by UEFA in May 2016 and only had to wait another 10 days before FIFA acceptance. An association in a region which has not yet gained full independence must seek the authorisation of the association "in the country on which it is dependent" before application. This last point is of course the contentious one, considering Serbia still believes Kosovo to be part of its own territory and refuses to recognise its move towards nationhood. FIFA, however, do not have the most consistent attitude when it comes to admitting smaller nations. The British overseas territory of Gibraltar was also admitted to FIFA at the same time as Kosovo (despite Spain's long standing historical claim to the area). There are still several nation states that currently have no formal membership of FIFA — mainly Pacific Island nations, as well as Monaco and the Vatican City.

The vote to accept Kosovo into football's governing bodies was not the processional celebration one could be forgiven for thinking. The UEFA vote or accession was passed by a 28/24 majority with two votes being declared invalid. The Serbian FA were understandably upset by the decision, with then President Tomislav

Karadžić declaring that "we must say no to politics" before giving a dire prediction that the vote could "create a tumult in the region and open a Pandora's Box throughout Europe" and that an appeal would be made to the Court of Arbitration for Sport. The Serbian government also stepped in to ensure that "the decision does not go smoothly and as the separatists may have imagined".

While some Swiss players are obviously unsure as to where their futures lie, others feel much more secure. Valon Behrami, who has a tattoo on his left arm of both the Kosovan and Swiss flags, was born in Mitrovica. In 1990, owing to the deteriorating political and economic situation in the region, his family moved to Ticino, a southern Swiss canton. After years of asylum rejections, the Swiss authorities decided in 1995 that the Behramis should leave Switzerland, however, the desperate family received help from an unusual quarter. The intervention of a local official, Alex Pedrazzini, was vital to their cause. Pedrazzini's son played for the same village team as Behrami and he immediately supported the family. "I did not do it for football, I did it for humanity," he later recounted. With the intervention of Pedrazzini, as well as a 200-signature petition, the Behramis were allowed to remain in Switzerland and two years later they received Swiss citizenship.

The fact that the family received so much help when they were at their lowest ebb may explain why Behrami has not been tempted to switch allegiance to the country of his birth. "I'm proud to wear the colours of Switzerland," he has said. "I can fight for a country that has given so much to my family". Behrami also goes a step further. Asked prior to the Euro 2016 tournament if he would celebrate scoring against Albania should he be lucky enough too, an emphatic Behrami declared that "celebrating a goal is part of football. When I score a goal, I want to celebrate".

For the Swiss national team, a side rich with a migrant culture, a haemorrhaging of some of their best players choosing to play for alternate national sides would be a change that could impact the team in the long term. Kubilay Türkyilmaz played 64 games for Switzerland between 1988 and 2001, scoring 34 goals. He was of Turkish descent, and would have been equally happy to have played for them as well, saying "I would have loved to have played for Turkey, but I was never offered the opportunity to do so". He also once refused to play for Switzerland in a game against Turkey. Murat and Hakan Yakin were both born in Basel to Turkish parents and won 136 caps between them and scored 24 goals for Switzerland. Despite both players being eligible to play for Turkey, Hakan turned down the opportunity when offered. He did however refuse to celebrate when scoring for Switzerland against Turkey in Euro 2008.

Switzerland is not the only national team that may have to compete with Kosovo for players now the latter has gained FIFA membership. Belgian international Adnan Januzaj was born in Brussels to Kosovan parents. His father fled to Belgium in 1992 rather than fight for the Yugoslav army in Bosnia, although several family members did fight for the Kosovo Liberation Army. The Yugoslav army entered the Januzaj's home village of Istog, razing 300 homes to the ground and murdering 17 civilians, though the Januzaj family home was spared, possibly due to its location set apart from the rest of the village.

Januzaj qualified to play for Belgium, Albania, Turkey, Serbia, Croatia and Kosovo, although the latter were yet to attain their FIFA or UEFA membership. In a bid to persuade Januzaj, Albanian television aired a programme called *Hero or Traitor*. The insinuations were obvious. Januzaj, however, eventually opted to play for Belgium. As of 2021, Januzaj has represented the Belgian national team only 13 times, failing to make both the delayed Euro 2020 and World Cup 2022 squads.

In September 2020, FIFA changed their eligibility rules. Players were no longer tied to a nation having made an appearance for that national side. Instead, if a player can prove that they were eligible to play for a second country at the time they made their debut for the first, they will be allowed to switch. There are still rules in place to police this new law: players cannot have played more than three times for the first national side, none of the matches can have been in the World Cup finals, and the player should not be older than 21. These new rules will be able to assist young players such as Januzaj whose families move due to political or humanitarian circumstances and feel conflicted about their background.

Albania are the other obvious candidates that could lose players to Kosovo. The elder brother of Granit Xhaka, Taulant, would qualify to switch nationalities. He chose Albania despite Switzerland being the country of his birth and having represented them up to and including under 21-level. The two brothers have their own little piece of history when in June 2016 they lined up against one another in the European Championships.

Kosovo began their inaugural qualification for the 2018 World Cup in Finland in September 2016 and were placed in a highly intriguing group. As well as the Finns, they played one of Euro 2016's surprise packages Iceland (who hold a team spirit Kosovo would surely want to emulate), Ukraine (a country with its own separatist issues and currently at war), former Yugoslav neighbours Croatia and finally Turkey. However, they gained just one point thanks to a 1-1 away draw with Finland.

They fared much better in Euro 2020 qualifying. When qualification was postponed due to the coronavirus pandemic, Kosovo sat third in Group A, having beaten Bulgaria, the Czech Republic and scored three goals against England at Wembley where they lost 5-3. While it is infeasible that Kosovo will attract all the players who are eligible, they will still be able to put together a competitive team, and may qualify to play at a future international tournament.

Despite Kosovo's recognition by football's governing bodies, it was not until the 2017/18 season that its teams were admitted to European club competitions. Initially, UEFA did not permit Football Superleague champions KF Feronikeli, nor domestic cup winners Pristina into the Champions League or Europa League, respectively. Artan Beris, Feronkeli's sporting director was quoted as saying that

UEFA "requested our financial reports for the past two years and we could not provide them so soon".

Former Yugoslav teams have not fared well in European competition since Red Star Belgrade's now almost mythical European Cup win in 1991. The following season, the defending champions reached the new group stage of the revamped competition, which would be renamed the Champions League the following season, having played two previous rounds. Their cause was not helped by being forced to play their home matches in Hungary and Bulgaria due to the escalation of the war in Yugoslavia. Without the atmosphere of the Marakana, they were not as formidable at home, but they still finished second in their group behind eventual finalists Sampdoria, whose team contained Roberto Mancini, Atillio Lombardo and Gianluca Vialli. However, it was not enough to progress under the format that year.

Due to sanctions, this was Yugoslavia's last foray into Europe's elite competition until the 1997/98 season, when the country was made up solely of Serbia and Montenegro (it was also be the first season that Macedonia would be represented in the Champions League). Other republics, however, were represented. Slovenian representatives Olimpija Ljubljana made it to the second round, before being trounced 7-0 on aggregate by AC Milan in the first qualifying round. The gulf in class was obvious for all to see and was exemplified by Demetrio Albertini's technically excellent goal in the second leg at Milan's Giuseppe Meazza stadium. A headed clearance by the Olimpija defence looped high in the air to Albertini on the edge of the area and he volleyed it straight past the goalkeeper into the top corner. It was symptomatic of the difference between the two sides and the lopsided aggregate score showed how much teams from the former Yugoslavia had to do to drag themselves to the same heights as Red Star had reached only a few years before.

Hajduk fared somewhat better in the 1994/95 season as they made their way to the quarter finals (the only time a former Yugoslav club has made it past the group stages thus far), losing

3-0 on aggregate to eventual winners Ajax. Meeting one of Europe's footballing giants, who went on to win the tournament that year, may be considered unlucky, however the decline of former Yugoslav clubs in European competition was a trend rather than a momentary blip. Since the inception of the Champions League in 1992 and up to the commencement of the 2023/24 competition, Yugoslav and former Yugoslav clubs have made the group stages 17 times, with Dinamo leading the way on seven appearances.

The defining factor in the reduction of the influence of former Yugoslav teams is the increased freedom of movement. During Tito's rule, players were unable to secure lucrative moves to the western European leagues until they were 28. Dr Richard Mills described the ruling to me as "one of brilliance" as it maintained a strong domestic league whilst also protecting young Yugoslav players from being swallowed up by the youth academies of Western Europe. One possible example would be Zoran Tošić, signed by Manchester United in 2009 as a young prospect in his early twenties. Tošić joined United in January 2009, making two league appearances that season before his career became stifled in the north west of England.

The following season he made two League Cup appearances, before spending the second half of the season on loan at Hertha Berlin. Following his return to United at the end of the 2009/10 season Tošić was subsequently sold to CSKA Moscow where he stayed until 2017, winning three Russian Premier League titles. His career subsequently took him back to Partizan, followed by short spells in China, Kazakhstan and Greece.

Tošić is clearly a player of some talent, winning leagues and cups in Serbia, Russia and Kazakhstan. He has also represented Serbia more than 70 times, however, it could be said that his move to United came too early. His lack of impact could be a sign that he was not ready to leave Serbia, especially not to a club the size of Manchester United. Had he stayed within his home country until he was 28, a transfer to one of Europe's elite may have been more successful.

As communism fell and Yugoslavia tore itself apart, the major European clubs began to snap up star players. The victorious Red Star team of 1991 began to disintegrate almost immediately, as three of the starting XI left the club the same year, with the remainder leaving in 1992. The players moved to clubs in a number of countries including Belgium, Sweden and the Czech Republic, yet seven of the team went straight to Italy and Spain. Serie A was the dominant European league at the time and was only a short hop over the Adriatic Sea from Yugoslavia. It was not long though before the players started to move to England.

By 1995, the first players made their way to the Premier League, with the Serb players leading from the front. Savo Milošević joined Aston Villa for £3.5m in the summer of 1995. He scored 29 goals in 90 appearances over three years, but his spell at the club ended in ignominy when he was transfer listed for spitting at his own fans in a Premier League match against Blackburn Rovers. One wag summed up the feeling that Villa fans felt towards him by suggesting that "knowing Savo, he would probably miss anyway".

For all his faults, Milošević showed players from Yugoslavia and its former states that it was possible to move away from the relative familiarity of Italy and Spain. By the turn of the century, players from all six republics had begun to play for English clubs. In January 2016, Bersant Celina became the first Kosovan to play in the Premier League when he came on as a substitute for Manchester City against Leicester City.

Serbia has had a high representation in England. After Milošević made his move to Aston Villa, several dozen more of his countrymen have made the journey to England with varying degrees of success. Some players became cult heroes for their clubs, like Saša Ćurčić (once described as the Serb George Best) at Bolton Wanderers. Others, like striker Milan Jovanović, were out-and-out flops. Signed for Liverpool from Standard Liege on a free transfer and with a healthy reputation, Jovanović stayed for just one season making just 10 goalless appearances before heading back to Belgium.

Others, such as Nemanja Vidić, were more successful. Vidić established himself as a legendary figure at Old Trafford, winning five Premier League titles and a Champions League medal with Manchester United, as well as becoming a worthy captain.

Croatia also has had significant representation within the Premier League. Igor Štimac was the first to make the move, joining Derby County in October 1995. He stayed for four years, pulling them up from the then First Division to mid-table respectability in the Premier League and was eventually voted the club's greatest cult hero in a poll by the BBC, winning 59% of the vote. In 2016, after the controversial sacking of Paul Clement while the club were in fifth place, Derby fans were understandably outraged. Štimac, however, wrote an open letter to the fans calling for calm and patience with both the club hierarchy and also rookie manager Darren Wassall. Referring to the fan base as "us" and "we" in the letter, it was obvious that Štimac still had positive feelings towards both Derby County and England.

The remaining republics have offered only a handful of players each, however they too have left an impact on the places they played. Slovenia's Robert Koren made positive impressions upon the fans of Hull City and West Bromwich Albion in a seven-year stint in the Premier League. Montenegro's Stevan Jovetić showed glimpses of how good he could be in a frustrating, injury-ravaged two years at Manchester City. Macedonia's Gjorgji Hristov upset the locals in Barnsley when he claimed that the "local girls are far uglier than the ones back in Belgrade or Skopje". The outburst was probably more an expression of his difficulty to adapt to his new surroundings as he "expected more of Barnsley as a town and as a club". He failed to find much sympathy in the local population with one of the town's female residents describing him as "no oil painting".

One uncompromising defender who did make a positive impact was Muhamed Konjić. The Bosnian played for Coventry City between 1999 and 2004 and was nicknamed "Big Mo" by the Sky Blues faithful for his no-nonsense approach. Konjić had taken the hard road to the Premier League. A former soldier in the Bosnian Army during the war, he was conscripted at the age of 21 for eight months' active duty, and he would often spend his spare time practising on the streets between the rubble and debris of the war. Eventually offered a trial at Croatian club NK Belišće, Konjić and a friend were driven the supposedly safer but longer way from Bosnia to Croatia. The car he was travelling in left the road and crashed into a ditch, leaving Konjić with two broken arms. Stuck between being unable to stay in a Croatian hospital owing to a lack of documentation and returning to the war in Bosnia, Konjić and his driver pressed ahead to Belišće. Just nine days after the accident and screaming in agony every time he played the ball, Konjić made his debut for Belišće and the local fans adored him for his ability to play through the pain barrier. Konjić also captained the Bosnian team who played Albania in their first match, only days after the Dayton Accord was signed.

Konjić came to the attention of then Coventry city manager Gordon Strachan who paid £2m for him, making him the first post-war Bosnian to play in English football, preceding the next by almost a decade. He subsequently joined Derby County and it was there that he sealed his place in Coventry City folklore. In 2005, he played for his new club in Coventry City's final game at Highfield Road before they moved to the new Ricoh Arena. Konjić had a disastrous game, conceding a penalty, and Coventry ran out 6-2 winners.

It is incredibly difficult to see how individual Balkan football leagues can begin to sustain themselves in the 2020s and beyond, let alone thrive. As the West opened up not only to young and hungry players wanting to succeed at Europe's highest level, but also as Balkan dreams of European Union membership are beginning to be realised, freedom of movement means that it is difficult to stop the haemorrhaging of players as they move further afield to improve themselves. The idea of a united Balkan football league is itself not a new one, but was debated as long ago as 2007 when delegates from Russia, Romania, Slovenia and Serbia convened for a conference to discuss the idea. There are precedents elsewhere, most notably in basketball and water polo. The latter features teams from Croatia, Serbia and Montenegro in the 2022/23 season and the former has featured teams from all six former Yugoslav republics. Common denominators which translate to football include clubs from Belgrade — Partizan and Crvena Zvezda — which are both multi-sport associations.

The basketball league in particular was created to fill the void left by the dissolution of the previous league in the aftermath of the wars. Formed in 2008, the Balkan International Basketball League (BIBL) featured teams from Serbia, Macedonia, Bulgaria and Romania (Bulgaria's Rilski Sportist were the league's inaugural winners). The league expanded the following season to include two teams from Montenegro with Croatia and Bosnia receiving representation in the league's third year. Kosovo received membership in the 2013/14 season and the Kosovan team Sigal Prishtina were back-to-back champions in 2015 and 2016.

One of the most obvious barriers to a united Balkan football league is the question of fan security, a concern that Croatian academic Dario Brentin believes is "legitimate". While the BIBL is pointed to as an example of Balkan nations working together to promote sport in the region, representation has at best been disjointed. Whilst Serb, Bosnian and Croat teams have all faced each other in the past, Kosovan teams have only faced opposition from Macedonia and Montenegro. Whether Serbia would accept a FIFA-recognised Kosovo into a prospective Balkan league remains to be seen.

In 2007, Partizan were expelled from the UEFA Cup following crowd violence in a qualifying game at HŠK Zrinjski Mostar. Having won the first leg 6-1, Partizan would have been confident of progression to the second qualifying phase, however, the game was suspended for 10 minutes in the first half as fans clashed with each other and the police. More than 30 fans were injured and six were arrested. Following the match, police used tear gas to disperse the rival fans. Ultimately, Partizan were expelled from European competition for a year and fined 50,000 Swiss Francs. And in 2011, a friendly celebrating Željezničar Sarajevo's 90th anniversary was cancelled after clashes between their Maniacs ultra group and the Torcida ultras of their opponents Hajduk Split.

Any new league system would possibly start with a minimal UEFA coefficient rating, thus making European club qualification even harder for the big four Croatian and Serb teams. This, Brentin believes, is another barrier as the big clubs in Croatia and Serbia, who at the moment have an excellent chance of earning European qualification and the related prize money, would be unwilling to dilute their chances for the sake of a Balkan league. "Football is not organised in a very democratic fashion," said Brentin in a depressingly accurate observation.

The promised land of the Champions League and the enormous revenues qualification brings are also a massive incentive for Balkan football associations too. According to the UEFA website: "Each of the 32 clubs that qualify for the group stage can expect to receive a group stage allocation of €15.64m, split into a down-payment of €14.8m and a balance of €840,000" for the 2022/23 season. For each draw a club will receive €930,000 and a win will net the club €2.8m. Should a team qualify for knockout stage they can expect to receive €9.6m for making it to the last 16 alone, with €15.5m given to the two clubs reaching the final and an additional €4.5m for the winners. Each club qualifying for the group stages of the Europa League will receive €3.63m and for the Conference League €2.94m." With these amounts of money involved, it is easy to see why the teams that currently have a monopoly on European qualification league positions in their own countries, would be reluctant to join a unified league where these places would suddenly become more competitive.

Bosnian football journalist Sasa Ibrulj told me that those who want a united Balkan league had a mix of "nostalgia and hope". It's easy to see why they would — there was a time just before the break-up of the country when a Yugoslavian team lifted the European Cup and the country had the makings of a phenomenally strong national side too. Overall, the national team competed at eight World Cups, four European Championships and were Olympic champions in 1960. At a club level, as well as Red Star's 1991 European Cup and Intercontinental Cup wins, Dinamo Zagreb won the Inter-Cities Fairs Cup in 1967. Partizan were European Cup finalists in 1967, losing 2-1 to Real Madrid in the final. Yugoslav teams were also perennial semi-finalists at the UEFA and Cup Winners Cups as well, at a time when the country was held together by Tito's all-embracing Brotherhood and Unity policy. Yugo-nostalgia refers to more than just football, not least because those who see poor regional economies and high youth unemployment in certain areas of the former Yugoslavia often hark back to the past.

The Yugo-nostalgia is also used as a stick with which to beat those who are far-sighted enough to call for regional change. When Dinamo's Vice President Zdravko Mamić advocated a regional league, he was denounced as an "opponent of Croatia". There seems to be a more vehement opposition to the regional league in Croatia than in other former republics. Slovenia made the first tentative steps to a united league in 2004 when they organised a conference with the help of an outside sports management company. The format, known as the Central European Football League, was two teams from the former Yugoslav republics followed by clubs from neighbouring countries which gave a total of 20 teams overall. Eventually the idea petered out, despite having wide support, with even the Croatian clubs feeling positive, Dinamo's representative at the conference stated that "the future is the creation of a regional league".

However, Hajduk's President Branko Grčić wanted nothing to do with the plan: "None of those interested want the regional league to overlap with the territory of Yugoslavia ... we are against restoring the Yugoslav league." By 2009, Hajduk's stance hadn't changed: "We have our Croatia, and our national league is entirely sufficient for the development of our clubs." There were even suggestions that Hajduk opposed the plans as they saw it as a way of re-establishing political connections between the former republics. Croatia had fought so hard for their independence that they didn't want to start giving it away in something that amounted to a reunification of Yugoslavia by stealth.

As Croatia looks west to its future and is now an EU member, it wants to distance itself from its eastern past and is maybe more amenable to a league involving both Balkan countries and other EU countries in their vicinity. Serbia, on the other hand, is either unwillingly shackled in the east due to its historic ties with Russia, or maybe identifies more with those countries in that area and so does not want a wider league and is happy with a purely Balkan one.

The use of the term 'Yugo-nostalgia' seems harsh in a footballing context, not least because there is a real sense of unfinished business. The country won the under-20 World Championship in 1987. Many of those players played for the senior national team that was cruelly eliminated from the Italia '90 World Cup on penalties at the hands of Argentina. Following Red Star's European Cup triumph a year later, it was felt that Yugoslav football was on the cusp of something extraordinary. Thus, the question of how far would Yugoslavia have gone in the 1992 European Championships had they not been expelled is one of football's great unknowns.

Their replacements Denmark went on to win the tournament and among the adulation that the Danes received, it is easy to forget Yugoslavia and their enforced absence. Yet this was supposed to be their destiny, the culmination of five years' hard work and effort for those boys who became youth world champions in Chile and failed so heartbreakingly at Italia '90.

Yugoslavian fans and the wider footballing world were denied the opportunity to see if the country's national team could achieve immortality; instead the country descended into violence and self-destruction. Red Star's 1991 European Cup win had rightfully been for its own fans and maybe to some extent Serbia, but a victory at Euro '92 could have been Yugoslavia's goodbye to itself.

Nevertheless, maybe glorious failure is Yugoslavia's specialism and what secretly it wanted for its football team. From Milos Obilić's martyrdom at the Battle of Kosovo through to penalty shootout heartbreak in Italia '90, has the psyche of those living in Yugoslavia always been that of spectacular implosions and glorious defeat? Anybody can aspire to be Germany and live through the dull metronome of continual tournament victories, yet real football emotion is that of pain and the wondering of what might have been, and the Yugoslavian football team gave their fans more than enough reasons to wonder.

On a beautiful, warm day in late May 2016, the Open Fun Football Schools held its sixth Mini Champions League in Bihać, Bosnia. Between June 1992 and August 1995, the town was in a state of siege, surrounded by Bosnian Serbs (Republika Srpska) to the east and Croat Serbs (Republic of Serbian Krajina) to the west; they were also helped by rebel groups in the area too. The town's Bosnian Muslim and Croat inhabitants suffered three years of artillery bombardment and air strikes, with Serb planes taking off from Krajina and bombarding the town before NATO planes could reach the area. Almost 5,000 civilians were killed or wounded in the siege, which ended when Croats and Bosniaks, keen to avoid another massacre similar to what had happened in Srebrenica, took back the town in a joint operation which formed part of the larger Operation Storm.

The ethnic demographics of the town are weighted largely towards the Muslim majority. The 2013 census saw 88% of respondents declare themselves Bosniaks, 5.8% as Croats and only 1.61% as Serb. It is a region ripe for Open Fun Football Schools' input.

On the day that OFFS arrived in Bihac, the town square was transformed into a series of small pitches, moulded into a variety of shapes by the inflatables marking out the edge of the pitch. Children were split into small groups and given balls of differing sizes to play with. Some participate in a traditional football match; some chase an oversized ball almost as big as themselves, using their hands to pat the ball around, while others hone their skills by pairing up and balancing balls between their foreheads. For younger children, there is the chance to meet a clown or simply just to sit and colour in and feel like they are taking part in something.

Having seen this footage, I asked Elezovic what moment has given her the most pleasure in all her time of working with the OFFS? "Every time I step out and I hear a roar of 200 kids from the pitch, I feel so completely overwhelmed," she said. "Not just because it is the crown of a year's work, but because it is so natural and simple, to be together and play and have fun, and yet so difficult to achieve in today's world, but we make it every time."

In the video, there's a group of young girls standing together, one of them wearing a broad smile. It's a young Bosniak girl, or perhaps she's Serb, or maybe Croatian. It's hard to tell, but then again there is no need to.

★

★
ACKNOWLEDGEMENTS

There are more people to thank that I can even begin to count so I apologise profusely if I forget to mention you by name, but please note that this book would be nothing without everybody who gave up their time for me.

I wish to thank Kirsten Schlewitz, Uros Popovic, Dario Brentin, James Montague and Anders Levinsen who all gave up their time to talk to me over Skype. Josip Šimunić, Gabriele Marcotti, Runar Nordvik, Vildana Delalic Elezovic and Sasa Ibrulj who all gave their time to answer questions over email.

To David Hartrick and Ockley Books for taking a chance on me and allowing me to scratch the writing itch I've had since I was 12 years old. And to Rob MacDonald and Adam Bushby from Halcyon Publishing for their tireless work in ensuring that the book got to the stage where it was able to be released, they've been trojans.

Thanks also to Ray Guzenda and Paul Downes from GD Associates for their cover concept and the outstanding Steve Leard for carrying this through in his design.

A thank you to the very patient Mark Godfrey formerly of *The Football Pink* for being the first to print my work and offer me sound advice which has helped enormously with this book.

A huge amount of gratitude to Laura Lawrence who has helped enormously during this process when at times things got too much.

A big, big thank you to my friends at the *Man On The Post* podcast who put up with me weekly and indulge my niche segways into the footballing unknown.

Finally the biggest of thanks of all to Charlotte, Georgia and Poppy. Both this book and myself would be nothing without the three of you. You are the reason I get up in the morning and make me want to do better.

★

BIBLIOGRAPHY

A Croatian Champion With A Croatian Name: National Identity And Uses Of History In Croatian Football Culture: The Case Of Dinamo Zagreb - Tea Sindbaek

A Lofty Battle For The Nation: The Social Roles Of Sport In Tudjman's Croatia - Dario Brentin

A New Look At Soccer Violence - Roy Hay

An Ex-Yu Football League: Will It Ever Happen? - Ante Raic

Behind The Curtain - Jonathan Wilson

Beyond The Pattern: Corruption, Hooligans And Football Governance In Croatia - Loic Tregoures

Black (Yellow Or Green) Bastards: Soccer Refereeing In Australia: A Much Maligned Position - Roy Hay

British Football, Wogball Or The World Game? Towards A Social History Of Victorian Soccer - Roy Hay

CCPA's Open Fun Football Schools Programme - The Danish Ministry Of Foreign Affairs

Commemorating A Disputed Past: Football Club And Supporters Group War Memorials In The Former Yugoslavia

Complicating The Relationship Between Sport And National Identity: The Case Of Post-Socialist Slovenia - Mojca Doupona Topic and Jay Coackley

Ethnicity & Soccer In Australia - ASSH Studies In Sports History 10

Fertile Land Or Mined Field? Peace-Building And Ethnic Tensions In Post War Bosnian Football - Davide Sterchele

FK Vojvodina, Red Firm And The Repercussions Of The Yoghurt Revolution - Richard Mills

Fighters, Footballers And Nation Builders: Wartime Football In The Serb Held Territories Of The Former Yugoslavia 1991-1996 - Richard Mills

Football After Yugoslavia: Conflict Reconciliation And The Regional Football League Debate - Shay Wood

Football Against The Enemy - Simon Kuper

Football And Reconciliation In Post-War Bosnia And Herzegovina - Dr Ionnis Armakolas

Football And War In Former Yugoslavia. Serbia And Croatia Two Decades After Break Up - Ivan Dordevic And Bojan Zikic

Football, Blood And War, The Observer

Football Fandom And Formation Of Cultural Differences In Bosnia: A Comparative Ethnographic Study On FK Zeljeznicar And FK Sarajevo Fans In Sarajevo - Ozgur Ozkan

Football In Bosnia: As An Aim Towards Reconciliation - Sebastian Dutz

Football Is War: Nationalism, National Identity And Football - Mette Wiggem

It All Ended In Such An Unsporting Way: Serbian Football And The Disintegration Of Yugoslavia 1989-2006 - Richard Mills

http://www.fifa.com/u20worldcup/news/y=2013/m=7/news=turkyilmaz-would-have-loved-play-for-turkey-2134375.html

http://www.howlermagazine.com/fifa-gets-right/

http://www.independent.co.uk/sport/football-new-start-for-depleted-germans-1177363.html

http://www.kosovodiaspora.org/saving-valon-behrami/

http://news.bbc.co.uk/1/hi/sport/football/45298.stm

http://www.nytimes.com/1998/01/21/sports/21iht-soccer.t_5.html

http://www.nytimes.com/2016/05/04/sports/soccer/uefa-recognizes-kosovo-paving-way-for-fifa-membership.html?_r=0

https://www.theguardian.com/football/2016/jun/03/valon-behrami-swiss-warrior-euro-2016

https://www.theguardian.com/observer/osm/story/0,6903,1123137,00.html

Kosovo: How Myths and Truths started a War - Julie A. Mertus

Modern Albania: From Dictatorship To Democracy In Europe - Fred Abrahams

Nations Of Former Yugoslavia Prove That Size Doesn't Matter - Jonathan Wilson, The Guardian

No Mans Land: Sinisa Mihajlovic, Vukovar And The Compromises Of War - Jonathan Wilson, The Blizzard

Ready For The Homeland? Ritual, Remembrance, And Political Extremism In Croatian Football - Dario Brentin

Saviours of the Nation?: Serbia's Intellectual Opposition and the Revival of Nationalism - Jasna Dragović-Soso

Slobodan Milosevic and the Destruction of Yugoslavia - Louis Sell

Soccer And Croatian Nationalism - Allen L Stack And Zeljan Suster

Sport And Peace Building In Post Conflict Societies: The Role Of Open Fun Football Schools In Kosovo - Sanije Krasniqi

The Antinomies Of Multicultural Sporting Nationalism: A Case Study Of Australia & South Africa - Douglas Booth

The Ball Is Round - David Goldblatt

The Curious Drama Of The President Of A Republic Versus A Football Fan Tribe - Srdjan Vrcan

The Death & Life Of Australian Soccer - Joe O'Gorman

The Death Of Yugoslavia - Laura Silber & Alan Little

The Fall Of Yugoslavia - Misha Glenny

The Game: Early Soccer Scenery In New South Wales - Philip Mosely

The Multi-Kulti Question - Mike Phillips, The Blizzard

The Origin Of Soccer In Serbia - Dejan Zec

The Paradoxes Of Politicisation: Football Supporters In Croatia - Andrew Hodges And Paul Stubbs

The Structure Of Football In The City Of Split - Slobodan Bjelajac

The War Is Dead, Long Live The War, Bosnia The Reckoning - Ed Vulliamy

Thirty-One Nil - James Montague

Transitions Online: Football Is War - Andrej Krickovic

Twenty Years Later: The War Did (Not) Begin At Maksimir - Ivan Dordevic

Velez Mostar Football Club And The Demise Of Brotherhood And Unity In Yugoslavia, 1922-2009 - Richard Mills

★

Printed in Great Britain
by Amazon